# The Scottish Smuggler

# The Scottish Smuggler

### Gavin D. Smith

**Birlinn**

First published in the UK in 2003 by
Birlinn Limited
West Newington House
10 Newington Road
Edinburgh
EH9 1QS

www.birlinn.co.uk

ISBN  1 84158 285 9

British Library Cataloguing-in-Publication Data
A catalogue record of this book is available from the British Library

Typeset by Edderston Book Design, Peebles
Printed and bound by Creative Print and Design, Ebbw Vale, Wales

# CONTENTS

# ACKNOWLEDGEMENTS

Thanks are due to the following people who have made various contributions to this book: Ron Barrie of HM Customs and Excise, Tom Bruce-Gardyne, Campbell Dewar of HM Customs and Excise, Dr Cathlin Macaulay of the School of Scottish Studies, Edinburgh University, Charles MacLean, Wanda Russell, Jacqui Seargeant, Donald Smith, Ruth Smith, and the staff of Birlinn Ltd.

I am also indebted to the staff of Aberdeen City Library, Aberdeenshire Council Archives, Angus Archives, Ayrshire Archive Centre, Dumfries and Galloway Archives, Dundee Central Library, Dundee City Archive and Record Office, Edinburgh City Archives, the Mitchell Library, Glasgow, the National Archives Scotland, Edinburgh, the National Library of Scotland, Edinburgh, Orkney Library and Archives, and Shetland Archives.

# INTRODUCTION

Today Britain seems less like an island than ever before. The skies overhead are filled with aircraft, and a Channel Tunnel links us to mainland Europe, so it is easy to forget the great importance that the sea has played in our history. We no longer think of the oceans as our main commercial arteries, but until comparatively recently Britain relied *totally* on the sea for trading.

A seafaring nation such as Britain was never going to find it too difficult to avoid paying high taxes imposed by government when the same dutiable commodities could be purchased at low prices in foreign ports. During the eighteenth and early nineteenth centuries, duty levels on many items rose dramatically, and smuggling became an everyday part of life in the British Isles. The Scots were as active and enthusiastic as anyone in evading duty, and as we shall see, in many cases had greater motivation for supporting smuggling than most.

Today few tangible reminders of Scotland's smuggling heritage remain. The occasional 'Smugglers' Cave' is marked on an Ordnance Survey map, and it is possible to stay in establishments such as the Uplawmoor Hotel in Renfrewshire, originally a coaching inn on the route from Glasgow to the Ayrshire coast, and a favourite haunt of smugglers. In the Fife port of Anstruther you can drink in the Smugglers' Tavern or even live in a modern housing development called Smugglers Gait. By and large, however, the significant part Scotland played in the 'free trade' is too often overlooked.

When we think of smuggling we tend to think of the coasts of Cornwall and Kent rather than Angus and Ayrshire. Certainly, most of the available published literature relating to smuggling concentrates on the south of England. This book is an attempt to redress the balance.

In the pages ahead we trace the rise and demise of Scottish smuggling and examine the kind of goods involved, before embarking on a geographically diverse tour of 'Scotland's smuggling country'. We look at the fascinating literary heritage of Scottish smuggling, and ultimately remind ourselves that Scottish smuggling is not a purely historical phenomenon.

Finally, this book is not the work of a disciplined, professional historian. For one thing, there are no footnotes. Using nothing but official historical records might provide a factually flawless book, but it would also provide a dull and one-sided one.

While it may be an old cliché to say that history is usually written by the victors, with regard to Scotland's smuggling story, it was usually the authorities who had the need to correspond and record, and the skills of literacy with which to do so. What follows, then, is a mixture of official records, letters, published accounts, fiction, myth, lore and legend . . . .

# 1

# A SHORT HISTORY
# OF SCOTTISH SMUGGLING

In his 1755 *Dictionary of the English Language* Dr Samuel Johnson defined a smuggler as 'a wretch who imports or exports goods without payment of customs'. However, he also defined 'excise' as 'a hateful tax levied upon commodities, and judged not by the common judges of property, but by wretches hired by those to whom excise is paid'. To Johnson, it seems, both the law-enforcers and the law-breakers were 'wretches'!

The *Oxford English Dictionary* defines customs as 'tribute, toll, impost, or duty, levied by the lord or local authority upon commodities on their way to market; esp. that levied in the name of the king or sovereign authority upon merchandise exported from or imported into his dominions; now levied only upon imports from foreign countries'. According to the *OED*, the first attestation of the word (as '*customarios*') occurred *c.* 1325.

The *OED* quotes the *Encyclopaedia Britannica* definition of excise: 'A duty charged on home goods, either in the process of their manufacture or before their sale to the home consumers'. The *OED* adds: 'In England this kind of taxation was first adopted in 1643, in acknowledged imitation of the example of Holland. The taxes levied under the name of Excise by the Ordinance of 1643 included certain duties imposed, in addition to the customs, on various foreign products; it was not until the present century that the actual use of the word became strictly conformed to the preceding definition.' With the sense of any toll or tax, the word excise (as '*excisas*') was first recorded in 1490, while with the specific *Encyclopaedia Britannica* definition it was initially used by Edmund Spenser in his 1596 book, *A View of the Present State of Ireland*: 'All the townes of the Lowe-Countreyes doe cutt upon themselves an excise of all thinges towarde the mayntenaunce of the warre'.

The word 'smuggler' was probably introduced into the English language during the Civil War of 1642–49. On 9 August 1661 – after the restoration of Charles II to the throne – a royal proclamation was issued '. . . for the prevention and punishment of all frauds on the Customs committed by . . . a sort of lewd people called "Smuckellors," never heard of before the late disordered times, who make it their trade . . . to steal and defraud His Majesty of His Customs'. Charles II can also be credited with creating the Board of Customs, in 1671.

It may not have been until the Restoration period that these 'lewd people' were referred to as smugglers, but they had been defrauding the Customs for several centuries prior to the Civil War. English smuggling had begun in the reign of Edward I (1272–1307) when English wool was bought by French weavers who sold their cloth for lower prices than those commanded by English textiles. The king was responsible for developing the basic system of 'British' customs duties, imposing a tax on wool and woollen products leaving England. This hit the French merchants hard, but some English traders offered to supply them with wool at something close to the previous prices. These wool smugglers were mainly based in Kent and Sussex, and became known as 'owlers', because they smuggled their contraband goods out of the country by 'owl-light'.

According to Gilbert Denton (*A Brief History of HM Customs & Excise*), 'to King John in 1203 goes the credit for establishing a Customs service on a national scale responsible directly to the crown. At all the ports he required 6 or 7 "wise and substantial men, well versed in the law" to account to him for the revenue; and he divided the control between assessment, collection and accounting to guard against bribery or collusion – a system which has survived into the twentieth century and the computer era.'

In Scotland, there had been occasional bouts of taxation, notably during the reign of King William I (1165–1214), while customs duties were a part of commercial life by the reign of King David (1329–71). In 1357, a council at Scone, near Perth, ordered a series of new taxes and a reassessment of existing ones. Subsequently, customs duties quadrupled.

In *Clyde Coast Smuggling*, J.R.D. Campbell observes that 'when we look back at the years preceding the reign of James VI and I, smuggling had not been regarded too seriously. The first duty levied was on the export of sheep and horses etc. Later revenue laws were intended both to restrict English trade, and to confine foreign traffic to the Scottish Royal Burghs . . .'.

After the Union of the Crowns in 1603, when James VI of Scotland also became James I of England, increasingly large sums of money were required to sustain the economy, so customs and excise legislation began to grow. When money was required at short notice to bankroll the Scottish troops fighting alongside the English parliamentarians against King Charles I, the Scottish Parliament introduced a number of new taxes. Most significantly, they passed an 'Act of Excyse' in January

1644, which imposed a duty of 2s. 8d. on 'everie pynt of aquavytie or strong watteris sold within the countrey'.

Scottish traders had been selling hides, wool and fish in northern Europe during the thirteenth century, and by the late seventeenth century comparatively large quantities of wool from Scotland were being exported to France and the Netherlands, while timber and iron were among the principal legal imports, along with Biscay salt, tobacco and sugar.

T.C. Smout (*A History of the Scottish People 1560–1830*) notes that 'Edinburgh (using the dependent port of Leith), Dundee and Aberdeen sent their ships every year along the trade routes from Trondheim in Northern Norway and Danzig in the inner Baltic, to Rotterdam and Veere, to Normandy and La Rochelle and Bordeaux in Biscay and sometimes as far as Spain; ships even from quite small towns like Crail and Pittenweem in Fife, Dunbar in East Lothian and Montrose in Angus appeared with the greatest regularity in the delta of the Scheldt, in the Norwegian fjords or the Danish Sound.'

Smout points out that Crail-based herring boats would bring cargoes of Swedish iron home in return after selling their fish in Danzig or Stockholm, before severe winter weather closed the Danish Sound to shipping. West coast merchants traded with Ireland and France, and later with North America and the West Indies, but they also began to trade with Norway and the Baltic, sending boats through the frequently perilous waters of the Minch.

Scots had a particular connection with the port of Bordeaux, due to the special privileges they had long enjoyed in wine-trading there, as well as with Stockholm, from where Swedish iron was regularly transported.

It is often stated that Scottish smuggling really began in the aftermath of the 1707 Act of Union, which united Scotland and England, and was accepted by the Scots as the only way of avoiding impending economic ruin. As T.C. Smout observes, however, 'the Scots were already large-scale smugglers, and the union merely allowed them to marry their long-held dislike of customs and excise duties and the officials who enforced their collection with the conveniently patriotic concept of cheating the English.'

Before the union, a series of Navigation Acts, principally the Navigation Act of 1660, caused a great deal of resentment in Scotland. This stipulated that only English ships could trade in England's colonies, and that ships trading with the colonies must have a crew that was at least 75 per cent English in its composition.

An ordnance of 1650 forbade foreign vessels from trading in the colonies, and another, a year later, stipulated that colonial goods had to be carried in English or colonial ships with 75 per cent English crews. The 1660 Act was based on these earlier ordnances, but also required that colonial goods were only shipped to England. This 'mercantilism', or protectionism, was principally directed against the Dutch, but the end of mercantilism was signalled by Sir Robert Walpole's reforms of 1722, when over a hundred export duties, as well as tariffs on the import of raw materials and semi-finished goods were abolished.

If the Navigation Acts displeased Scottish traders, then the immediate effects of the Act of Union must have displeased them far more. Article VI of the *Act Ratifying and Approving the Treaty of Union of the Two Kingdoms of Scotland and England* (1706) stated 'That all parts of the United Kingdom for ever from and after the Union shall have the same Allowances, Encouragements and Drawbacks, and be under the same Prohibitions, Restrictions and Regulations of Trade and lyable to the same Customs and Duties on Import and Export'.

Scottish import duties subsequently increased until they were in line with those south of the border, and in some instances the new rates were as much as seven times their pre-union levels. In *The Heart of Midlothian*, Sir Walter Scott commented that the people of Scotland were not accustomed to imposts, and regarded them as 'an unjust aggression upon their ancient liberties'.

There were, however, a number of exceptions to the increased levels of duty, including commodities such as salt, which was essential to the economically very important Scottish fishing industry. *The Act Ratifying and Approving the Treaty of Union of the Two Kingdoms of Scotland and England* stated that 'Scotland shall for the space of seven Years from the said Union be Exempted from paying in Scotland for Salt made there the Dutie or Excise now payable for Salt made in England'.

The revised levels of duty meant that some commodities which had previously been widely affordable in Scotland now effectively became unattainable luxuries, unless, of course, they were acquired without the tiresome business of paying duty at all. The Act of Union was therefore little short of a smuggler's charter in Scotland. The sort of goods involved included not only wines, spirits, tobacco and tea, but candles, glassware, notepaper, playing cards, soap, silks and sugar, all of which were the subject of increased duty.

However, Richard Platt (*Ordnance Survey Guide to Smugglers' Britain*) suggests that there was not the same demand for luxury goods in Scotland as there was in England, due to general poverty and sparse population, so Scottish smugglers tended to concentrate on bringing in heavily-taxed 'staple' items such as salt, which was essential not only for the fishing industry, but also for preserving meat.

There was great popular resistance to new and increased duties imposed after the Act of Union, exacerbated by a series of poor harvests and consequent food shortages which did little to make the union seem like a step forward for the ordinary people of Scotland.

As David Stevenson (*The Beggar's Benison*) puts it 'All over Scotland the duties were the most widespread, concrete causes of discontent with the post-union regime, and of active defiance of the law by men of all ranks . . . Scottish duties had traditionally been low, collection ramshackle and indirect. The new "English" duties were sometimes higher than the old ones by several hundred *per cent.*'

There was, as Stevenson notes, a basic conflict of interest between English duties, which were designed to help shield English manufacturing from foreign competition, and the situation in Scotland, where the economy was less manufacturing-based and more geared to the export of raw materials and the import of finished goods.

In *From Esk to Tweed*, Bruce Lenman notes that under English law the export of wool to the Netherlands was illegal, in order to deprive the Leyden cloth industry of raw material, as it was a major rival to the East Anglian trade. After 1707, new laws and customs enforcement attempted to stop the old Scots' trade of wool from Dundee and other east-coast ports to the Netherlands. Such legal barriers imposed on well-established and lucrative Scottish trade were another cause of resentment, and a great deal of wool was smuggled along the old trade routes despite the new laws.

The Shawfield Riots in 1725 and the Porteous Riots of 1736 (see pp. 109–100 and 165–167) were two high-profile examples of situations where popular resistance to the duty changes that followed the Act of Union was at its most extreme.

In 1713 the English Malt Tax had been extended to Scotland, though only at half the English rate, and this tax was widely evaded and rarely enforced. Twelve years later, however, the tax was raised to 6d. per bushel, in line with the English level, and the result was civil unrest, with eleven people being killed in June during Glasgow's Shawfield Riots. This was a tax on the everyday drink of 'twopenny ale', and the Scottish people were not amused.

Observing that 'twopenny' ale was the most popular Scottish beverage until around 1750 – '. . . made in every farm, manse and mansion, drunk in the dining-room and in the change-house' – H. Grey Graham (*The Social Life of Scotland in the Eighteenth Century*) wrote that 'in 1725 Parliament . . . enforced an impost, which had been hitherto evaded, of 6d. on every bushel of malt. At this tyrannical interference with their favourite drink the people arose in wild indignation. The Jacobites adroitly raised the cry, "No Union, no malt tax, no salt tax!" The decline of "twopenny" can be charted from that date, with whisky gradually coming to the fore as the popular drink of the people.'

The Jacobite supporters of the House of Stuart were opposed to the Protestant 'United Kingdom', and therefore to the customs and excise duties imposed in its name. David Stevenson declares '. . . to Jacobites buying smuggled goods became almost a moral obligation'.

Richard Platt (*Smugglers' Britain*) makes the interesting point that Jacobite-related smuggling activities were not confined to Scotland. The Oak and Ivy Inn in Kent which acted as headquarters for the Hawkhurst Gang took its name from the Jacobite emblem, and south-coast smuggling vessels often carried Jacobite activists and sympathisers to and from France, while smugglers sometimes even acted as spies and double agents for the Jacobite cause.

Though the volume of trade in Scotland increased after the Act of Union, revenue declined, chiefly due to the increase in smuggling. Post-union, as Sir John Clerk of Penicuik noted in his *General Observations on the two Branches of the Revenues of Scotland the Customs and Excise*, comparatively high levels of duty precipitated '. . . the running of goods into this part of Britain, which is a practice carried on here both by the English and us and is almost impracticable to prevent because of the convenience and multitude of our ports'.

Clerk backed up his view with some persuasive statistics (*Abstract of the General Accounts of the Customs in Scotland from Michaelmas 1715 to Michaelmas 1731*). In 1715–16 the net yield of customs in Scotland was £17,767, but by 1729–30 it had fallen to £6,481, despite Walpole's various reforms intended to curb smuggling. As Clerk also stated, the yield of customs was '. . . scarce sufficient to defray the Charge of Management'.

The Union of 1707 came about, and while the English despised the alliance, which a southern Commissioner superciliously likened to wedding a beggar with a louse for her portion, the Scots denounced it as destructive of Scottish independence, Scottish trade, Scottish pride – in short, of every glory and appendage that was Scottish. From the south came custom officers, whose very accent and presence were hateful; they watched every transaction with a keen suspicion, so different from the manner of the easy times in which the revenues of £160,000 had been collected when a Scotsman farmed them; and the nation bitterly complained that their money was used to feed the families of needy English cormorants.

Heavy salt duties were levied, and the deep-sea fisheries were crushed . . . the trade well nigh became extinct on the east shores. Many a once flourishing fishing town fell into stagnation, while in the offing were Dutch busses with their broad-beamed hulls catching the cod before the fishermen's eyes. From lack of work, these places became haunts of smuggling, in which every man and woman felt it honourable to join in, and to despoil the English of their tribute.

One great privilege Scotland gained by the Union was the removing of the prohibition against trading with the English colonies . . . Now this embargo was lifted off, and within a generation the trade with Virginia and the Indies was to bring fortune to Glasgow, and a rich commerce was to rise which Scots Commissioners little foresaw . . .

The beneficial results of the Union were slow of being felt, and for some twenty years the people saw less of the advantages than of the hardships it entailed – heavier taxes, more duties, vexatious restrictions, and dangerous competition with the trade of England, and a lost trade with France.

We may by 1730, however, see the stirring of a new life in the country, the gradual awakening of the community from its long lethargy, for by that time the linen industry was felt to be a source of prosperity owing to its trade with England.

– *H. Grey Graham*, The Social Life of Scotland in the Eighteenth Century.

In his introduction to *The Heart of Midlothian* (1818), Sir Walter Scott wrote insightfully of the ways in which 'union' was initially perceived, and the changes in that perception as Scotland began to see its commercial benefits.

In 1707 the vote for a new incorporating Union of England and Scotland was pushed through the Estates, partly by bribery in the manner of the age, by upper-class groups who expected to profit by new flows of patronage and trade and who in their turn orientated themselves to London. In the early days of the Union various pieces of Westminster legislation offended Scottish opinion: modernization of the taxes to meet the cost of eighteenth-century wars; the 'abjuration oath', which both asserted power over the Church and restricted succession to the throne to members of the Church of England; the imposition of royal or seigneurial 'patronage' of Church appointments over the established mode of selection by the middling landowners of a parish in conjunction with the Kirk-session of ministers and elders. Meanwhile the religious and political tension between the Protestant/Presbyterian/Whig/Hanoverian interest and the Catholic/Episcopalian/Tory/Stuart one remained more acute in Scotland than elsewhere, especially in the north, and fuelled successive

Jacobite insurrections, notably those of 1715 and 1745 – the latter being put down with genocidal brutality. As the century wore on, low-keyed indirect government through a 'manager' and the economic benefits of the First British Empire to Scottish trade and industry, notably through the American tobacco trade in the Glasgow area, made the Union a less sensitive question; agricultural 'improvement' and city-building typical of Enlightenment Europe both brought about and reflected stages of economic, social and intellectual modernization.

Nonetheless, even as the economic benefits of the union were being experienced, smuggling flourished in Scotland as never before. According to David Stevenson, 'smuggling was Scotland's biggest and most profitable service industry'.

As taxation levels rose during the eighteenth century, principally to pay for a succession of European wars, smuggling became progressively more lucrative. The risks involved were worth taking when large profits were to be made, and for many people living in poverty smuggled goods were an essential part of life. They could not have afforded duty-paid tea or tobacco, even if they had been inclined to pay 'legal' prices.

Duty levels rose to finance the War of Jenkins' Ear against Spain in 1739, the War of the Austrian Succession, and the Jacobite rising in 1745–46. During the Seven Years War (from 1756) various taxes were raised to pay for the 200,000 British troops who were in action. Some £60m was also borrowed, but import duties, such as that on tea, were raised significantly. The tax on tea had been cut from 4s. 9d. to 1s. in 1745 to deter smuggling, but when it rose again in 1759 it once again became an attractive commodity to smuggle.

Throughout the period when smuggling was most prevalent, participants would choose whichever commodities yielded the greatest profit at the time, switching merchandise as duty on individual items rose and fell.

As Richard Platt points out, tea could be bought for 7d. a pound on the Continent, and sold in Britain for 5s. Tobacco cost a similar amount and sold for 2s. 6d. Brandy and gin profit margins were even more attractive – a £1 cask could sell for £4, and if 'cut' to drinking strength before sale, the margins must have been significantly higher.

In *Reminiscences of Smugglers and Smuggling*, John Banks wrote

> To show the profit connected with smuggling, take for example a single tub of spirits; its cost in France was from ten shillings and sixpence to thirteen shillings – fourteen to sixteen shillings would be thought dear. A tub of spirits contained three and a half gallons of spirit so much over-proof that it would bear the addition of two and a half gallons of water,

and the six gallons would sell easily for three or even four pounds or guineas. (Our forefathers had a great love for guineas.) Here was a profit of from four to five hundred percent! After paying out of this the cost of transport, wages of the look-out men, etc the profits were so good that I have heard it said that if one cargo out of three was saved, there was then a profit.

Not only did smuggling flourish, but it flourished with the support of all sections of society. However, it is worth noting that while many 'respectable' people were involved in the activity in various ways, farmers, for example, who refused to loan horses to help retrieve smuggled cargoes or who would not allow their workers to participate, would often find animals killed, haystacks fired, or even worse.

To their supporters, smugglers became known, ironically, as 'fair traders' or 'free traders', and H. Grey Graham wrote 'In all transactions the "free trader" was a hero; to "jink the gauger" was an honourable exploit. If custom officers tried to search they found the country people in hundreds ready to oppose them, and before they could carry off a captured cargo a detachment of soldiers was required to support them.'

In a speech in the House of Lords, delivered in July 1805, Lord Holland noted that 'It is impossible totally to prevent smuggling; all that the legislature can do is to compromise with a crime which, whatever laws may be made to constitute it a high offence, the mind of man can never conceive as at all equalling in turpitude those acts which are breaches of clear moral virtues.'

As William Ferguson observes in *Scotland 1689 to the Present*, 'A chronic complaint was of the defects of customs and excise . . . Smuggling was accepted by high and low alike and even connived at by judges, not *ex officio* but in their private capacities'.

As the demand for ale decreased, [principally as a result of the Malt Tax of 1725] what drink was taking its place in a much-imbibing age? It was chiefly smuggled spirits. From Holland, France, and Spain luggers brought their contraband cargoes of wine, tea, cambric, and brandy. No crime was so respectable as 'fair trading'; none was so widely spread. Along the quiet bays of the Solway, into caves under the rocky cliffs of Forfarshire, to remote lochs of Ross-shire, and even to the open shores of Fife, boats came with fine impunity and perfect confidence. Bakers, shoemakers and farmers, schoolmasters and fishermen, and lairds, were interested in a traffic in which they all had shares and reaped rich profits. Gentlemen holding high position in the country and offices of justices of the peace joined the smugglers in their ventures of running in the cargoes, while excisemen were hopelessly baffled.

The signal of a white sheet or shirt out to dry on thatched roofs or corn-stacks was the reassuring sign by day, and bonfires on cliffs were timely warnings at night. So soon as news arrived of a lugger in the offing, all in silent confederacy – men, women, and children – prepared to help in the unloading. The kirk was poorly attended on the Fast day if confidential tidings arrived. In records of Kirk-Sessions occur frequent penalties on offenders who on a Fast day, ere twelve o'clock had struck, yoked their horses to convey the goods run in; but the discipline was not so much because they had broken the law, as because they had broken the Fast. The General Assembly might issue stern comminations on the demoralising traffic, which were read from the pulpits: not merely by magistrates was it winked at, but sometimes by ministers too. When the communion was at hand, and the minister had his elders and brethren to entertain, a mysterious anker of brandy might arrive at the manse, of which the clerical party drank gratefully, asking no questions – for conscience' sake. It even happened that in the far North smuggled goods were deposited occasionally in a kirk for safety, but with whose cognisance is not certain. It is significant of the public feeling that the eminently respectable firm of Coutts and Co. of Edinburgh, bankers and traders, had one member of the house a partner in a firm at Rotterdam, whose chief business consisted in furnishing goods for the smugglers who ran their cargoes on the north and east coasts of Scotland; and it was only after big profits had been made that Coutts was withdrawn from a line of business which ruffled the growing conscience of a most prosperous and honourable company. In the south counties were corporations of these smugglers who, as cover, took farms, and farmed them admirably, to the great benefit of agriculture.

– *H. Grey Graham*, The Social Life of Scotland in the Eighteenth Century.

Duncan Forbes of Culloden (1685–1747) served as Lord President of the Court of Session from 1737 until his death, having previously acted as Lord Advocate. In 1744 he wrote to the Commissioners and Trustees for Improving Fisheries and Manufactures regarding *Some Considerations on the Present State of Scotland*, and his virulent anti-smuggling stance can partly be explained by the anti-Union and pro-Jacobite connotations of smuggling. He had a well-known hatred of tea and considered its consumption a very great evil. This may not have been entirely unconnected with the fact that tea-drinking adversely affected his family's whisky distilling enterprise (see p. 52).

Forbes wrote passionately about smuggling in *Some Considerations*, and was clearly of the opinion that respectable citizens were not doing their duty as vigorously as they ought to in attempting to stamp out the illicit trade:

If the *Smuggler* cannot depend on having *Boats* to receive his goods from the *hovering* vessel, – and if he can hope for no *shelter* to cover them when landed; if he is to have no *protection* or assistance from the *Farmer*, but, on the contrary, is to look upon every *Farmer* as an *Informer*, and as an *assistant* to the officer, he must be very *mad* indeed if he persist in *running* ... did gentlemen in the different districts along the coast form themselves into small *societies* shall I call them, confederacies which should correspond with one another ... *Smuggling* must receive its Death Wound, and the country be delivered from its present distress.

In most cases, especially where smuggling was operating on a large scale, well-to-do, apparently respectable local families financed smuggling operations in return for a substantial share of the profits. The 'gentlemen' referred to by Forbes were frequently ill-disposed towards the authorities with regard to smuggling, as they had seen their powers of control over local customs affairs usurped by the Act of Union. Many were Justices of the Peace, and convictions for smuggling in their courts were few and far between.

Smuggling, for which the Isle of Man then afforded peculiar facilities, was general, or rather universal, all along the south-western coast of Scotland. Almost all of the common people were engaged in these practices; the gentry connived at them, and the officers of the revenue were frequently discountenanced in the exercise of their duty, by those who should have protected them.

– *Sir Walter Scott*, Guy Mannering.

Duncan Forbes was a notable critic of the poor performance and corruptibility of the customs and excise personnel, and William Ferguson writes (*Scotland 1689 to the Present Day*) that 'the excise service was notoriously corrupt, tide-waiter and collectors having a tariff on their remissness as well as on excisable commodities. Thus, in the 1730s William Somerville, a merchant of Renfrew, was daunting the other "free traders" on the west coast with vast quantities of Marseilles brandy at ten shillings the gallon.'

As early as 1721 there were complaints to parliament from English merchants that the Scots, as Ferguson puts it, 'constantly evaded the customs, helped by the corruption of the local customs officers'. These allegations were not without foundation, but applied equally to English ports.

Ferguson adds that 'the customs service in Scotland was nevertheless purged, and in 1723 new officers were appointed to the ports of

Greenock and Port Glasgow. In 1722 total imports of tobacco had been four and a half million lbs, but by 1725 they had dropped to four million.' However, 'the decline was not necessarily due to reform of the customs', according to Ferguson, who noted that a general depression affected trade during the period in question.

There are many documented examples of corruption concerning customs officials, with the Inverness Collector of Customs receiving a letter from the Board of Customs in Edinburgh during May 1788 informing him that they planned to remove the Lossiemouth 'tidesman', John Fordyce. This was not unreasonable, given that '. . . a cask of Geneva' was seized from his house by other officers, it being '. . . the property of his daughter who deals in uncustomed and prohibited goods'.

In September 1783, the Elgin-based tidesman Andrew Simpson wrote to the Collector of Customs in Inverness regarding fellow tidesman James Hutcheon, alleging that he had '. . . improper connection with dealers and has been acting in collusion with smugglers, by whom he is said to be frequently bribed'.

From 'A Letter from the Annual Committee of the Convention of Royal Boroughs of Scotland, by Order of the General Convention, for preventing the pernicious practice of smuggling', 3 September 1736:

> The strong expectations of gain, from the strictness of the duty, which was all to be saved, drew multitudes of persons with small stocks, and smaller correspondence, into the trade. Saving the whole duty on goods that pay so high as brandy, tea and wine, yields a glowing prospect. [However,] . . . the unhappy smuggler does not consider, or bring into account, the expense of running, the correspondence he must maintain with officers, and with the country, the frequent occasions for hush money and the accidental losses by seizure.

Smuggling operations varied greatly in scale, from the very localised and opportunistic to the well co-ordinated, professional ventures backed by significant sums of merchants' or gentlemen's money. With increasing sophistication, bankers' drafts replaced cash as a parallel to legitimate business practice.

Vessels employed in smuggling ranged from small fishing boats manned by a few local men at one extreme, to what were known as 'Flushing cutters', large and heavily-armed vessels, originating in the Dutch port of Flushing.

In a letter of October 1773, Duncan Aire, captain of the excise cutter *Royal Charlotte* described an encounter with '. . . a large lugger belonging to Flushing . . .' off the north-east coast. The vessel was carrying a cargo of spirits and tea, and '. . . bids defiance to all the yachts in the revenue of customs and excise'. Aire noted that the Flushing cutter was armed with '. . . six large carriage-guns and twenty swivels' and that during a pursuit she was taken alongside the excise cutter, '. . . the tampions out of her guns and every man a lighted flare in his hand ready to engage'. Discretion clearly being the better part of valour in this situation, the excisemen withdrew.

A common practice was for large smuggling vessels to lay offshore and allow local fishing boats to go alongside and buy goods, which they then ran ashore. Around 1800, Norwegian vessels carrying spirits from Holland were known to be particularly active in this type of smuggling.

Most smuggling was, however, more clandestine and less brazen. Vessels with legitimate cargoes would also carry contraband, often cunningly hidden in secret compartments behind bulkheads and between decks. Casks with false bottoms were used, with the brandy or gin hidden beneath water or perhaps wine, which attracted a lower level of tax than spirits. Tobacco might even be processed into thick 'rope', which would arouse little suspicion on board the smuggling vessels.

Many of the best stories of ingenuity and audacity in the face of customs and excise officers turn up in the south of England as well as in Scotland. The use of coffins and mock funerals to transport contraband was widespread, and regularly employed by Scottish whisky smugglers (see *Whisky Smuggling*). However, there are also several smuggling tales involving the use of hearses attributed to Cornwall, and a coffin was used by smugglers on the East Anglian coast to bring in lace and silk, according to Athol Forbes (*The Romance of Smuggling*). The pretence was that an English sailor serving on a French lugger had died, and his last request was to be buried in his native soil. The coffin was duly brought ashore and buried, with the local chief officer of the Coastguard being an unwitting mourner.

In *Some Considerations on the Present State of Scotland*, Duncan Forbes pointed out that smuggling was causing significant damage to the Scottish economy. He observed that grain prices were falling, which affected the incomes of 'gentlemen', as many owned large lowland estates geared to arable agriculture. Grain prices had begun to fall because less brewing and distilling were taking place in Scotland. Cheap smuggled tea was replacing ale as a staple common drink, and there were also large quantities of smuggled spirits available. Forbes wrote

> To trace the *disease*, under which we at present labour, to its *source*, we must look back to the *Union* of the Kingdoms. The Treaty for that Union was carried on and concluded much against the inclination of the generality of the people of *Scotland*; and the only popular topick produced for rendering it palatable now the great advantage that must accrue to *Scotland* from the *communications of trade* to which by the *union* it was to be admitted. This consideration was surely weighty; and, had the people honestly made use of that privilege to which they were invited, the complaints under which we now suffer, would not have had a being. But, unfortunately, the people took the most mischievous of all turns. In place of pursuing *fair* trade, they universally, with the Exception of *Glasgow, Aberdeen,* and one or two Places more, took to *smuggling*; their small stocks they invested in Goods that bore *high Duties*, and under the Flavour of *running* those securely on our wide and ill-guarded coasts, they flattered themselves they should soon grow rich, profiting at least of the high Duty, which by running they were to save.
>
> Though this Scheme proved *destructive* to almost every Adventurer who entered upon it, though it was bottomed on Fraud and Dishonesty, and though it had evidently tended to what it has very nearly accomplished, the total Ruin of the country; yet so blind, or rather perverse, were the People, that they, without Hesitation, and almost without Exception, gave in to it. – The *smuggler* was the Favourite. – His prohibited or high Duty goods were run ashore by the *Boats* of whatever part of the coast he came near; when ashore, they were guarded by the country from the customhouse-officer; if seized, they were rescued; – and if any seizure was returned and tried, the *Juries* seldom failed to find for the Defendant. These circumstances gave the *Running* Trade the Appearance of absolute Security; and have so *thoroughly* destroyed the Revenue, that the Customs are hardly able to pay the Salaries of their own Officers.
>
> Gain expected was the *Temptation* that drew the Traders into this villainous Project; and a *Dislike* to the *Union,* an *ill Opinion* conceived of the first sett of Customhouse-officers that were sent down hither, an *Unwillingness* to favour the Revenue, on a supposal that the Money thence arising was to be remitted to *England*, and the *Partiality* to their unhappy countrymen who were dipt in this Trade, together with small Bounties and Presents received from the *smuggler*, drew the Bulk of the People in, to favour them.

Forbes noted that for twenty years after the union

> By much the *greatest* part of the wine brought into the out-ports paid no duty, – and none paid higher than the *Spanish*; Brandy in vast quantities was imported without paying *any*: And by those means the consumption of beer and ale was in *some* degree impaired, and the use of home-made spirits *almost universally* laid aside. – But as the price of wine never came

so *low* as to bring it within the *reach* of the *populace*, as the *vice* of *punch-drinking* had not prevailed over the *meanest* sort, who were accustomed to no better liquor than twopenny; and as the *more pernicious* practice of *tea-drinking* was confined to what may be called people of condition: our grain still bore some price, because the Consumption of malt liquors was considerable. – The excise, though lower than it had formerly been, produced sums fit to answer the expence of the civil government and such cities and towns as had an impost on beer and ale granted to them, found no *considerable* diminution of their revenues.

But when the opening a Trade with the *East-Indies*, first at *Ostend*, and afterwards in *Sweden*, brought the Price of Tea in the Northern parts of *Europe* so low, that the *meanest* labouring Men could compass the Purchase of it; when the Connection which the Dealers in this country had with many *Scotsmen* in the Service of the *Swedish* company at *Gottenburg*, introduced the Common Use of the *Drug* amongst the *lowest* of the People; – when *Sugar*, the inseparable Companion of *Tea*, came to be in the Possession of the very *poorest* Housewife, where formerly it had been a great Rarity; – and thereby was *at hand*, to mix with Water and Brandy, or Rum; – and when *Tea* and *Punch* became thus the *Diet* and *Debauch* of *all* the *Beer* and *Ale* Drinkers, the Effects were very *suddenly* and very *severely* felt.

The excise sank in proportion as the abuses grew; the malt duty kept pace with it; the imposts in cities and towns fell still lower, as these vices prevailed more in towns than in the open Country: – Grain yielded no price; and at present, the melancholy experience of every man informs him that there is no *Bullion* left in the country, at least none in proportion to what was some years ago.

Wide and ill-guarded as the coasts of *Scotland* are, the *Running* Trade could never have succeeded without the Assistance of the Inhabitants of the Sea-Coast. – The *Smuggler* must have *Boats* to lay his goods on land; – he must have *carriages* to transport them by Land; he must have *Cover* to shelter them in, until *Carriages* are provided; he must be possessed to the *favourable* Disposition of the People, to secure against *Informations* to the Customhouse; nay, he must be confident of their *Power* to protect his goods from Seizure, or to *rescue* them, if by Accident they should be seized. – all these Aids are *indispensibly* necessary, and yet all of these Aids the *Felon*, who has been *murdering* his country, has hitherto had.

*Boats*, if the weather permit, the *smuggler* is absolutely sure of, whatever part of the coast he touch at. Our fishermen, everybody knows, have for the most part left off their *proper* Business, and dedicated their Time and *Industry* to the Assistance of the *Runner*; in so much that our Markets are far from being so well supplied with fresh fish as heretofore.

*Gentlemen* and *Farmers* go on in the usual Train, – cherishing and hugging to their Bosom the *Smuggler*, that *Leech* that lives by sucking their *Heart's Blood*.

. . . What makes the most *ridiculous* figure in all this matter, is the silliness of the temptation that prevails with them, so notoriously to give up their own interests, and those of their Country; which, besides the prejudices already stated amounts to no more than this. That the Gentleman has his Rum and Brandy, and his Lady Tea and Coffee, at very reasonable Rates, and the Farmer has small Presents of these precious Drugs made him . . .

In England . . . the goods run are a *trifle*, compared with the *regular importation*. But, in *Scotland*, every body knows that the matter stands *quite* otherwise. The *Smuggling* Trade is much *overdone*. The Facility of Running has invited every *petty* Dealer to try it. No foreign spirits *are*, and no Tea can be regularly imported into this country.

Five years after Duncan Forbes wrote so passionately to the Commissioners and Trustees for Improving Fisheries and Manufactures on the topic of smuggling, that body issued the following letter.

Trustees Office
Edinburgh, June 23 1749

Sir,
The Commissioners and Trustees for improving Fisheries and Manufactures in Scotland, considering the great loss and prejudice that arise to the Fisheries and Improvements through Smuggling, and the extravagant use of smuggled foreign spirits and other foreign liquors; the consumpt of our malt liquors, and consequently the malt duty, from which the funds for improvement arise, being thereby lessened; which disables the Trustees from giving such Encouragement as the State of the Fisheries and Manufactures requires, and has brought a reproach upon the Country, greatly to our Prejudice in many respects have therefore resolved to discourage and discountenance the pernicious Practice of Smuggling, and all concerned in or promoting the same, as far as in them lies. And as all the Offices and others employed by them hold Commissions during Pleasure, they have resolved to dismiss from their Service, every Officer, and other Person whatever now employed by them, who shall be a smuggler, or who shall be *aiding* or *assisting* in smuggling, or who shall themselves *use* or *consume*, or suffer to be used or consumed in their Families, any smuggled Foreign spirits or other smuggled liquors, knowing them to have been smuggled, or who shall be any way concerned in degrading his Majesty's Revenue in the Payment of any Duty whatsoever. And they have resolved to make it a Condition of Forfeiture of all premiums to be hereafter granted by them, that the Person or Persons claiming, or who might otherwise be intitled to the same, is or shall be a smuggler, or shall have been any way *aiding* or *assisting* in smuggling, or shall have *used* or *consumed* themselves, or suffered to be used or consumed by their Families, and smuggled foreign spirits or other smuggled liquors, knowing them to have been smuggled, or shall

have been any way concerned in degrading his Majesty's Revenue in the Payment of any Duty whatever. Which Resolutions are thus signified to you, by Order of the Trustees, not only that you may demean yourself agreeably thereto; but that you may, in your Station, exert yourself, and take every proper Opportunity to quash and discourage smuggling, and the consumption of smuggled foreign spirits and other smuggled liquors, as you regard the Interest and Prosperity of your Country, the Extension and Improvement of the Fisheries and Manufactures, and the Favour of the Trustees. I am,

Sir,

Your most humble Servant,

∽

In March 1783, George Bishop submitted a pamphlet for consideration by His Majesty's government on the subject of smuggling. The thrust of Bishop's argument was that duties should be lowered in order to curb smuggling, and while much of what he wrote had a southern English perceptive, with the leading smuggling county of Kent frequently featuring in examples, the statistics which he quoted refer to Britain as a whole, and not just England. Numerous specific references to Scotland were made within the pamphlet:

> *Observations, Remarks and Means, to Prevent Smuggling, Humbly Submitted to the Consideration of the Rt. Hon. The House of Peers and the Hon. House of Commons in Parliament Assembled* – George Bishop, Maidstone, March 1783.

The practice of smuggling has of late years, made such rapid and gigantic strides from the sea coasts, into the very heart of the country, pervading every city, town, and village, as to have brought universal distress upon the fair traders, from the most opulent and respectable, even to the smallest shopkeeper, and requires the united efforts of every honest man to aim at the suppression of it; foreign states having been enriched at the expence of this country, and the destruction of many fair traders.

There are many thousands of sailors employed in this illicit traffick, most of whom are victualled and cloathed, and their vessels repaired in foreign countries, who would otherwise become fishermen, and useful members of the community, thereby greatly enriching the sea coasts, training up a hardy race of sailors and enabling the sea ports, as heretofore, to assist the state in furnishing both ships and men; but so long as that pernicious practice continues, so long will the parish rates remain high and a burthen upon the fair dealer, and the sea ports be unable to afford any real assistance.

The smuggling-cutters are not only large, full of men and well armed, but so well constructed for sailing, that seldom one of them is captured in a year, and those which are taken are frequently permitted to depart with the loss only of part of their cargoes, as an additional encouragement for them to continue the same trade; this conduct is productive of many inconveniencies, and particularly to the farmer, who in many places near the sea, is unable to find hands to do his work, whilst great numbers are employed in removing smuggled goods from one part of the country to another . . .

. . . From the best accounts, there are employed in smuggling sixty thousand of the youngest men and best able to labour, which we may calculate at 1-25th part of the whole of the labourers in the kingdom; and one hundred thousand women and children in retailing and hawking about the country spirits and tea.

Smuggling is one great cause of the high price of provisions, as 1-5th or 1-6th part of all the horses kept are for smuggling, which horses consume more corn than is used in the distillery; if there was no smuggling we should have no occasion for an importation of oats at any time. The charge of maintaining, suppose one hundred thousand horses at one shilling per day each horse, annually amounts to 1,820,000l.

Instead of a contraband let us have a legal trade with all our neighbours, and treat with them, to lower the duties on the manufactures of these kingdoms, by lowering and permitting the manufactures and produce of their countries to be imported here, on paying small duties, which will increase the trade and commerce of this country, employ the poor and lessen the parish rates, to the very great interest of the landed property.

By lowering the duties on tea, coffee, and spirits, the West India trade will be promoted by an increase of the consumption of rum, sugar, and molasses, and in consequence the West Indies will take more goods from hence.

The consumption of rum may be increased to four times the present importation, if the making spirits privately in England and Scotland, and the smuggling of foreign spirits is prevented, and it will greatly promote the use of malt liquors, and of course increase the consumption of malt and hops.

I presume that smuggling is so much increased, the revenue will lose this year full three millions, which renders the taxes very unequal and more burthensome to the inland parts of the kingdom, as the inhabitants on the sea coast have their tea, spirits, wine, currants, raisins, starch, soap, china, glass, and tobacco, mostly smuggled, they contribute nothing to the public for those articles, and of course all the inland counties must be taxed double in order to raise the taxes, which is a very great hardship. If all his Majesty's subjects were taxed alike it would make their burthens much lighter . . .

. . . If the fisheries were encouraged, nature has been very bountiful to Great Britain, as no other part of the globe has such quantities of fish on their coast, and yet she profits but little of that blessing; the people on the Western isles want to be assisted with salt, casks, and small boats, and they would take immense quantities of herrings; the Orkneys abound with lobsters enough to serve all the markets in Europe, but have not boats to catch them, a little assistance would enable them to establish a considerable fishery; if carried on as it might be, we should have such a numerous race of hardy sailors as would make us superior to all the world by sea, and our poor be better fed, clothed and employed in carrying fish to foreign markets, which would be a great encouragement to trade . . .

. . . Both in England and Scotland smuggling in now carried on to a considerable extent, greatly promoted by the high duties on British spirits; in London and Bristol are many private distillers who make large quantities of spirits without paying any duties, and in Scotland there are upwards of ten thousand private stills which make and send immense quantities of spirits to London with some other that have paid the duties, to the very great hurt of the honest trader, by which practice the revenue has been defrauded of upwards of 100,000l this year; if some mode is not found to put a stop to this illicit trade the duties on spirits will come very short . . .

. . . In the year 1777 there were smuggled from Dunkirk 2,500,000 gallons of geneva, about which time there were established at Gottenburg, Newport, Ostend, Dunkirk, and Calais distilleries for making geneva to supply our smugglers with. Geneva is prohibited to be used in the French dominions in favour of their brandies. Upwards of 4,000,000 gallons of geneva are annually smuggled, and about half the quantity of brandy, besides rum and other spirits; there were employed twelve ships of 200 tons burthen each, to fetch rum from the Danish West India islands for Guernsey to smuggle into England . . .

. . . If the 160,000 that now carry on this trade [i.e. British smuggling generally] were employed in fishing, agriculture, &c. the labour of 60,000 men at one shilling and sixpence per day, and the women and children at sixpence per day each, amount to 2,464,000l annually, what an emolument to the trade and commerce of the kingdom! from those who are now supported in drunkenness, rioting, and debauchery by this iniquitous traffic, obviously productive of so numerous a train of evils, that prudence, common honesty, decency, order, and civil government united, cry loudly for redress.

Forbes, Bishop, and their anti-smuggling ilk found solid support from the hierarchy of the established churches, though it should be remembered that many individual clergymen were at best ambivalent about smuggling, and that Forbes himself was not above enjoying a glass of duty-free claret (see p. 135).

Ecclesiastical contributors to the vast undertaking that was the *Statistical Account of Scotland* were almost unanimous in their condemnation of smuggling, as is apparent in numerous quotations from the *Account* in the chapters that follow.

The Reverend John Newton had served as a Tide-Surveyor in

Liverpool before joining the ministry in 1764, and the Glasgow Religious Tract Society subsequently published his 'A Letter on the Sin and Pernicious Effects of Smuggling':

> Dear Sir,
>
> It is suspected, (or rather it is too certainly known), that, among those who are deemed gospel-professors, there are some persons who allow themselves in the practice of dealing in prohibited, uncustomed, or, (as the common phrase is) smuggled goods, to the prejudice of the public revenue, and the detriment of the fair trader . . . there is hardly any set of men more lost to society, or in a situation more dangerous to themselves and others, than the people who are called smugglers. Frequent fighting, and sometimes murder itself, are the consequence of their illicit commerce. Their money is ill-gotten, and it is generally ill-spent. They are greatly to be pitied.

Later lay commentators such as H. Grey Graham were keen to point out the harmful effects of smuggling, even if they appear to have had a sympathetic understanding of its causes:

> Smuggling was carried on far more largely in Scotland than in England, for the Scots fair-traders were satisfied with far smaller profits, and it was executed with more security, as the people helped and encouraged them in resisting customs that were imposed by the English. A vast deal of harm was done by this illicit trade to the inhabitants of the sea-coast – it encouraged a spirit of gambling in their life, it demoralised their tone, it discouraged all active, steady pursuit among those who might have lived by honest fishing in the sea or working on the land. But still the trade went on. In vain the Church denounced it; and also in vain town councils and country gentlemen in several districts of ill repute bound themselves in meetings assembled to discourage with all their strength the equally hurtful 'prevalence of smuggling and tea drinking', for not a third of the tea imported had ever passed a custom-house. It was not till 1806 that enactment against smuggling foreign spirits and the lowering of the duty began to crush a demoralising trade, which had in many places spoiled the industrial life of small towns, like those on the Solway, which were reduced to hopeless inactivity.

It may seem from much of the above that smuggling went unchecked, that the Customs and Excise services were entirely ineffective. Certainly there was incompetence and corruption, but the enormity of the task faced by their officers should not be underestimated.

The sheer physical area covered by the customs' team of each designated 'outport' was vast. For example, on the whole of the north-east coast there were only outports at Montrose, Aberdeen and Inverness in 1707. With the best will in the world, the officers employed could not hope to prevent the landing of contraband along lengthy expanses of frequently unpopulated and remote coastline. Intelligence sources were vital if captures were to be made, and as we know, a high percentage of the population of the country seems to have been pro-smuggler and anti-enforcement. Reliable intelligence was difficult to come by.

The customs service at sea also faced significant difficulties. The revenue cutters were often slower and less manoeuvrable than the smugglers' vessels, and their captains and frequently 'pressed' crew-members were not necessarily the best seamen or the bravest. By contrast, smugglers such as Jack Yawkins (pp. 71 and 154–5) were extremely skilful, and had incentive and motivation on their side.

Convictions for smuggling were rare, since there was such general approval of the activity that evidence was almost impossible to obtain. When smuggled goods were seized, it was not unknown for the smugglers or their accomplices to assemble a mob to seize the contraband from the warehouses where the customs officers had stored it.

The usual procedure, following a seizure, was that the items in question were assessed by Customs or Excise officers, and a 'return of seizure' notice was sent to the Board of Customs in Edinburgh, detailing the capture. The smuggled goods were then either sold or destroyed, with tobacco being burnt. The proceeds of any sales were used to cover any expenses incurred, and the balance was then divided between the exchequer and those officers involved in making the seizure. However, in a market frequently well supplied with the same goods at 'smuggled' prices, it was often difficult for the customs service to find buyers for seized items when they were offered for sale.

According to David Stevenson (*The Beggar's Benison*), in the wake of the Act of Union 'a new bureaucracy of customs and excise officials – comptrollers, surveyors, clerks, tide waiters – quickly spread across Scotland'. Centralisation of control was also a key feature of the changes. Locally-based customs officers were paid by, and reported directly to, the Board of Customs in Edinburgh, whereas previously local councils and landowners had enforced – or chosen not to enforce – payment of duties.

In *A Brief History of HM Customs & Excise*, Gilbert Denton notes that 'the English and Scottish Boards of Customs were combined in 1723 but the assimilation of the two tax systems into a single administration was difficult and the Boards separated in 1742. They were to come together again in 1823, this time to include the Irish Customs.'

'There were also at various periods, even after the Union of 1707, separate Boards of Excise for England and Scotland and another Revenue Board for Ireland. In 1823 one Board of Customs and one Board of Excise were empanelled for the United Kingdom . . . In 1909 the Excise was separated from the Inland Revenue and amalgamated by Order in Council with Customs to become the Board of Customs and Excise.'

On the ground, each outport and its environs was administered by the resident Collector of Customs, whose role was to manage his staff, deal with merchants, ship owners and captains. He was answerable to the Board of Customs for all activities within his remit. His deputy was the Comptroller of Customs, who was also in charge of the accounting and financing functions of the outport. In the mid-1770s the Collector received an annual salary of £50, while the Comptroller received £40.

As J.R.D. Campbell explains in *Clyde Coast Smuggling*, 'from about 1700, the outdoor service in the ports had been organised in three lines; (1) the preventive and cruiser service afloat; (2) the "waiting" staff on the coast: and (3) the corps of riding officers, inland.'

One division of the 'waiting staff' was the Tide-Waiters, under the command of the Tide-Surveyor. The Tide-Surveyor was in charge of the 'king's boat' where an outport was equipped with one. Not every outport had its own boat, and sometimes vessels were hired locally when required.

The Tide-Waiter's job was to meet the vessels 'on the tide', board them, and make sure that all goods brought 'within the limits' were discharged under the jurisdiction of the Land-Waiting staff. The Tide-Waiter – or Tidewatcher – was the lowest grade of official in the service, and his annual salary during the later eighteenth century was £15. Boatmen earned the same salary, and were also known as Tidesmen. They were stationed at creeks throughout the area commanded by the Collector.

Land-Waiters, under the command of the Land-Surveyor, oversaw all goods landed, calculated duties payable and ensured that no goods were released until duty had been paid or acceptable security given. Riding Officers – also known as Coastwaiters – each patrolled a designated ten miles stretch of coast, often on horseback.

The crews of the 'king's boats' received comparatively modest salaries, but these were boosted substantially by bounty payments for smuggling vessels and cargoes captured. In 1750 the captain of such a vessel earned slightly in excess of £24 per year, but J.R.D. Campbell estimates that with their share of bounty payments, which amounted to half of all smuggled goods intercepted, they could have been earning up to the present-day equivalent of £250,000.

In 1809 the Preventive Water Guard was established using Royal Navy sailors to augment the revenue cruisers in their attempts to stop smuggling. The Guard's main role became the protection of cargoes at sea, and it failed to make much of an impact on smuggling. Then, in 1817, the Coast Blockade was formed, consisting of a number of Royal Navy ships, though it later became part of the Coastguard Service. Six Leith-based vessels were active during the 1820s around Scottish coasts, and in addition there were a dozen Admiralty revenue cruisers, plus two cruisers under the control of the Boards of Customs and Excise.

In 1822 the Coastguard Service was formed, when the Riding Officers who undertook anti-smuggling duties on land were combined with the Preventive Water Guard and the naval cruisers which worked further out to sea. The Coastguard Service Act 1856 gave the Admiralty control of the organisation, by which time it had already proved to be a useful reserve for the Royal Navy.

However effective the efforts of the Customs and Excise services, the reality was that smuggling was never going to be defeated, or even severely restricted, by their work. Only changes to legislation relating to duty payments could render smuggling uneconomic.

In an attempt to curb smuggling, Walpole proposed an excise scheme to replace customs duty on wine, spirits and tobacco in 1733. The plan was that these goods could be imported freely, but had to be stored in bonded warehouses until distributed, when an excise tax would be imposed. Walpole had decided that excise officers were more efficient than customs officers, but the public rebelled against the idea. They associated excise with governments of France and of the English Commonwealth period, and both were hated regimes in Britain at that time.

Walpole abandoned his plans in the face of such public opposition, but he appointed Sir John Cope to head a committee which would examine the smuggling problem. The new act of 1736 which followed, toughened the penalties for smuggling, but it had little real effect.

The White Paper produced by Cope's committee noted that 'the number of Custom House Officers who have been beaten, abused and wounded since Christmas 1723 being no less than 250, besides six others who have been actually murdered in the execution of their duty'.

By the time George III came to the throne in 1760, some 800 items existed on which duty had to be paid, but during the next few years more than 1,000 were added.

Financing the American War of Independence from 1775 to 1783 also led to the raising of import duties, and there was the additional encouragement to smugglers that troops who had been used in peacetime to help in the fight against their activities were now being posted to America.

It was clear to most observers that the customs laws were in desperate need of rationalisation and simplification. These laws were contained in no fewer than twenty-seven volumes and were not available for public scrutiny. Many goods were liable to duty under twelve or eighteen separate Acts, and there were a hundred different branches of duty for value, imports and accounts.

When William Pitt the Younger became Prime Minister in 1783 he proposed a straightforward solution to the problem of smuggling, simply cutting levels of duty, as advocated by George Bishop in his pamphlet of March 1783. In 1784 duty on tea was reduced from 119 per cent to just 12.5 per cent. He also pioneered the development of one single duty for each article. An extraordinary 2,615 different resolutions were approved by the House of Commons during one sitting in 1787. Pitt's measures were partially effective, though tea smugglers simply switched to other, high-duty merchandise.

L.M. Cullen (*Smuggling and the Ayrshire Economic Boom*) notes that in the early 1770s, the 'preventative service organised and coordinated their vessels effectively . . . and had a very high rate of success in 1771, 1772 and 1773.' This also played a part in reducing the activities of smugglers.

In *An Inquiry into the Nature and Causes of the Wealth of Nations*, published in 1776 as the smuggling boom was coming to an end, the great free-trade advocate Adam Smith wrote

> Bankruptcies are most frequent in the most hazardous trades. The most hazardous of all trades, that of a smuggler, though when the adventure succeeds it is likewise the most profitable, is the infallible road to bankruptcy. The presumptuous hope of success seems to act here as upon all other occasions, and to entice so many adventurers into those hazardous trades, that their competition reduces their profit below what is sufficient to compensate the risk. To compensate it completely, the common returns ought, over and above the ordinary profits of stock, not only to make up for all occasional losses, but to afford a surplus profit to the adventurers of the same nature with the profit of insurers. But if the common returns were sufficient for all this, bankruptcies would not be more frequent than in other trades.

Cullen also quotes John Galt, who, in his 1821 novel *Annals of the Parish* (see pp. 162–164), chronicled the change in smuggling fortunes.

Referring to the year 1770, Galt's narrator observed that '. . . the darkest cloud of the smuggling had past over, at least from my people . . .'

But the smuggling trade in Scotland was far from dead. Regarding 1778, the narrator wrote about '. . . a revival of that wicked mother of many mischiefs, the smuggling trade, which concerned me greatly'.

What finally killed smuggling was Britain's free-trade policy of the 1840s, which cut import duties to comparatively low levels. This was principally the work of Sir Robert Peel, who became Prime Minister in 1841. His tariff reforms ended with repeal of the Corn Laws in 1846. Peel said of the Customs Service in 1843: 'I confess I distrust everything about the Customs, so far as to feel assured that a vast many have been dishonest and none have been vigilant.'

Peel chose to follow Pitt's example and lower duties rather than raise them, in order to encourage people to buy more dutiable goods. Received wisdom had always been to raise levels of duty and increase the range of goods to which they applied.

By the time Peel became Prime Minister the country was nearly bankrupt, and duties collected by the Customs and the Excise services were vital to the economy. Peel's tactics were therefore notably bold. He abolished duty on more than 600 items, and reduced it on many others. To make up the fiscal shortfall – at least until the situation stabilised and people were buying more dutiable goods – he reintroduced income tax, first levied by Pitt during Britain's war with Napoleonic France, and abandoned in 1816. This enabled Peel to balance his budgets, while the smuggling trade declined dramatically.

The 1911 edition of the *Encyclopaedia Britannica* outlined the main provisions of the 1876 Customs Consolidation Act, which illustrates by its very existence that smuggling had not been totally eradicated at that time.

Vessels engaged in smuggling are liable to forfeiture and their owners and masters to a penalty not exceeding £500. Smuggled and prohibited goods are liable to forfeiture. Officers of customs have a right of search of vessels and persons. Fraudulent evasion or attempted evasion of customs duties renders the offender subject to forfeit either treble the value of the goods or £100 at the election of the commissioners of customs. Heavy penalties are incurred by resistance to officers of Customs, rescue of persons or goods, assembling to run goods, signalling smuggling vessels, shooting at vessels, boats, or officers of the naval or revenue service, cutting adrift customs vessels, offering goods for sale under pretence of being smuggled, &c.

However, in 1887 the Board of Customs in Edinburgh issued a report that noted:

With the reduction of duties and the removal of all needless and vexatious restrictions, smuggling has greatly diminished and the public sentiments with regard to it have undergone a very creditable change. The smuggler is no longer an object of public sympathy, or a hero of romance, and people are beginning to awake to the perception of the fact that the offence is less a fraud on the Revenue than a robbery of the fair trader. Smuggling proper is almost entirely confined to tobacco, spirits and watches . . .'

# 2

# SMUGGLED GOODS

Having examined the circumstances in which smuggling took place, attitudes towards it, and attempts to curb it by enforcement and legislation, it is interesting to take a look at some of the commodities which were regularly smuggled. More details about these commodities and the manner of their smuggling will be found in the geographically-based chapters that follow. As whisky smuggling, in all its many guises, was such an important part of Scottish economic and social life for the best part of two centuries, a separate chapter has been devoted to it.

As has already been noted, smugglers would deal in any commodities that were sufficiently highly taxed to make the risks worthwhile, and the list of goods that were smuggled into Scotland at one time or another is a very long one. It includes corn and cattle, which were regularly smuggled from Ireland, silks, lace and linen, along with such apparently unlikely items as nutmegs, liquorice, coffee cups, hair powder, starch, sealing wax, vinegar, syrup of maiden hair and coffin nails, not to mention playing cards.

During the eighteenth century, a pack of playing cards carried a duty of 6d., but only when complete with the fifty-second card, the Ace of Spades, which was elaborately embossed to deter forgery. Forging an Ace of Spades was punishable by hanging, which is why the Ace of Spades became known colloquially as 'the Hanging Card'.

Tobacco, tea, wine and spirits were particularly attractive to smugglers as they were valuable relative to their bulkiness, and in Scotland these were the most commonly smuggled types of contraband, along with salt.

## Tobacco

Tobacco smuggling dated from the imposition of a high level of duty by that great tobacco-hater, King James I, and during much of the eighteenth century, tobacco was one of the most significant high-duty, legal trading commodities in Scotland. Unsurprisingly then, it was very attractive to smugglers. It became even more attractive after 1784, when duty on tea was significantly reduced, and smugglers required another commodity which promised large profits.

In *A History of the Scottish People 1560-1830*, T.C. Smout notes that 'imports of tobacco from Chesapeake Bay in America increased . . . from eight million pounds in 1741 to forty-seven million pounds in 1771: the Scottish share of the tobacco trade similarly rose from ten per cent in 1738 to fifty-two per cent in 1769 largely because Scottish enterprise proved better fitted than English to meet the rising tide of demand for tobacco from the French.'

In 1762, tobacco accounted for eighty-five per cent of Scottish imports and fifty-two per cent of the country's exports. Writing of Glasgow's 'Tobacco Lords', Henry Grey Graham (*The Social Life of Scotland in the Eighteenth Century*) observed that 'by 1760 wealth [in Glasgow] had grown apace; the cargoes of rum and tobacco from Virginia and Maryland and the West Indies were bringing fortunes to traders.

'Everything seemed in their favour till the American war in 1776 broke out and ruined the great Virginian trade. Disastrous failures followed, princely fortunes were lost, and many who had dominated society for thirty or forty years had to struggle on with small incomes and to sink into obscurity.'

Tobacco smuggling tended to involve a network of couriers organised by the merchants who ran the smuggling operations, as tobacco was distributed widely, unlike salt, for example, which was usually used close to the places where it was brought ashore.

David Staig, the Collector of Customs at Dumfries, reported in March 1787 that he believed at Langholm '. . . there is a great deal of tobacco smuggled and manufactured under cover of one or two real certificates . . .'.

In other words, the tobacco had actually been smuggled, but was processed – or 'manufactured' with proper authority, as though it was duty-paid 'unmanufactured' tobacco. '. . . under the protection of which [certificates] they manufacture only smuggled tobacco'. Staig recalled raiding premises in Langholm the previous year with a party of twenty dragoons, and seizing 7,000lb of '. . . manufactured and unmanufactured tobacco'.

## TEA

While the notion of smuggling spirits and tobacco seems perfectly understandable to us today, we tend to be surprised at the idea of what to us is a cheap, innocuous beverage like tea being the subject of major smuggling operations.

Formal tea cultivation began in China, around AD350, and it was first taxed in that country in 780, due to its popularity. In 1610 tea appeared in Europe with Dutch traders, and in 1652 it arrived in Britain, courtesy of the Dutch East India Company. A mere eight years later the government saw fit to tax it, with a duty of 8d. per gallon being imposed on tea sold in coffee-houses, and in 1680 customs duty of 5s. per pound was introduced.

By the middle of the eighteenth century, the tea tax had risen to an extraordinary 119 per cent, which not surprisingly made it a prime smuggling commodity. Because of the cross-section of society who drank tea, the smuggling operations involved everyone from farm-workers and fishermen to priests and politicians. Syndicates were formed to 'import' and distribute smuggled tea within communities. Up to 70 per cent of the tea drunk in Britain had been smuggled, according to contemporary calculations, but even smuggled tea could cost up to 10s. 6d. (53p.) per pound by the 1770s – one-third of the average weekly wage at the time.

Holland and the countries of Scandinavia were the main sources of tea smuggled into England and Scotland, and during the late eighteenth century the Dutch port of Flushing (now Vlissingen) was the principal centre for the trade.

Merchant ships from the countries supplying smuggled tea would anchor off the coast of England or Scotland in order to allow local fishing boats to transport the tea ashore.

According to Jan Fairley (*Chambers' Scottish Drink Book*), the fishermen involved in smuggling '. . . hid their boats in caves connected to remote lanes, snickets and bridleways which can still be found in the Fife ports of Pittenweem, Anstruther and St Monans today'.

In addition to smuggling, adulteration of tea was common, much as it is with illegal drugs today. Old, used tea-leaves might be mixed with fresh leaves, while willow or liquorice would be added to black tea. Least palatable of all was the additive known as 'smouch' – a subtle blend of ash leaf and sheep dung!

Tea smuggling continued to increase, until in 1784 Prime Minister William Pitt the Younger's Commutation Act was passed by parliament. This reduced tax from 119 per cent to just 12.5 per cent, and tea smug-gling ended virtually overnight. An influential figure in this dramatic cut was the grandson of the first tea shop proprietor in England, Thomas Twining, who had a substantial vested interest in the subject, as Twinings had become leading tea merchants by that time.

Tea was first introduced to Scotland, it is believed, by James, Duke of York, brother to Charles II, on a visit to Holyrood Palace during the seventeenth century, and the popularity of tea increased after the imposition of the Malt Tax in Scotland in 1725 (see p. 65).

In May 1675 it is recorded that Provost Robert Mylne of Linlithgow legally imported 4lb of tea for the Duchess of Linlithgow – at a cost of 88 guilders. Tea was so highly taxed, however, that even the upper echelons of society only bought small quantities.

The first legal British importation of tea not to be shipped into London docks arrived at Leith in April 1735. Leading Edinburgh tea merchant Andrew Melrose had chartered the 422-ton schooner *Isabella*, which set off to Canton in China in December 1833. When the vessel arrived in her home port sixteen months later, she was carrying 7,000 chests of tea.

According to H. Grey Graham, 'the fashion of tea-drinking, becoming common about 1720, had to make its way against vehement opposition. The patriotic condemned tea as a foreign drink hurtful to national industry; the old-fashioned protested against it as a new-fangled folly; the robust scorned it as an effeminate practice; magistrates, ministers, and energetic laymen put it in the same category as smuggled spirits, anathematised its use by the poor, among whom (they warned them) it would assuredly produce "corruption of morals and debility of constitution".'

In a footnote to the text, Graham added that 'medical men regarded tea with disfavour. Commended in lethargic diseases, headaches, gouts, and gravel, it was considered hurtful to weak constitutions if much used . . .'.

Along with whisky [observed Graham] tea came into vogue as a dangerous rival to ale . . . The introduction of tea was met with animosity by the haters of new-fashioned beverages and the patriotic lovers of old native products. Town councils, heritors, and ministers equally denounced it, and parishes afflicted with smuggling entered into resolutions to abstain from tea, just as people take pledges today against alcoholic drinks. In 1744 the heritors of East Lothian complained that 'the luxurious and expensive way of living has shamefully crept in upon all classes of the people, who, neglecting the good and wholesome produce of our own country, are got into the habits of an immoderate use of French wines and spirits'; as also, 'that the drinking of tea, and especially among people of the lower rank, has arrived at an extravagant excess to the hurt of private families by loss of their time, increase of their expense, and negligence of a diet more suitable to their health and station'. Farmers and lairds in parishes entered into solemn bonds, under self-imposed penalties, not to drink a drug so demoralising and pernicious. But in spite of all opposition, in spite of its cost, it won its way into the affections and homes of all classes – not to the hurt, but to the advantage of the people, who found in it a substitute for far less innocent drink . . . by 1750 the most stalwart and conservative had succumbed to its attractions, and tea (tempered with brandy) took the place of ale as a necessity at every breakfast table.

In *Highland Folk Ways*, Dr I.F. Grant wrote that 'tea-drinking was sometimes preached against as an effeminate habit and I was given a small earthenware jar in which an old lady of long ago in North Uist had kept her supply of tea carefully hidden away in a cranny in the wall. Nevertheless, all through the eighteenth century, it was steadily making its way into the regular dietary of the Highlanders.'

She also noted 'tea was, however, still an expensive luxury at the end of the century, for it cost 5s. or 7s. 6d. a lb. Whereas port and Malaga [sweet, dark, fortified dessert wine from southern Spain] could be bought for 15s. a dozen bottles, and a sheep cost from 3s. 6d. to 8s.'.

## WINE

Wine was being imported to Scotland by the mid-thirteenth century, and tax was imposed on it for the first time in 1612 by James VI. In that year alone the tax generated revenue of £32,000. Astonishingly, one-third of Edinburgh's corporate income was provided by duty paid on Leith-imported wine.

Claret was a great Scottish favourite; indeed it was almost a national drink for people of all classes before whisky-drinking became widespread outside the Highlands. Claret was even shipped directly into Inverness during the first half of the eighteenth century, so it was not just Edinburgh sophisticates who were drinking it. Traditionally, Scottish judges would have an open bottle of claret in front of them in court, which would be emptied during the course of the session.

Wine-drinking had become very common in the Highlands and Islands by the late sixteenth century, and smuggling of wine into the Hebrides and the north-west mainland was in full flow during the first half of the seventeenth century.

After the Act of Union in 1707 the tax on claret was increased significantly, because the English wished to antagonise the French, and so taxed their wines much more highly than those of Portugal and Spain. During times of war with France, the importation of French wine was banned completely.

As a result of the Treaty of Methuen between England and Portugal in 1703 the import of British textiles into Portugal was allowed in return for a significantly lower level of import duty on port wine from Portugal than that which applied to French wine.

Despite the high level of taxation, however, great quantities of claret continued to be drunk in Scotland, and inevitably much of it was smuggled. Prince Charles Edward Stuart was a great claret drinker, and it remained a favourite drink of the nobility until Victorian times.

Smugglers did not just try to transport cargoes of wine without payment of duty, they also tried to pass French wine off as the product of countries with which trade was allowed during the numerous Anglo-French conflicts of the eighteenth and early nineteenth centuries.

In February 1710 the Board of Customs in Edinburgh wrote to the various Collectors of Customs in the outports:

> The season of the year now approaching in which we are to expect wines to be imported from Portugal, Spain and the Levant and there being great reason to believe that the merchants will use the same endeavours and industry as they have formerly done to import French wines under the denominations of wines of those countries we therefore think fit to give you this timely advise for your government and for preventing the damage the revenue has hitherto suffered by irregular proceedings of officers. When any ship arrives with wines, after the wines are entered and landed (and not before) you are with great care and circumspection to view and taste. All the wines you find cause to believe are French or have any mixture of French wines in them you are to lay your hands upon them and give us notice thereof with the particular circumstance of the case.

Quite how the Collectors were meant to tell French wines from those of other countries is not explained, unless their palates were more experienced and discriminating than might have been expected. Presumably, however, they often had fun viewing and tasting, 'with great care and circumspection'.

There is evidence of vessels supposedly sailing from Spain to Scotland, and landing cargoes of wine at ports on the Forth, when in fact they had come directly from Bordeaux with cargoes of French wine. Claret from Bordeaux would be shipped to Inverness for the leading merchant Bailie Steuart (see pp. 134–7) via Dutch ports in order to lessen the likelihood of ships carrying it being seized by customs officers. It was then 're-exported' from Amsterdam and Rotterdam to the Moray Firth.

In *Knee Deep in Claret*, Billy Kay notes that a letter written in 1710 by the Elgin merchant William Sutherland to Archibald Dunbar of Thunderton, the provost of Elgin, regarding a shipment of French wine, gives a good insight into how the mechanics of landing smuggled goods might work. It also reminds us that respectable public office was no barrier to involvement with smuggled goods:

> I have ventured to order Skipper Watt, how soon it pleases God he come to the firth, to call at Caussie and cruise betwixt that and Burgh-head,

until you order boats to waite him. He is to give half of what I have of the same sort with his last cargoe, to any having your order. Its not amiss to secure one boat at Caussie as well as the burgh boats. The signall he makes will be all his sails furled, except his main Topsaile; and the boats you order to him are to lower their saile when within musket shott, and then hoist it again; this, least he should be surprised with catch poles. He is to write you before he sails to Bordeaux.

On one occasion in the spring of 1716 a cargo of claret destined for Dunbar was seized, but he managed to retrieve it by the simple expedient of having the lock of the cellar where it was being stored in Elgin smashed open. Alexander Erskine, Collector of Customs at Inverness, protested furiously in a letter of April 1716, but Dunbar escaped censure, perhaps due to the intervention of Charles Eyre, solicitor to HM Customs, and a man who, Kay suggests, '. . . was a great lover of claret, and probably not averse to accepting cheap contraband wine when it came his way'.

Two government cruisers were stationed in the Moray Firth in 1725 in an attempt to curb smuggling, but, as Billy Kay writes, 'with the men of power and influence in the Highlands, such as Duncan Forbes of Culloden, if not actively involved in the activity, then certainly turning a blind eye to it, feeble gestures of this sort were doomed to failure. Cheap claret, free of duty, retained its privileged position on Highland tables for the remainder of the century.'

The Scots had long been famous for their wine and for their ability to consume it. 'Bacchus hath great guiding here,' wrote the English ambassador from Edinburgh with regard to the court, when James VI was entertaining his wife's brother, the Duke of Holstein, in 1598.

The wine bills [in a 'nobleman's establishment'] were out of all proportion to the other expenditure, though wine was cheap compared to articles of food, which were dear considering their price in other countries and the high value of money. Before the Customs were made uniform in England and Scotland, Annan was the headquarters of an extensive smuggling trade for carrying wine, brandy, and other foreign goods into Cumberland, often on men's backs concealed in loads of hay, sacks of wool, or sheafs of wheat. The coast was covered with small ships in the service of smugglers, and in 1711 a Custom-house officer writes to his superior in Edinburgh that at Ruthwell [a small village just north of the Solway Firth, six miles west of Annan] the people are such friends to the traffic, 'no one can be found to lodge a Government officer for a night.'

– *C. L. Johnstone*, The Historical Families of Dumfriesshire and the Border Wars
(1878)

## SPIRITS

The importation of foreign spirits into Scotland commenced considerably later than the importation of wine. Gin was a favourite with smugglers, and large quantities found their way from the 'gin capital' of Rotterdam into Scotland, with the Northern Isles being particularly enthusiastic importers (see *The North and Northern Isles*, Chapter 6). The popularity of gin had developed in Britain during the reign of Dutch-born William III (from 1689). When he declared war on France soon after taking the throne, French imports were banned, which affected not only wine but also brandy, so gin – originally known as genever, and often referred to as such in contemporary documents – became one of Britain's leading spirits. Excessive gin consumption led to a series of acts, from 1729 onwards, designed to restrict gin distillation and sales, which only made the situation more attractive for the smuggling fraternity.

Brandy, principally from France and the Mediterranean countries, was smuggled in 'half-ankers' – known as kegs – holding around four and a half imperial gallons, and as Frances Wilkins writes in *Dumfries & Galloway's Smuggling Story*, 'by the 1750s the market was flooded with various cheap brandies'. She notes that on 27 December 1750 George Moore, a merchant in the Isle of Man involved in the smuggling trade, wrote to Mr Gerard van Hoogmorf in Rochelle on the subject of 'cognac brandy'. Moore declared that 'the price exceeds the market of this Isle, which is becoming glutted with brandy from Cette and from a different party in Spain, where the cheapness is inviting'. According to Dr Johnson, 'Claret is the liquor for boys; port for men; but he who aspires to be a hero must drink brandy'.

Rum was a comparative newcomer to the British drinker, only being imported in significant amounts from the West Indies after the end of the Seven Years War (1756–63). It proved notably popular in Scotland, often being preferred to French brandy and to native whisky. Inevitably, it was smuggled into the country, especially onto the west coast, where vessels from the West Indies usually made landfall.

## SALT

Salt was extremely important to the Scottish economy, as it was an essential preservative for the fishing industry and for meat, which was preserved in brine. Pickled herrings and salt beef were exported from Scotland to the tobacco plantations of the American southern states, where they provided nourishment for the tobacco barons' slave workforces.

Salt was an easy target for taxation, being such an essential commodity; but there was also an import duty on salt in order to protect the domestic salt-producing industry from foreign competition. In the articles of the Act of Union of 1707, salt was one of the commodities which was not initially taxed at the higher rate prevailing in England (see p. 4).

To encourage the Scottish fishing industry, and the vast herring fishery in particular, any duty paid on salt used for herring pickling could be recovered from the government. Inevitably, smuggled salt was frequently used, and if the users then 'reclaimed' duty on it – duty which they had never paid – herring fishing became a lucrative business.

The collection of 'salt duties' occupied a large part of the customs officers' working hours in most outports. There were stringent regulations regarding the way in which various salted commodities were packed into barrels, and this required officers to observe relevant transactions in every herring port with great care.

During the latter part of the eighteenth century the 36-ton wherry, *Prince of Wales*, was posted to the Clyde, where its principal duty was to deter smuggling of salt from Ireland onto the Scottish west coast.

Salt was often smuggled from Ireland and the Isle of Man because it attracted a high level of duty in order to protect the trade of salt-making areas in the west of Scotland. Smuggling was attractive for this reason, but also because the illegally imported salt was of far better quality than that produced domestically.

In the *Statistical Account of Scotland* (1791-99), Isaac Davidson, DD, minister of the Parish of Whithorn in Galloway, wrote that

> Rock salt refined, and made into white salt is eight times as strong as that made in the frith of Forth; and at Liverpool the former is sold, the best at 8d. and small at 5d. per bushel, exclusive of duties; while that made in the frith of Forth is sold at 1s. 3d. Here is a temptation to smuggling, which cannot be resisted; and this ruinous contraband trade flourishes in the west of England and Scotland . . . Almost all our salt being smuggled, there is a dependence upon a precarious supply at the time of laying in our winter provision; and I have known of poor people losing that provision . . . The duty on English salt is 5s. per bushel, weighing 56lb.; but I never heard of 1s. of duty being received, it being all smuggled. Make the duty lower, and it will be paid.

Writing of the towns on the southern shores of the Firth of Forth during the mid-1720s, Daniel Defoe (*A Tour Through the Whole Island of Britain*) noted the availability of coal in the nearby hills. 'The coal being thus at hand, they make very good salt at almost all the towns upon the shore of the Forth; as at Seaton, Cockenny,

Preston, and several others, too many to name: They have a very great trade for this salt to Norway, Hamburgh, Bremen, and the Baltick; and the number of ships loaded there with salt every year is very considerable . . .' Although he does not name Prestonpans, the name of the village betrays its origins. In *Place-Names of Scotland*, James B. Johnston noted that Preston means 'priest's village', and that by 1611 the settlement was named Prestounepannis. 'Salt pans made here by Newbattle monks, *a.* 1200'.

In 1670 there were no fewer than fifteen coal mines in the area around the Firth of Forth, and while some coal was exported, much was used to boil the water off the salt pans. Domestic salt was of poorer quality than air-evaporated Biscay salt, but it was cheaper, and was widely used in Scotland, and some was even exported. The Biscay salt was a much more efficient preservative, and was imported to Scotland in considerable quantities.

In *The Book of Arran*, W.M. Mackenzie declared that 'no impost was so iniquitous as that upon salt, which restricted a necessity, starved the fishing industry, and gave an unwholesome stimulus to the manufacture of kelp. In the circumstances its record, while quite as serious, is even more repellent than that of the others. When a salt-boat was captured it was usually scuttled, sometimes even by the occupants, which disposed of the salt, not so easy to transfer as kegs of liquor; but not infrequently there was more serious business toward, as we here see.' There follows an extract from the *Edinburgh Advertiser* for 22 October 1796:

> On Wednesday evening a young man was shot in a salt boat, between the Isles of Pladda and Arran, by a boat's crew belonging to Captain Dowie, of the *Prince Augustus Frederick*, Revenue Cutter. The crew of the smuggling boat having with their oars opposed that of the Revenue's boat making a seizure of it. It is to be lamented that the poor people on the coast should persevere in a trade which by the laws of our country subjects their property to seizure, and exposes their lives to destruction if they make any opposition to the officers of Revenue – There have of late years been several instances where the lives of these unfortunate persons have been sacrificed when attempting a feeble resistance to preserve a few bolls of salt.

In his *Journal of a Tour in Scotland 1819*, the author Robert Southey made some interesting observations regarding salt smuggling. Writing about Fort Augustus, he noted for Friday, 17 September:

> When we went down stairs in the morning some half dozen sacks of salt were lying just within the door, which 'the Gauger' had seized in the night. About half of them were reprieved during the day by the summary mode of carrying them off. This illicit trade in salt grows out

of the indulgence of Government in allowing it duty-free for the fisheries. The people are not content with obtaining it for this purpose, and for their own domestic use: they carry on an extensive contraband trade in it with the Lowlands, and this will probably render it necessary to deprive them of an indulgence which, being reasonable in itself, is thus grossly abused.

Later, regarding the Moor of Rannoch, he observed that

A great contraband salt trade is carried on upon these roads. Garrow told us of an instance which had lately occurred within his knowledge. A man who had formerly worked on the roads, but who found that the illicit salt-trade was a more gainful occupation, made a bargain at the Kings House to give six bolls of salt for a new cart, and deliver four of them at Tynedrum, and the other two at Balachulish. The value of the cart was six or seven pound, the salt had cost him 7s. 6d. per boll, and he estimated the charge of delivering it as 10s. so the bargain on his side was a good one. On the other hand the purchaser sold it again for 2£ per boll, and thus made more than an equal profit. His market for the four bolls was at Killin; I did not learn whither the rest was conveyed from Balachulish. The Excise officers give very little interruption to this trade, because the value of a seizure is far from being an adequate compensation for the trouble and risque of making it. There is a great profit to be made by dealing in smuggled salt, and very little by seizing it. The Landlord of the Kings House took that Inn ten years ago, and had only a capital of 70£ to begin with. This year he has taken a large farm, and laid out 1500£ in stocking it.

For many years salt, like whisky, was more highly taxed in England than it was in Scotland. In 1822, a farmer called Harding was shot by an excise officer at Great Corby in Cumberland while smuggling three stones of salt from Scotland, destined for pig-curing purposes. Salt duty was reduced the following year, and repealed in 1825.

## Coal

The situation regarding coal was the reverse to most Scottish smuggling in that it was 'export smuggling'. A high level of duty was payable on coal being exported from Scotland, and one of the ways in which coal was successfully smuggled was for the skipper of a coal-carrying vessel to claim his journey was to take place in British waters, for example from Alloa to Dundee. Bad weather would then supposedly force the vessel out into the open sea, sometimes allegedly lasting until the vessel was forced into a port in Sweden or Holland!

There were various documents designed to ensure that coal was not smuggled abroad, but stayed within British waters, giving permission for the voyage, noting 'clearance' from port, and listing the contents of the vessel for verification upon arrival. A financial bond also had to be paid by the skipper or the owner of the cargo in question, redeemable only when the customs authorities were satisfied that all the paperwork was in order.

However, the skippers of smaller vessels plying their trade on the Firth of Forth were not required to have formal 'clearance' regarding the quantity of coal they had on board their vessels, so inevitably the true cargoes might be fifty per cent greater than that noted in the skipper's 'sufferance'. The skipper might then apply to change the nature of his voyage to an overseas destination, paying duty on the amount of coal noted in the sufferance, rather than on the actual cargo. This was then exported duty-free, and a useful profit was made in the process. Another ruse was to take on extra coal at sea from coasters after the original cargo had been cleared, then return to port and pay duty to export the quantity of cargo specified in the clearance.

# 3

# WHISKY SMUGGLING

The smuggling of whisky was unique compared to other commodities in Scotland. It was smuggled *within* Scotland, *out* of Scotland into England, and occasionally to Ireland.

With regard to whisky, the term 'smuggling' has a much broader definition than in more general usage. Here 'smuggling' refers not only to the transportation and distribution of illicit spirit, but also to its manufacture. When reference is made to 'whisky smugglers', the intention is usually to embrace those engaged in producing it, as well as in transporting and supplying it to the customer.

Illicit distilling tended to take place in comparatively remote locations, where the approach of an excise officer would be preceded by plenty of warning, though urban stills were far from uncommon. In his 1799 *History of Edinburgh*, Hugo Arnot noted that a few years previously it had been estimated that the capital possessed some four hundred stills. Alas, for the government, only eleven of them held licences.

The famous district of Glenlivet on Speyside was a notably popular location for illicit whisky distilling during the eighteenth and early nineteenth centuries, having the optimum assets of an excellent fresh water supply, abundant peat to fuel the stills, and ready access to barley for malting. It was remote, yet not too remote from towns and villages thirsty for its 'make'. It is often said that during the late eighteenth century no fewer than two hundred illicit stills were operating in Glenlivet, and though such a figure seems remarkably high, the glen was clearly well-favoured by whisky smugglers. 'Glenlivet' whisky came to have a real cachet about it, and sold for a higher price than illicit whisky made elsewhere.

In *The Whisky Distilleries of the United Kingdom*, Alfred Barnard noted, after visiting Glenlivet, that 'formerly smuggling houses were scattered on every rill, all over the mountain glens, and at that time the smugglers used to lash the kegs of spirit on their backs, and take them all the way to Aberdeen and Perth for disposal'.

'Disposal' was frequently the most risky stage of the entire smuggling venture, and smugglers often resorted to subterfuges, such as mock funerals, with coffins full of illicit spirit, in order to outwit the excisemen.

In 1953 the great folklorist, songwriter and poet, Hamish Henderson, recorded the reminiscences of an old man on Speyside for Edinburgh University's School of Scottish Studies. According to the interviewee, when illicitly-distilled whisky was smuggled from Greenmire, in the Glenlivet area, straw ropes were sometimes put around the wheels of the carts and the feet of the horses to muffle them. The theory was that anyone observing the silently-moving vehicles would imagine they had seen a ghost and do nothing for fear of ridicule.

Sometimes concealment and subterfuge were scorned by the bolder smugglers, and 'pony trains' laden with whisky would travel quite openly, as Thomas Guthrie recalled in his autobiography, published in 1874:

> They [smugglers] rode on Highland ponies, carrying on each side of their small, shaggy but brave and hardy steeds, a small cask or 'keg' as it was called, of illicit whisky, manufactured amid the wilds of Aberdeenshire or the glens of the Grampians. They took up a position on some commanding eminence during the day, where they could, as from a watch-tower, descry the distant approach of the enemy, the exciseman or gauger: then, when night fell, every man to horse, descending the mountains only six miles from Brechin, they scoured the plains, rattled into villages and towns, disposing of their whisky, and as they rode leisurely along, beating time with their formidable cudgels on the empty barrels to the great amusement of the public and the mortification of the excisemen, who had nothing for it but to bite their nails and stand, as best they could, the raillery of the smugglers and the laughter of the people.

Usually the whisky was distributed in towns and cities by 'bladdermen', so named because they would conceal bladders filled with whisky about their persons. In other cases metal 'dogs' strapped to their chests fulfilled the same function. Women made good couriers, as considerable quantities of spirit could be concealed beneath their voluminous skirts, and excise officers would, in theory at least, be less likely to undertake body searches.

Speyside was undoubtedly the highest-profile area in Scotland for illicit distilling, but there is no shortage of tales relating to whisky smuggling from all corners of the country. In the far north, for example, George Fraser was notorious as one of the leading distillers and whisky smugglers in Caithness during the second half of the nineteenth century.

Fraser, of Broubster, near Reay, reputedly ran a total of eleven stills, and the abandoned church of Shurrery was used for the storage of his illicit spirit. On one occasion, being chased by an excise officer, Fraser waded out into Loch Tormaid and deposited his still so that there was no incriminating evidence of his activities.

The small island of Stroma lies in the Pentland Firth, between Caithness and the Orkney Isles, and illicit distilling was rife there, with even a local schoolmaster playing a part at one stage, by selling smuggled whisky from his schoolhouse.

In *A Wild and Open Sea*, James Miller tells how the revenue cutter *Prince of Wales* took part in a raid on Stroma in May 1816, during which two stills were captured and destroyed. In March 1837 revenue-man Terence Macmahon led a party which captured two working stills and 150 bushels of malt. The distiller, Peter Green, was arrested and charged, as reported in the *Northern Star* during March of 1837. Macmahon devoted much attention to Stroma and the nearby island of Swona, in the Pentland Firth, often using fog as a cover for early-morning raids. In 1838 the *John o' Groat Journal* reported he had been so successful in his efforts that as a result the people of the island had become '. . . steady, sober and discreet'. The same newspaper, however, reported that Macmahon and a party of fellow officers were forced to flee the island of Shapinsay in January 1840 due to threats of violence from distillers and their henchmen, as reported in the *John O'Groat Journal* for 24 January 1840.

In common with many places in rural Scotland, the population of Stroma actually fell as smuggling was suppressed, as it formed a vital source of income for many island families. People were forced to find work on the mainland, and some opted for emigration, ending up in Canada, New Zealand and Australia.

In November 1841 coastguard officers seized whisky on the tiny islands of the Skerries, east of Stroma, and the pilots of Stroma, who guided vessels through the treacherous waters of the Pentland Firth, were suspected of involvement. One was Peter Green, the illicit distiller. Four suspects, including Green, were told to report to Burwick in Orkney to be interviewed about their involvement in the seizure, but during the voyage their boat sank, and all four men drowned.

A recording made by the folklorist Calum MacLean in 1953 for the School of Scottish Studies tells the tale of 'Hairy Donald', a whisky smuggler on the island of Shuna, south-west of Oban. On one occasion, when being pursued by excise officers, Donald hid in a shallow cave surrounded by bushes and heather. His face was sticking out of the cave, but it was so heavily whiskered that it blended perfectly with the heather, and the gaugers failed to spot him. A great deal of 'shebeen whisky', as it was known, was distilled on Shuna.

The same was certainly true of the Isle of Arran, which possessed the virtue of remoteness, along with plentiful supplies of barley and peat, not to mention a thirsty eager market in the growing towns of the mainland across the Firth of Clyde. In *The Book of Arran*, W.M. Mackenzie wrote:

> With the decrease of duties and the relaxation of restrictions so that small distilleries became possible, the temptations to smuggling fell off, while the watchfulness of officers, grown as astute as the smugglers themselves, increased the risks as the possible profits decreased. By 1793 three licensed distilleries were at work in the island, and besides what was consumed in these, the islanders found it the better bargain to send their barley to similar establishments at Campbeltown or to Ayr, Irvine, Saltcoats, and Greenock. Much furtive distilling, however, continued, though the art must have degenerated, when they took to distilling from sour beer imported from Ireland.
>
> Still it must have proved profitable. In 1826 a father, son, and daughter from Arran were convicted, before the Excise court in Rothesay, of illicit distillation. They 'bore the appearance of great destitution,' nevertheless, by the end of the week they had paid their huge fine of £60 . . .
>
> Craigdhu was a namely place for secret distilling, where one practitioner was a muscular lady with a hug like a bear, who once nearly squeezed the life out of a gauger when she received his intrusion with an embrace.
>
> By 1840 illicit distillation had been almost entirely suppressed so far as Kilmorie, the worst offender, was concerned. In 1822 the smuggling of whisky was still well in vogue, as we can judge from the misfortune that befell Malcolm and Angus 'Sellers' and Alexander Crawford with their cargo of twelve casks from Brodick on the night of November 27. A wrecked boat, 'her mast broken by the beam,' and loose casks floated ashore between Ardrossan and Saltcoats next morning, telling all of the disaster that could ever be known. As late as 1860 we have a story of the landing in the south end of three casks of whisky that had paid no duty, which were pounced upon by the Excise officers. Invited to a friendly glass by a brother of the consignee in the inn at Lag, they returned to carry away the casks, from which, however, the whisky had in the interval been run into washing tubs, and replaced with salt water.

The excise officers, or 'gaugers' as they were often known, were just as unpopular with the population at large as their counterparts in the customs service. They were at a perpetual disadvantage, as they were usually operating in terrain that was far more familiar to their adversaries than it was to them, and where they had few friends or potential informers.

Once apprehended, whisky smugglers, like smugglers of most

commodities, often appeared before magistrates who were at worst sympathetic to their plight, and at best were regular customers. Apart from the apparent futility of much of their work, excise officers also frequently faced great danger from whisky smugglers. Serious assaults were common, and a number of officers were killed.

William Nimmo's *History of Stirlingshire* was first published in 1777, and the edition of 1880 was 'Revised, Enlarged, and brought down to the Present Time' by R. Gillespie.

Gillespie noted the existence '. . . some seventy years ago' of James Gilfillan, of the parish of Killearn. Gilfillan was a whisky smuggler with a formidable reputation who was summoned to attend a sheriff court in Drymen for what appeared to be a trivial matter. What Gilfillan did not know, however, was that the local excise officer, one 'Mr Hosie of Bucklyvie', had set a trap, not daring to try to capture him in open country. Hosie had brought in a number of sailors from the revenue cutter which operated on Loch Lomond to help him to apprehend Gilfillan, having obtained information about his smuggling activities that would surely see him sent to jail. The smuggler, however, noticed the blue uniforms of the men through the panels of a door in the court building, and realising what was happening, he turned the key in the door, locking the men inside, and pocketed the key.

He entered the courtroom and found officer Hosie sitting by the window, while two officers moved to guard the door after his entry. Hosie was, according to Nimmo, '. . . somewhat short built, but was of a proud disposition, and waged war against the smugglers with considerable vigour'.

Seeing that he was trapped, Gilfillan '. . . seized the lower sash of the window, pulled it to him, and dashed it with great violence over the officer's head; then vaulting into the road below, walked quietly away, none daring to follow him . . . Hosie was rather seriously cut, and some difficulty was experienced in getting his head extricated from the pane.'

Gillespie also tells of a Stirlingshire smuggling episode that ended in the violent death of an excise officer:

Stationed over the country to assist the regular excisemen were officers, with smaller or larger bodies of assistants, as the necessity of the district might require. These were commonly called 'rangers,' chief of whom was an officer of the name of Dougal. He was a very quiet and inoffensive man, but powerful and of a self-reliant nature. He was much liked by the smugglers, and often told them that a smuggler deserved to be taken if he did not keep smuggler's hours. Mr. Dougal had been repeatedly warned of the threatening character of one of the most villainous of the class, but treated these warning lightly, and said he was a match for him at any time. Once when riding between the villages of Arnprior and Fintry, and on looking accidentally round, he observed this wretch priming his pistol behind a dyke on the roadside. Being at the time unarmed, but possessed of considerable presence of mind, he suddenly dashed his hand into his pocket and took out a small spy-glass. Springing from his horse, he rushed to the place where the ruffian lay concealed, crying, 'Come on, I am ready for you, my lad.' The would-be assassin, taking the spy-glass for a pistol, fled into the wood, and Mr. Dougal rode on his way to Fintry. Some short time after this the officer went amissing, and dark suspicions floated about that he had been the victim of foul play. Ultimately, his body was discovered on the farm of Glins. Traces of a scuffle, and some articles identified as his, were found on the shores of Loch Laggan, and it is believed he was murdered there and his body carried to where it was found, upwards of a mile. Well-grounded suspicion soon fell upon this man, who was afterwards totally rejected by his former companions, and died a wandering outcast.

It was not all doom and gloom for the excise officers, however. They did have their successes, and sometimes it was the smugglers who paid with their lives. According to the *Dundee Advertiser* on 26 July 1816: 'Wm. Dick in the Parish of Blairgowrie, and two others, attempted to bring some whisky they had made into Dundee, but when at Logie Farm were met by Custom House boatmen, who fired at them, wounding Dick it is feared mortally.'

During the summer of 1816, a group of seven men from the Highlands smuggled casks of whisky across the Tay to woodland near Birkhill House, where they waited in the woodland to transport the casks further south on a cart. Customs officers arrived at Balmerino, captured the kegs, and took them back to their boat. While they were doing this, the smugglers recruited eleven local men, and together they attacked the officers, but their stones and sticks were no match for the officers' guns and cutlasses, and the whisky was forfeited.

Sometimes the actions of excise officers were deemed to be too heavy-handed, and in the 1926 publication *The Story of Glenisla: traditional, historical, social*, David Grewar gave an interesting account of a controversial excise raid aimed at whisky smugglers in the glen:

There is at least one raid of which there is documentary evidence to prove its authenticity. Certain events, however, preceded it. Dalnamer, near the head of the glen, was occupied by three or four families, all of whom took an active part in smuggling. Before the illicit distillers were driven to the remoter corries, operations were carried on at Dalnamer in a sheep-cot, in close proximity to the houses. The excisemen found out this, and oftener than once favoured it with their attentions. On one occasion tidings were received of their approach. A considerable quantity of barley lay fermenting in the barn, and if the officers saw this, trouble was sure to follow. The barley was too bulky to be easily hidden, and the excise were at hand. It seemed as if the avoidance of a seizure was impossible. At last one of the smugglers had a bright idea. It was spring-time, and a field of lea was ready for the seed. Why not sack up the barley and dump it down at regular intervals, as if for sowing? Willing hands at once proceeded to fill the sacks, while others yoked a cart. Every trace of its presence was removed, and the cart was going through the field depositing the sacks when the excisemen arrived. They found nothing of an illicit nature, and never once suspected the ruse, which they actually witnessed, being carried into effect.

At a later date a couple of excisemen again put in an appearance. There was no intimation of their approach until they were seen within a few hundred yards of the place. Distillation had recently been engaged in, but everything had been removed except the sma' still. To lose the valuable 'head' and 'worm,' which were of expensive copper, would be a great misfortune to the smugglers, but such seemed inevitable. The quick wit of a smuggler saved the situation. Seizing an old pitcher he rushed up the steep rocky face of Craig-en-Gash, in front of the house. The excisemen saw him, as they were meant to do, and noting that he was carrying something at once concluded that it was the coveted 'head.' Jumping off their horses they at once gave chase. The smuggler gave them a good long run before being overtaken. When the excisemen knew they had been tricked, their wrath knew no bounds. They accused the man of smuggling, which he denied. Asked why he had run if innocent, he replied that he knew of no law preventing him from running with his own flagon on his own ground when he felt inclined to do so. Again, failure had to be recorded! No trace of illicit distillation could be found.

Such tales of 'decoys' relating to whisky smuggling are common throughout Scotland, but the local excise supervisor in Coupar Angus, Macleod, was determined to do something about Dalnamer. That autumn he and a number of troopers descended on the settlement one night, and the events that took place so outraged the local people that they drafted the following letter, a copy of which survives, though sadly it is undated:

Dalnamer.

To his Majesty's Justice of the piece, Colector of Exise and gentlemen of the County –

We, the poor pendiculars in Dalnamer, in Glenisla, doth find ourselves under the Disagreeable needsesity of giving you our complaint on the misconduct of a party of Exise and Dragouns that came to our Countray on the neight of — under the command of McLoud, Supervisor in Couparangus, who came not as Exise, But as plunderers and thieves of the neight. they went to our stack yeards and pulled down our corn stacks, fas[tened] there horses to the number of Eleven, they thrang more of our Corn before them than was Sufficient for six times the number.

they then went to a sheep cote, where they some time before had found some smuggled stuff, and when not finding anything belonging smuggling, they went to the said sheep-cote carrying pe[a]ts and hether to it, and then set it aburning, which, had it not been the goodness of providence in turning the wind from the north to the north-east our whole houses, ourselves, Wives, and Children, along with our corn and cattle, being in the Dead of neight, had all been burned to ashes.

What the monsters' desire was we know not, only they could have no ground for so baise an action, nor doth the Laws of our Countray alow such practises, and if the county gentlemen dos not pay, or cause to be pay'd. the Loss of our corn, of course we must aplay to the fiscal of the county to look after such thifts and volinces.

true, there were smugglers in our countray, yet such as was not cannot be robed by the Exise – nor do we deserve such usag from them, for had they call'd on us, and asked it of us, we would have given them as at other times, meat for themselves and corn or hay for there horses. But in place of that the Serjeant of the Dragouns threatened us with a drawn sword in his hand, that if we said aney more about our corn he would setesfy himself with our blood.

So if the fiscal of the county doth not put a stope to such Barbarus practices, Blood for Blood must be allowed.

As Grewar noted, 'It does not appear whether a copy of the above letter was forwarded to the authorities or not; neither is any mention made of subsequent proceedings. It seems probable that when the indignation of the injured parties had cooled down no further active steps were taken. That does not, however, mean that any of the offending party would go scatheless, if opportunity offered, in any of their subsequent visits to the glen.'

The first excise duty was placed on Scotch whisky on 31 January 1644, the rate being 2s. 8d. on 'everie pynt of aquavytie or strong watteris sold within the countrey'. As with so many taxes, it was a war which led to this imposition. The Scots required funds to pay for their army which was supporting the parliamentarian forces opposing King Charles I.

Once in place, excise duty on whisky stayed, regardless of peace or war, and many and varied pieces of legislation were subsequently introduced, all with the intention of maximising revenue for the government. Many of them were, however, ill-conceived, and were more likely to increase illicit distilling than suppress it. In some instances, taxes were lowered in the Highlands in order to try to stimulate legal distilling and curb smuggling, but the outbreak of war with France in 1795 led to a trebling of duty, and further increases followed.

Illicit whisky-making therefore became more profitable than ever, and, as with all other smuggled commodities, when the reward was high enough the risk would be taken, and in truth the risks for whisky smugglers were frequently very small. Illicit distilling became something of an epidemic, and the protests of licensed distillers grew ever louder. Even lairds and clergymen who had previously been at best ambiguous about illicit distilling began to think that the situation was getting out of hand.

Once Britain was no longer at war it was possible to contemplate reducing duty to more reasonable levels, which would have the effect of making illicit distilling less lucrative. The quality of much legal whisky had also greatly improved by the early 1820s.

It was the Excise Act of 1823 that dealt illicit distilling the blow from which it would never recover. Among the provisions of the Act were a cut in duty of more than fifty per cent to 2s. 5d. a gallon, while a minimum legal still size of forty gallons was stipulated.

The Act was extremely successful at stimulating the legal whisky industry in Scotland, making reasonably-priced, high-quality whisky a very viable alternative to the product of the illicit stills. The end was in sight for all but a few comparatively isolated illicit operations, with the number of detections falling from around 14,000 in 1823 to 692 by 1834, and just six in 1874. In 1823 Scotland boasted 111 licensed distilleries, but just two years later that figure had risen to 263.

David Grewar noted that the demise of illicit distilling in Glenisla, Angus, '. . . really proved a blessing to the people. How great the change was is shown in the different Statistical Accounts. In that of 1791–92 it is stated that: 'The grain produced in this district is not sufficient for the consumption of the inhabitants'. In the Account of 1842 it is said: 'Several thousand bolls of it [grain] are now, unless in very favourable seasons, annually sent to the market'.

While a number of other factors, such as improvements in agricultural methods, mean that the comparison may not be as straightforward as it at first appears, the virtual ending of illicit distilling certainly helped to improve the situation dramatically. Historical accounts of the Scottish Highlands and Islands frequently lament the fact that so much grain went for illicit distillation rather than into the mouths of the people, and during times of bad harvests, especially during the late eighteenth and early nineteenth centuries, all distilling was sometimes banned in badly affected areas.

In his 1800 *Journal of a Tour in the Highlands and Islands of Western*

*Scotland*, Dr John Leyden observed that '. . . distillation had a most ruinous effect in increasing the scarcity of grain last year, particularly in Isla and Tiree, where the people subsisted chiefly on fish and potatoes'.

If large-scale whisky smuggling within Scotland declined rapidly in the years following the 1823 Excise Act, then a brisk cross-border trade into England continued for another three decades.

Although whisky-drinking was not generally common in England during the eighteenth century and the first half of the nineteenth century, the practice had penetrated into the border county of Northumberland, where both drinking it and illicitly distilling it were common. Illicit whisky made in Northumberland was known colloquially as 'innocent', because it was innocent of duty.

Cross-border smuggling was lucrative because for many years duty on whisky was higher in England than it was in Scotland. It has been estimated that some 300,000 gallons of whisky were smuggled across the border into England in 1784. As much as 11,000 gallons was said to have been smuggled each *week* during the 1820s, and smugglers even trained dogs to swim across the rivers Esk and Eden, carrying pigs' bladders filled with contraband spirit.

People carried concealed bladders of whisky too, and in some cases iron canteens were fabricated and strapped to the stomachs of young women to make them appear heavily pregnant. In that way up to two gallons of spirit could be transported across the border.

John Dalgleish of Glencaple, south of Dumfries, wrote in a letter of 5 January 1820 to the Collector of Customs in Dumfries that '. . . a number of persons both of the Scotch and English side of the water are in the habit of carrying whisky in tin cases from this neighbourhood into Cumberland'.

From 1824 onwards, excise officers were based in towns close to the border, and the following year duty on spirits in England was cut from 11s. 9d. to 7s., while in Scotland it was raised to 2s. 10d.

The Excise Board set up a sixty-strong special force to counter smuggling in 1830, and in the spring of that year, Charles W. Biggs, Chairman of the Northumberland Quarter Sessions, wrote to the Chancellor of the Exchequer about cross-border smuggling: '[spirits] are conveyed in tin cases upon the shoulders of men, who being well acquainted with the mosses and infrequented tracks, which are impassible for horses, are thus enabled on foot to evade the watch of the officers . . . [The smugglers] have now so organized their system that they frequently go in bands and armed with pistols in order to terrify and dismay the officers in the execution of their duty.'

Sometimes, however, the approach was more low-profile. One summer in 1825 a funeral cortège was making its way from the village of Newcastleton towards the English border to collect the body of a Scottish smuggler who had drowned during an attempt to ford the Esk river. He was to be brought home for burial in Scotland. As the cortège approached the border it was halted by a pair of excise officers, who proceeded to make themselves deeply unpopular by insisting on opening the coffin. This must have been a high-risk strategy for them, but they were rewarded by the discovery in the coffin of thirty gallons of whisky.

On 23 July 1832 the people of Berwick-upon-Tweed petitioned the House of Commons on the issue of cross-border smuggling, noting that,

> Ever since the distinction made in the Scottish and English rates of duty upon whiskey, the offence of smuggling from Scotland into England has arisen to a most alarming height on the Borders, and seems constantly increasing in spite of the exertions of a large body of officers kept at a great expense to the revenue . . . The offenders chiefly consist of persons in abject poverty, and among them children and very old people, chosen to convey the smuggled spirits in order to evade the levying of any pecuniary penalty.

When the west coast railway line opened in 1847, followed by the east coast railway line two years later, the 'Border Control' presented a bigger problem than ever. Excise posts were set up at Carlisle and Berwick-upon-Tweed railway stations, and the luggage and clothing of all passengers travelling from Scotland into England was searched at the border.

Merchants in small towns and villages on the Scottish side of the border tended to hold stocks of legally-distilled whisky far in excess of anything they could ever have hoped to sell for local consumption. English smugglers would buy from them, and sell the whisky in Northumberland, making a useful profit in the process. Stephen Oliver wrote in his 1835 volume *Rambles in Northumberland* that

> The smuggling trade on the border is at present, however, in a very depressed state. As the duty is only four shillings a gallon higher in England than in Scotland, and as the excise officers on both sides of the border have, for the last seven years, been much more vigilant than formerly, the risk of loss is greater than the chance of gain. There is still a little business done, though more cautiously and in a smaller way; and the angler who happens to be near the head of Coquet or Kail-water in

the grey of the morning, about a week before Stagshaw-bank fair, may sometimes observe a man driving a cart, or leading a horse, seemingly loaded with a sack of corn, who, by suddenly halting or altering his course, on the appearance of a stranger, shows that he is anxious to avoid a meeting.

According to the *Weekly Scotsman* for 6 June 1908, looking back to the years following the Excise Act of 1823,

> The great reduction of duties in 1823 nearly knocked up smuggling in Scotland, but while it has done so in the Highland districts, the high duties still in force in England have brought the centre of active operations to the Borders. Smugglers from the northern and middle reaches of Scotland have marched almost together to the Border districts, where a fine field is open to their talents in introducing spirits legally made in Scotland, not England. The difference in duty is 8s. 6d. a gallon. On the line of county between Annan and Berwick, from 6,000–7,000 gallons of whisky are smuggled across the border every week. The whisky that can be bought in Scotland for 5s. or 6s. per gallon can be retailed over the Border to 10s. or 11s. The vendors are all bold and hardy peasants. Each person is loaded with a tin canister fitted to his person holding on average 8–10 gallons and as they travel in parlee of from 8–14 armed with bludgeons the excise officers are afraid to interfere.

It was William Gladstone, in his role as Chancellor of the Exchequer in Lord Aberdeen's coalition administration, who finally brought cross-border whisky smuggling to an end in 1855 by introducing a universal rate of eight shillings duty per proof gallon.

Just as smuggling in general was not seen as a great offence, and was engaged in by people of all ranks and occupations, the making of whisky was viewed by many in Scotland, and in the Highlands in particular, as an inalienable right, indeed, almost a duty.

Writing of whisky smuggling, W.M. Mackenzie in *The Book of Arran*, observed that

> Rich and poor, high and low, for profit as agents, for cheapness as buyers, were implicated in the method of a traffic which, from its conditions and gambling nature, was subtly demoralising. At the same time to the people it seemed as if they were maintaining a fight against an oppression which sought to deprive them of a legitimate method of turning their industry to account in the only way possible to them, and by which alone they could secure the means of meeting the rent which provided an income for the very men who, as magistrates, had to convict them. Hence too, no little connivance and laxity on the part of these same authorities.

In *Mountain Spirits*, Joseph Earl Dabnie writes that 'the smuggler of Scotland . . . became a highly respected citizen and not only had the sympathy of the people but their total cooperation. It was said that Scotland's illicit whiskey enterprise was "the secret half a country keeps." A special "smugglers' loft" was reserved in the Dundonald parish church [between Kilmarnock and Troon in Ayrshire] where the free-traders sat on Sunday "with their wives gay in silks, highly respected by all the worshippers".'

Alfred Barnard offers a relevant tale in his *Whisky Distilleries of the United Kingdom*, when chronicling the distilleries of Campbeltown. 'A capital story is told of an aged woman who resided near Hazelburn. She was of a rather doubtful character and was charged before the Sheriff with smuggling. The charge being held proven, it fell to his lordship to pronounce sentence. When about to do so he thus addressed the culprit, "I daresay my poor woman it is not often you have been guilty of this fault," "deed no Sheriff" she readily replied "I haena made a drap since youn wee keg I sent to yersel."'

In his fascinating book *A Hundred Years in the Highlands* (1921) Osgood Mackenzie quoted from an unpublished manuscript written by his uncle, Dr John Mackenzie:

> Even so late as then, say 1820, one would go a long way before one met a person who shrank from smuggling. My father never tasted any but smuggled whisky, and when every mortal that called for him – they were legion daily – had a dram instantly poured into him, the ankers of whisky emptied yearly must have been numerous indeed. I don't believe my mother or he ever dreamed that smuggling was a crime. Ere I was twenty I had paid £1,000 for the 'superiority' of Platlock, at Fortrose, to make me a commissioner of supply and consequently a Justice of the Peace, and one of the about thirty or forty electors of the county of Ross; and before it had occurred to me that smuggling was really a serious breach of the law, I had from the bench fined many a poor smuggler as the law directs. Then I began to see that the 'receiver' – myself, for instance, as I drank only 'mountain dew' then – was worse than the smugglers. So ended all my connection with smuggling except in my capacity as magistrate, to the grief of at least one of my old friends and visitors, the Dean of Ross and Argyle, who scoffed at my resolution and looked sorrowfully back on the happy times when he was young and his father distilled every Saturday what was needed for the following week.

In *The Story of Glenisla: traditional, historical, social*, David Grewar told the tale of the Reverend Andrew Burns, minister of Glenisla. Burns lived in a manse which looked out upon the glen's hotel, where excise officers would stay while searching for illicit stills in the area. When he saw a group of officers enter the hotel he would fetch his pony and set off at a relaxed pace up into the glen, leading the animal, as though taking it to graze there. Once out of sight of the hotel he would leap onto it and ride bareback and fast up the glen, waving his hat at each cottage where he knew an illicit still to be situated, shouting 'the Philistines be upon thee, Samson'. The Rev Alisdair Hutcheson of Kiltarlity near Inverness went a stage further, and actually distilled and sold his own whisky for a while.

In one instance, a family whose members were considered to be pillars of the establishment distilled and sold whisky without payment of any duty, but they managed to do so while remaining on the right side of the law.

Duncan Forbes of Culloden (see pp. 10 and 11) was head of the Forbes family from 1734, and his energetic anti-smuggling stance was undoubtedly influenced by the fact that his family was notable for making high-quality whisky. The family did, however, share with the smugglers they so despised the advantage of not having to pay duty on the whisky they distilled.

By the late seventeenth century the Forbes' Ferintosh distillery near Dingwall was one of the larger commercial distilling enterprises in Scotland, with the estates being in the hands of Forbes' father, also Duncan.

He was a staunch supporter of the Protestant King William III, who deposed the Catholic James II in 1688, and his estates were ransacked during the Jacobite rising in favour of James the following year. Forbes claimed compensation of £54,000 from the government for fire damage caused to Ferintosh distillery, and by way of settlement, and also in recognition of his loyal service, the Scottish parliament granted Forbes the right to distill at Ferintosh free of duty in perpetuity on payment of 400 marks Scots per year. During the ensuing century while this exemption was in force the Forbes family became very wealthy.

It seems that the rise of illicit distillation during the half-century after Duncan Forbes' death in 1747 did little to damage the business. Ferintosh whisky enjoyed a very high reputation, and it is said that Prince Charles Edward Stuart drowned his sorrows in Ferintosh after the defeat of his Jacobite army at Culloden. Presumably at the same time the Forbes family would have been happily toasting the defeat of the prince with the same spirit.

During the 1760s Ferintosh was enlarged, and a further three distilleries were built on the estate. More land was also acquired on which to grow barley in order to qualify for the continuing exemption from duty payments. By the late 1760s the Forbes family were making the vast profit of £18,000 per year from their whisky, and a few years later were reported to be distilling almost 90,000 gallons per year.

It is hardly surprising that the legal distillers who had to pay duty on their whisky were vociferous in their condemnation of the Forbes exemption, which must have seemed to them much like legalised smuggling. Both Ferintosh and the smugglers represented 'unfair' competition.

When new excise legislation was introduced in 1784 the exemption ended, and the Forbes family was awarded £21,580 in compensation. Robert Burns, for one, was outraged by the ending of the Ferintosh privilege, and his poem *Scotch Drink* (1785) and *The Author's Earnest Cry and Prayer* of the following year articulate his feelings at the loss of Ferintosh's unique status in particular, and the repressive state of the excise laws relating to whisky in general:

> Thee, *Ferintosh!* Oh, sadly lost!
> Scotland lament frae coast tae coast!
> Now colic grips, and barkin' hoast
>                           May kill us a';
> For loyal Forbes's charter'd boast
>                           Is ta'en awa'!
> Thae curst horse-leeches o' th' Excise,
> Wha mak the whisky stills their prize!
> Haud up thy han' Deil! . . . ance, twice, thrice!
>                           Their seize the blinkers!
> An bake them up in brunstane pies
>                           For poor d' . . n'd Drinkers.

Scotch whisky was unique in that it featured in an extremely late flowering of large-scale smuggling, during the 1920s and '30s, when the spirit was smuggled into North America.

Prohibition came into force in the USA on 16 January 1920, and lasted for fourteen years. It helped corruption to become endemic in the USA, as gangsters found that fortunes could be made smuggling 'bootleg' liquor into the States and distributing it during the 'great experiment'. Most famously, Al Capone in Chicago grew rich on the profits of bootlegging and associated activities. Overall, prohibition brought bribery, extortion and levels of violence unparalleled in the history of British smuggling.

Although they did not presume to challenge prohibition directly, many high-profile Scottish distillers were more than happy to supply their product for consumption by the American people, working hard to get it into a position from which it could be 'run' into the USA. Agencies were established by respectable Scotch 'whisky barons' in Canada, Cuba, British Honduras and the Bahamas.

For example, Nassau, the capital of the Bahamas, was British territory, yet it was conveniently located only 175 miles from the Florida coast. There was nothing unlawful about filling warehouses in Nassau with good Scotch whisky and selling it to dealers. They proceeded to smuggle it into Florida, or take it on the lengthier trip to 'Rum Row' – a 150-miles-long stretch of international water between Atlantic City and New York. In Rum Row vessels filled with Scotch and other spirits would lie at anchor, legally selling it to daring 'entrepreneurs' who would then run it ashore for distribution. In 1918, the Bahamas imported less than 1,000 gallons of whisky, yet four years later, with prohibition in place, the group of islands imported 386,000 gallons.

The tiny French islands of Miquelon and St Pierre, on the Gulf of St Lawrence, imported in excess of 16,000 gallons of Scotch whisky during 1922; quite an amount for a combined population of 6,000 people, who would each have had to consume twenty gallons of the spirit during that year if all had actually been for domestic consumption!

The blended whisky 'Cutty Sark' was formulated in 1923, specifically to appeal to the American market, being deliberately light in colour and character. Its creators, the ultra-respectable London firm of Berry Bros & Rudd were keenly aware that vast quantities of Canadian whisky were being consumed in prohibition USA, and saw their new Scotch as a means of penetrating that market. One of the entrepreneurs who imported Canadian whisky into the States was Samuel Bronfman, owner of the Seagram company in Ontario, while the Hiram Walker company, based on the Canadian side of the Detroit River, similarly profited by prohibition.

Francis Berry, of Berry Bros & Rudd, linked up with one of the principal 'rum runners' during a fact-finding mission to Nassau. The runner was a certain Captain Bill McCoy, who had a reputation for integrity which was rare among those of his calling. He was the ideal man to ensure that what Berry's customers got to drink in the USA had not been cut with water or adulterated with industrial alcohol to make it go further. Cutty Sark was to became known as 'the real McCoy', and when prohibition ended it went on to become one of the best-selling Scotch whiskies in the USA, a position it still holds today.

William Whiteley, who owned the tiny Edradour distillery in Perthshire and the King's Ransom blended brand, developed an 'arrangement' with the mobster and bootlegger Frank Costello, supplying King's Ransom in robust, square bottles, which were transported by sea and then fired from torpedoes onto the beaches of Long Island, from where they were carried in laundry baskets to the drinkers of New York.

A number of British-registered vessels were seized or sunk by US coastguard vessels while smuggling Scotch whisky, and on one occasion a boat carrying rubbish from New York was found to contain some $90,000-worth of Scotch whisky, apparently due for delivery to Frank Costello.

In 1925 the *Record* noted regarding the US market: 'With American whisky out of the way and an ever-increasing demand for good Scotch brands, there must be a greatly increased business, seeing that prior to Prohibition the amount of Scotch whisky consumed in the States in comparison to American was, we believe, somewhere in the region of five per cent'.

In 1924 Britain signed a Liquor Treaty with the USA, but in November 1930 Sir Alexander Walker of John Walker & Sons was cross-examined in some detail regarding the sale of Scotch whisky to US markets by the Rev Henry Carter, while giving evidence during a royal commission on licensing.

The Rev Carter asked Sir Alexander, 'Could you, if you would, as whisky distillers, stop a large proportion of the export of liquors to the United States?'

'Certainly not!' retorted Sir Alexander.

Most of the whisky barons were engaged in ensuring that their brands reached the US, or at the very least were less than fastidious in preventing them doing so. Then, of course, there were the large quantities of whisky which were imported legally for 'medicinal purposes'. Indeed, in Chicago alone, doctors prescribed around 200,000 gallons of whisky during 1922. Quite a sick country.

Inevitably it became possible to obtain 'medicinal' whisky without first seeing a doctor. The great whisky entrepreneur and all-round showman, Tommy Dewar, delighted in telling a story on the subject, relating to a visit to Canada, undertaken during his second 'world tour' of 1898, and subsequently published in his book *A Ramble Round The Globe* (1904):

Prohibition has been tried in several parts of Canada, but has not found much favour. I may mention a rather amusing experience here. I was going through a 'prohibition' state, and tried to get some whisky from the conductor of the train, but without success. 'Can't do it, boss; we're in a prohibition state, and I can't do it.' However, he eventually advised me to try a store at the next stopping place, and this I did. 'Do you sell whisky?' 'Are you sick mister, or got a medical certificate?' 'No.' 'Then I can't do it. See, this is a prohibition state, so I can't sell it; but I reckon our cholera mixture'll bout fix you. Try a bottle of that.' I did, but to my great astonishment received a very familiar bottle, which, although it was labelled on one side 'Cholera Mixture: a wineglassful to be taken every two hours, or oftener as required,' had upon the other side the well-known label of a firm of Scotch whisky distillers, whose name modesty requires me to suppress!

The Scotch whisky distillers' desire to sell their product in the USA was not just based on the undoubtedly attractive short-term profits to be made, but also because with no bourbon or rye whiskey being distilled in the USA there was a golden opportunity to get Americans drinking Scotch, with the not unreasonable expectation that when prohibition ended they would continue to drink the imported product. As the example of Cutty Sark illustrates, in this they were absolutely correct.

Whisky smuggling did not end completely with the repeal of prohibition in the USA, and the highest-profile example in history of Scottish smuggling came in 1941, with a drama which was subsequently immortalised in novel form by Sir Compton Mackenzie and in film as *Whisky Galore* (see pp. 167–8).

The events of *Whisky Galore* were inspired by the wrecking of the SS *Politician* off the Hebridean island of Eriskay in February 1941. Part of its cargo was 24,000 tons of spirits, principally whisky, and the islanders enthusiastically looted it, hiding bottles in peat bogs, haystacks, drain pipes, and even in babies' cots.

The whisky was removed from 'number five hold' of the vessel by eager parties of islanders, using their small fishing boats to ferry the cases ashore. Boats descended on the wreck once word got around about its magical cargo, coming from as far afield as Lewis in the north, and from mainland ports such as Oban, Mallaig and Gairloch.

Bottles were buried in small, shallow 'graves', with the sites marked perhaps by a bulrush or an iris for easy identification later. Some bottles were sunk in lobster creels in the sea, and there was barely an island peat- or hay-stack that did not contain a cache of 'Polly'. Even rabbit warrens were pressed into use. It is claimed that there was so much smuggled whisky that it was used as a rub for rheumatism and even to dose sickly cattle.

The Hebridean smugglers did not have everything their own way, however. The offensive against them was led by local customs officer Charles McColl, who was stationed in Lochmaddy, North Uist, and his superior, the Portree-based surveyor Ivan Gedhill.

Once the initial official salvage operation on the vessel was completed, when a large quantity of whisky was left on board, the pair put a customs seal on the hatch of the hold containing the whisky. This seal was subsequently, but not surprisingly, broken, and when McColl discovered the damage he commandeered a boat. With local police constable Donald Mackenzie, he then proceeded to apprehend the occupants of several vessels who were in possession of 'Polly' whisky. The culprits were caught red-handed, or rather black-handed, due to the quantities of oil leaking from the SS *Politician*.

According to a report written by McColl, the SS *Politician* held '21,000 cases and carton of whisky, all stowed in Number Five Hold'. He estimated that 'at least 500–1,000 cases' had been illegally removed from the ship, and noted 'it is believed that a considerable quantity of the looted spirits is buried in and around the shores of Eriskay and South Uist'. He later revised his estimate to 2,000 cases (an impressive 24,000 bottles). Crofts were searched by customs and excise officers and the police, but very little smuggled whisky was discovered. It was all much too well hidden.

Whisky was sold on to construction workers building an RAF station at Balivanich on Benbecula, while some was even posted to friends and family on the mainland. On one occasion an RAF lorry filled with 'Polly' whisky was pursued towards Balivanich by a police car, only for the RAF driver to swerve sharply onto the newly-constructed runway, causing the entire cargo of whisky to fall in front of a bulldozer that was levelling fresh tar. The 'evidence' was duly lost.

A number of the islanders who were caught smuggling whisky ashore from the wrecked vessel made appearances at Lochmaddy Sheriff Court, with fines ranging from £3 to £10. A number, however, were sent to prison in Inverness for two months.

Bottles of whisky from the SS *Politician* have been discovered from time to time over the years, with four bottles of White Horse being revealed under a neatly adapted floorboard hatch in a Barra croft in 1990.

In November 1987 eight bottles of 'Polly' whisky were auctioned by Christie's in Edinburgh, and such was the enduring fascination with this latter-day example of Scottish smuggling that they fetched a total of £4,000.

Most recently, in January 2003, a wooden panel from one of the cases of 'Polly' whisky was auctioned at Bonhams in London by the Liverpool-based Harrison Line, owners of the SS *Politician*. The panel was stencilled 'Ballantine's Liquer Scotch Whisky. George Ballantine & Son Limited, Distillers, Glasgow, Scotland. Established 1827'. The panel was estimated at £500, but actually sold for more than £1,500.

Whisky smuggling continues from time to time even today, as counterfeit whisky is occasionally smuggled into the UK. The Scotch Whisky

Association works hard to maintain the integrity of the product around the world, ensuring that what is marketed as Scotch whisky really *is* Scotch whisky.

During November 2002 warnings went out to the public to beware of smuggled whisky which purported to be Johnnie Walker Black Label, but originated in Spain and contained 2,000 times the usual level of methanol. Fifty bottles were seized in the London borough of Hackney, and such levels of methanol were said to be likely to cause blurred vision, possibly leading to blindness, breathing difficulties, severe abdominal pains, and even to make the hapless drinker lapse into a coma.

Tell-tale signs in what were otherwise plausible forgeries was the word 'Distilleries' instead of 'Distillers' on the royal warrant on the label, along with a less subtle Spanish-language rear label.

And the word 'smuggling' continues to be used by the press in relation to whisky. In April 2002, the *Aberdeen Press & Journal* newspaper ran a report by Natalie Walker headlined 'Customs seize £250,000 of Scotch'. This began 'Customs officers have seized more than £250,000 worth of smuggled whisky in one of the largest alcohol swoops in Scotland . . .'

In Glasgow, 18,000 bottles were recovered from a 40-ft trailer. According to Customs Scottish detection chief, Dave Clark, 'The seizure of 1,540 cases of smuggled Scotch whisky from one curtained-sided trailer shows how easily large quantities of illicit goods can be moved around UK roads'.

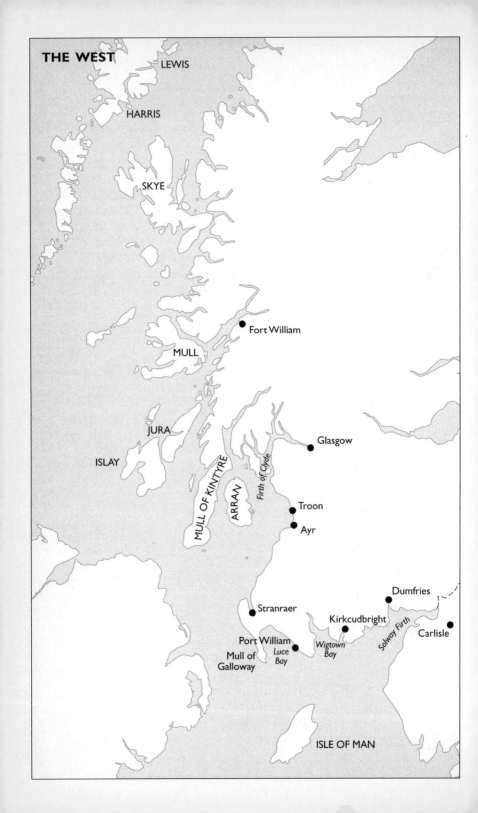

# 4

# THE WEST COAST

Economically speaking, the west coast of Scotland developed more slowly than the east. In the east, Leith and Aberdeen merchants traded with France, which encouraged economic growth from the late seventeenth century, while only trade with Ireland and America brought the focus to bear on the west. During the mid-eighteenth century the economic shift from east to west coast was pronounced. Much of the legitimate trade was in highly taxed goods such as tea, tobacco and spirits, so it is hardly surprising that this spurned a thriving 'black economy' concerned with smuggling such commodities.

Although most of the motivations and mechanics of smuggling were very similar, no matter where in Scotland it was taking place, the principal differences concerned the types of goods being smuggled. As we have seen, these varied according to the levels of duty levied upon them at various times, but geography also played a part. More smuggled tobacco was landed on the west coast than on the east, for example, as vessels carrying tobacco from America made landfall on the west first.

Foreign ports regularly involved with smuggling goods onto the Scottish west coast included Dunkirk and Roscoff in France, and Rotterdam and Campvere in Holland. Campvere was a port which had long associations with Scotland, and it provided tea and tobacco for smuggling, while Ostend and Gothenburg supplied spices, teas and silks, known as 'East India Goods'. When legally sold, these commodities were totally out of the price-range of most people in Britain, as they were very heavily taxed and only officially imported into London by the East India Company, who had a monopoly on the trade.

Silk, linen and lace items were smuggled from Spanish ports, and wine also came from Portugal. Gin and brandy were smuggled from Holland, France and other European destinations, while tobacco sometimes came in directly from America, as did rum and sugar from the West Indies. During the mid-eighteenth century, the port of Liverpool was also a place from which cargoes of tobacco, salt and sugar were often smuggled into Scotland.

Wool was smuggled out of the west of Scotland into Ireland, at times when its sale overseas was banned, and there was a large-scale, lucrative trade in it with Ireland from a number of west coast ports. The route from the Mull of Kintyre to the Antrim coast was frequently favoured, and as the Collector of Customs for Campbeltown noted in a letter of 20 July 1785, 'the vicinity of the south end of Kintyre to Ireland makes it very difficult and perhaps scarcely possible to prevent the exportation of wool from it to that kingdom'.

Along with such obvious commodities as tobacco, tea and alcohol, salt was also smuggled onto the west coast of Scotland, either directly from Ireland or the Isle of Man. Salt smuggling was usually undertaken by the fishermen themselves, who made their own profit. If the salt came in from Ireland or Man it rarely travelled far from its point of landing, being used in situ for fishing purposes.

As well as its role in salt smuggling, Ireland also acted as an important 'staging post' for vessels from further afield with cargoes destined to be smuggled into Scotland. If Ireland was an important factor in the prosperity of west coast smuggling, then the Isle of Man was an even greater influence on the 'free trade' activity of the west during much of its eighteenth-century golden age. The island was just thirty miles from parts of the west coast mainland, and was owned by the Duke of Atholl, who acquired it as a dowry. He imposed his own levels of duty, not being constrained to follow those set by the government in London.

The Isle of Man was a constant thorn in the side of the British government, as its duty levels were so low. Duty of up to 4s. 6d. was imposed on spirits on the mainland, while the Duke's levy on rum and brandy was just 1d. Successive dukes of Atholl seem to have been quite happy to allow the status quo to prevail, as their income was considerably augmented by duty from the smuggling trade. Man was an attractive base for merchants who traded with Scotland, as they could sell commodities that were dutiable in Britain but not under Isle of Man legislation, to Scottish customers without breaking the law.

During the early 1760s, the Isle of Man was importing rum from the West Indies, gin and refined sugar from Holland, tea from Gothenburg, silks and brandy from the Mediterranean, and brandy, wine and silks from France. Wool and coal were imported from Britain and sold to France, while tobacco exported from Britain to ports such as Dunkirk and Campvere found its way to the Isle of Man and was then smuggled into Britain and Ireland.

Significant quantities of rum, brandy, claret, tea and 'East India goods' were smuggled from Man to the Clyde coast, to Galloway, the Solway coast, and north-west England.

According to L.M. Cullen, in *Ayrshire and the Economic Boom*, 'in a technical sense, the advantage of the island was its proximity to the final market. Thus, large vessels brought cargoes on the long haul from continental Europe; paying low duties in the Isle of Man, bulk was broken there, and the goods could be carried on very small craft to the adjacent shores of Scotland, Ireland and north-west England. The operation thus minimised costs for the long voyage from Europe, and reduced to a minimum both the journey and size of craft for the high-risk final run'.

It is estimated that when the smuggling trade with the Isle of Man was at its height around the middle of the eighteenth century, the loss of duty to the British government was probably some £1m per annum.

Something clearly had to be done to curtail this illegal trade, and in 1765 the Revestment Act was passed, by which the British government purchased the sovereign rights to the island for £70,000, plus an annual annuity for the remainder of the Duke of Atholl's life.

Existing Dumfries customs records date back to 1708, in the form of letters from the local Collector of Customs to the Board of Customs in Edinburgh, and on 6 December 1708 the Collector wrote that

> This is to acquaint your honours that on Saturday last about fourteen miles from this, at a place called Casthorne [Carsethorn] was seized by Mr Grearson our riding surveyor and one of our tidewaiters a Manx boat about ten tunns burthen with three tuns of brandy and one tun of wine and some coarse Irish lenning [linen] we had information of it and that it was to be run in a creek near Abbey home in the precinct of Carlile, which we informed that office of, and advised said Mr Grearson to be upon his round on this coast, and all our other officers to be on there [sic] guard, the barke was lying for the tyde to goe to that place aforementioned on Saturday last there touched at Kircubright that American marchant of Whitehaven from Virgina bound for Leverpoole with tobacco, we sent a waiter on board which was all wee had there, and shall order an other in his place. I have given the warrant for apprehending the people that insulted the officers at Wigtown as directed and it will be taken care of, wee are just taken horse to order the securing of the goods and barke seized, and shall give a further account in our next.

The Dumfries Collector wrote to the Board on 24 April 1710, stating that the principal role of the service there was to '. . . prevent running of goods from the Isle of Man, Ireland and other parts'.

In *The Statistical Account of Scotland* (1791-99), the Reverend Mr

James Little, Minister of the Parishes of Colvend and Southwick, on the northern shore of the Solway Firth, observed that,

> The Isle of Man, which lies two leagues distant to the S. W. the higher ground of which are in sight here, is well known, before the lordship of it was purchased by government in 1765, to have been the great channel of a contraband trade with France, to the secret operation of which, the nature of this country as above described, but then in a still more unpolished state, was oft favourable. Having the advantage of many secret caverns, impervious thickets, devious paths and unfrequented tracts, which afforded innumerable and secure hiding places, it is not to be wondered at, if the inhabitants were generally and deeply engaged in it, and consequently addicted to idleness, and to the staple of that trade immediately ministered. But the abolition of that trade has had a happy effect upon the improvement of the country, and the manner of the people in this corner; and the traces of the more licentious times, which were a proverbial reproach to this parish, are now almost wholly obliterated.

Once fiscal control of the Isle of Man was in the hands of the British government, smugglers had to find new 'entrepots'. The *Penguin Dictionary of Human Geography* defines an entrepot as 'a specialized port with external trade relations of a re-export form. It acts as an intermediary centre for trade between foreign countries to which goods in transit are brought for temporary storage before re-export'.

Initially, the favoured replacement for the Isle of Man was St Peter Port in Guernsey, as it boasted the same sort of fiscal immunity that Man had previously enjoyed. However, Man carried on being a source of wine and brandy from France and for salt for many years afterwards, despite the government's best efforts.

Surviving records give a vivid account of an encounter between the customs service and a Guernsey smuggler. The following is from a letter dated 6 February from the Campbeltown Collector to the Board of Customs.

> Permit us to acquaint your Honours that on Tuesday the 31st ult, the wind south-west, about four o'clock in the afternoon of that day, the *Stag* cutter commanded by – Taylor and a lugger commanded by Kennedy Scott [of Guernsey], both smugglers, and the former pierced for eighteen guns, were lying off Ballycastle Bay in Ireland and the *Porcupine* frigate, Mr Martin commander having that day sailed from Belfast came round the Fair Head and gave chase. The lugger made a few tacks towards the land, by which she effected her escape, and the smuggling cutter having stood to the westward the frigate captured her by 12 o'clock that night off Ansturhull on the Irish coast and the first Lieut. Mr McKellar being put

on board the cutter as prize master to carry her to Belfast but it having come on a severe gale she was forced into this harbour the 2nd and sailed the 4th – her cargo consists of about three hundred matts tobacco, some rum Geneva and a few boxes tea in all six hundred parcels. The frigate was put into Lochindale in Islay and we learn that the lugger landed the greatest part of her cargo near Turnberry the night of 31st ult.

Many of the Scottish merchants involved with smuggling established links with Guernsey, and even placed staff there. Tobacco and rum passed through the island, along with other spirits and tea, and whatever regulations existed relating to potentially smuggled goods tended not to be enforced. Even the placement of a Custom House officer in the island during late 1767 served merely to interrupt the trade, not end it, as his stay was only temporary.

However, the officer's presence did cause merchants to look at other locations, with Dunkirk being favoured for a range of commodities including tobacco and tea, while there are records of sizeable rum transactions being conducted there in 1768. Roscoff was also popular for trading tea and spirits, while Norwegian ports such as Bergen and Trondheim were noted centres for tobacco destined to be smuggled into Scotland.

The Faroe Islands were also used, being usefully remote, and accessible via the sea to the north of Scotland, where interception was unlikely, though rough seas meant that smuggling operations tended to be suspended during the winter months.

The Faroes were also used as a fictitious destination for what the customs service referred to as 'pretended-bound' voyages. Vessels sailing from French ports, to land smuggled goods in Ireland or Scotland, carried false papers specifying the Faroes as their intended destination.

Guernsey had an advantage over ports in Holland, France, Norway and the Faroes, however, in that it usually boasted a wide range of goods which were legally traded, including wine. These goods provided vessels involved in supplying smuggled goods with the return cargoes necessary to make their ventures profitable. It was much more difficult to guarantee return cargoes from most of the other ports which were used.

## 1. Dumfries and Galloway

A great deal of Scotland's smuggled goods were landed on the Solway coast. The long, low north coast of the Solway Firth is geographically perfect for smuggling, being pitted with creeks and mud flats. It is also little more than thirty miles from the Isle of Man.

Much of the merchandise smuggled onto the coast of south-west Scotland was then transported across the Solway Firth into Cumberland, Northumberland, and further afield. The Solway, between Scotland and England, was in places very narrow, and it was therefore comparatively easy to ship smuggled goods into England without too much fear of being caught by the overstretched customs service.

As the Collector of Customs in the Cumberland port of Whitehaven reported in June 1746, the smuggling trade at that time was principally carried on '. . . between Blackshaw and Redkirk on the Scotch side and Flimby and Rockcliffe on the English'. He noted that at its narrowest the distance of sea between Flimby and the Scottish coast . . . 'not above four or five leagues over', adding '. . . these coasts . . . extend above one hundred and sixteen miles . . .'

According to Daniel Defoe in his *A Tour Through the Whole Island of Great Britain* (1724–26), Whitehaven had '. . . grown up from a small place to be very considerable by the coal trade, which is encreased so considerably of late, that it is now the most eminent port in England for shipping off coals, except Newcastle and Sunderland . . .'

Later in the century Whitehaven was second only to London as a port, having twice the tonnage of Liverpool and Bristol, exporting coal and importing tobacco from Virginia.

The long sea coast and good anchorage between the Esk and Dumfries produced hardy fishermen at Annan, Redkirk, Locharwood, Newbie, and Saltcoats; and these were turned to account by some of the landowners in a brisk trade which grew up during the 17th century between the West of Scotland and the Isle of Man, Holland, and the West Indies. A Government vessel was kept at Dumfries, but appears to have been far from vigilant; so when high duties were put upon foreign and colonial goods, this trade degenerated into smuggling, which was extended across the Esk into England, and continued a source of great profit until comparatively recent times.

– *C.L. Johnstone*, The Historical Families of Dumfriesshire and the Border Wars (*1878*)

In *A Tour Through the Whole Island of Great Britain*, Daniel Defoe wrote of Dumfries that 'here, indeed, as in some other ports on this side the island, the benefits of commerce, obtain'd to Scotland by the Union, appear visible; and that much more than on the east side, where they seem to be little, if anything mended, I mean in their trade'.

Large quantities of tobacco from Virginia, along with wine and Baltic timber, were legally landed at Dumfries, but by 1760 smuggled tobacco had effectively killed off the legitimate trade.

The Dumfries Collector of Customs wrote in 1761 regarding '. . . the insolence and audacity of the smugglers', who '. . . ride openly thro the country with their goods in troops of 20, 30, 40 and sometimes upwards 50 horses suffering no officer to come near to try to discover who they are, far less to seize their goods'.

In his entry on 'the Town and Parish of Dumfries' in the *Statistical Account of Scotland*, the Reverend Mr William Burnside, Minister of Divinity, wrote that 'forty years ago a considerable tobacco trade was carried on from Dumfries. At an average of four years, 1250 hogsheads were then annually imported. It is alledged, [sic] that the importation was considerably greater, and that in consequence of the detection of some attempts at smuggling, the trade in this article came to be discouraged.'

In reply to a circular letter requesting information regarding smuggling activity within his jurisdiction, the Dumfries Collector of Customs replied to the Board on 7 November 1785. He stated that

> We . . . beg leave to inform you that we know of no vesels in this district employed and carrying on an illicit trade. We have no doubt a good deal of smuggling business is carried on both by land and on water and principally tobacco brandy salt etc but the importations we understand are generally made a good deal to the westward of us and the quantities destined for this part of the coast and all the way to the English Borders are either sent up the firth in pretty large boats or wherries or transported by horses by land. We have indeed within these few days heard of a sloop that came to the neighbourhood of the Water of Urr within these few weeks and discharged tobacco and brandy in open day, and we wrote to our tidesman stationed in that neighbourhood if he knew or had heard anything of the matter and he gave us the particulars as well as a description of the vesell and to whom the cargo belonged if he could learn, but there being no regular post to that part of the country, it may be some days before he can find an opportunity of giving us an answer.

In October of the following year, the Collector at Dumfries reported that there was a significant smuggling trade being carried out at Sarkfoot, near Gretna, where the River Esk enters the Solway, and added that it would be difficult to halt this trade without military support, with '. . . the whole country being in favour of the smugglers and being a lawless set of people . . .'.

In August 1786 the Dumfries Collector noted that the previous April a vessel had made five runs into Sarkfoot from foreign ports, carrying around 500 ten-gallon ankers of spirits on each trip. A number of other boats, each carrying some 300 ankers had also discharged contraband spirits at the Water of Urr within the previous few months. He estimated that '. . . upwards of 20,000 gallons of spirits have been smuggled into this district in the course of the last seven months'.

Robert McDowall was a leading Sarkfoot smuggler, and on 2 August 1786 the Dumfries Collector wrote that a number of boats had been observed

> Passing up the Firth towards Leehouses and Sarkfoot, and at the latter place we understand a smuggling company have established themselves under pretence of carrying on a fair trade. To these and other places on that part of the coast the tobacco, spirits etc are carried and from thence through the country to the northern counties of England. This day we have had an information of a smuggler about ten days ago from Guernsey to Jersey direct to the company (McDowal [sic] & Co) at Sarkfoot consisting of one hundred packages of tobacco and a good deal of spirits. The vessel was about 25 tuns burthen.

A principal smuggled cargo at Sarkfoot was salt, from Ireland and the Isle of Man, and Southerness, a remote point some fifteen miles south of Dumfries, was similarly used. In October 1789, the Collector of Customs at Kirkcudbright wrote to the Dumfries Collector, warning him to be on the lookout for a ship which had recently docked at Southerness, with a substantial cargo of salt on board. The local tidewaiter, James Hunter, went to investigate, only to be taken prisoner by the crew, '. . . and detained there till the tide came, when the boat went off again, and we hear she has since landed her cargo in this Firth'.

The Collector in Dumfries observed in a letter of 1786 that once duty had been removed from tea, then tobacco soon replaced it as a smuggled commodity, making the point that most ships engaged in the smuggling trade in his area carried cargoes of spirits along with some tobacco. 'This smuggling business', he wrote, 'is carried on chiefly betwixt Irvine and the Water of Urr'.

The ships involved were usually loaded with their cargoes of contraband in Guernsey or at Ostend, though some of the smaller ones originated in the Isle of Man and Ireland. An average cargo, he noted, would consist of between 200 and 300 ankers of spirit and 100 to 150 bales of tobacco.

He also reported that some ships had been carrying cargoes consisting principally of tobacco, which was landed and then transported overland to 'Edinburgh, Glasgow, Paisley, Ayr . . .', while a considerable quantity was also shipped to 'Whitehaven and the Cumberland coast, from whence it is again carried further into the country'.

Rum and tobacco came in from Ireland, too, he noted. 'All the rum exported to that country is returned smuggled in small quantities. And this is chiefly carried on in the neighbourhood of Kirkcudbright.'

When I was a very small boy, an old man living in a snug little wood-begirt cottage near Lochenbreck Spa, told me a story of his youth, associated with the remnant of smugglers of whisky, brandy and tobacco. In a smaller way than was the custom of the earlier smugglers, they disposed of illicit cargoes among the hills of Galloway and Ayrshire, in what might be called a retail way.

Blether Jock was looked upon by everyone who knew him, not as a gangrel or half-witted beggar, but rather as a well-to-do pedlar, with a curious eccentricity of unwillingness to show his pack of goods. He made periodical visits over his own particular route among the wilder parts of the country, and was rarely observed moving about during the day, but usually 'daunert in aboot the gloamin'.

He was in the habit of carrying on his back and upon his person what he termed his 'ain bedding', which looked like a huge pack. This, Jock was always careful to keep under his keen eye at all times when unburdened of his load. A large, round bundle, it was wrapped in a blue home-made blanket. The contents of this pack was nothing less than a basket made from dried rushes, constructed somewhat on the plan of a wasp's nest. Each cell contained a bladder of whisky or brandy. The inside of his long shaggy coat was also a stowing-place for tobacco, or any small pieces of stuff he could pick up from the curious ports where he got his wholesale supplies.

Jock would call at one of the moor houses, usually shepherds' cottages, and in due time he snugly stowed in the byre or barn for the night. The shepherd would say nothing till Jock was supposed to be asleep, when he would make an errand to the byre to see that all the cattle were right before he would retire. This was to get his two or three bladders of whisky, etc, from Jock and to pay for the same. Next day Jock would wander over the hills to another customer, and thus dispose of his cargo, his blanket pack never to appearance altering in bulk, if lighter in weight. Jock, the old man told me, was one of a numerous gang who plied this kind of trade all over Scotland, and did so successfully for many years after the Solway was supposed to be cleared of the smugglers.

– *William S. Thomson* The Smuggling Era in Scotland, (*1910*)

Some communities in the south-west, such as Sarkfoot, seem to have specialised in smuggling, but it was not just the inhabitants of coastal settlements who indulged in the activity. In the *Statistical Account of Scotland*, the Reverend Mr John Johnstone of the parish of Crossmichael wrote that '... smuggling for which our local situation is but too favourable, tends to relax every moral obligation.' Crossmichael is close to the east shore of Loch Ken, some five miles north-west of Castle Douglas, and fifteen from the nearest port of Kirkcudbright.

Sometimes the smugglers operated much further inland. In March 1783 it was noted by Nish Armstrong – chief supervisor of the Newcastle-based contingent of riding officers – that significant quantities of tea and spirits from Gothenburg were being smuggled onto the south-west coast of Scotland. Much of this contraband was then purchased by '... the smugglers of Langholm in Scotland and the borders thereof, who have associated themselves into formidable bodies to carry and convey these goods through the country into Cumberland, Northumberland, Newcastle and the Southern Counties with firearms, threatening the riding officers in this port with murder whenever they meet them.'

In a letter of 21 March 1787 the Collector of Customs at Dumfries, David Staig, stated that cargoes of smuggled goods landed on the Ayrshire coast '... are generally sent towards Edinburgh or carried across the country by Langholm towards Northumberland'.

In his *Ordnance Survey Guide to Smugglers' Britain*, Richard Platt notes that a minister of Anwoth, near Gatehouse-of-Fleet, just to the north of Fleet Bay, was removed from his post for his active involvement in the local smuggling trade. He observes that 'the whole area around Kirkcudbright has a reputation for the free trade, but Rascarrel Bay and Abbey Head were particularly notable'. There is, supposedly, a smuggler's cave at Auchencairn, east of Kirkcudbright, where Auchencairn Bay provides a perfect landing place for smuggled goods.

Balcary House, which overlooks Balcary Bay, two miles south-east of Auchencairn, dates back to 1625, and was built by a company of smugglers who went by the name of Messrs Clark, Crain & Quirk. The house was equipped with vast cellars capable of holding the proceeds of a large-scale smuggle. It overlooks Hestan Isle, which was a hiding place for smugglers and a 'warehouse' for smuggled goods. The property is now a country-house hotel.

In the *Statistical Account of Scotland*, the Reverend Robert Muter, DD, of Kirkcudbright wrote 'would government take off the high duty upon the importation of coals, which is the only fuel used in the place, it would afford great encouragement to these manufactures [cotton, woollen, candle and soap factories] and turn the attention of the people to a more certain profit, than they can expect from pecuniary advantages which result from smuggling'.

Two fellow ministers in the area also made interesting points regarding smuggling. The Reverend James Thomson of Rerrick bemoaned the '. . . variety and abundance of foreign spirits, illegally imported on the coast . . .', while the Reverend Mr Henry Blain of Stoneykirk noted that 'some years ago, salt was manufactured at two places in this parish; but the practice is now discontinued, probably because it was found easier to smuggle that article from Ireland'.

Kirkcudbright features in a customs report relating to the notorious Captain Jack Yawkins, the model for Dirk Hatteraick in Sir Walter Scott's novel *Guy Mannering* (see pp. 154–6). A letter of June 1787 from the Collector of Customs at Kirkcudbright to the Liverpool Collector described how, having landed seventeen boxes of tea, a vessel was intercepted off Abbey Burn by the revenue cutter *Pilote*, and escorted to Liverpool. Her cargo consisted of '. . . between eighty and ninety boxes of tea, four hundred ankers of spirits and a quantity of silks and tobacco being the most valuable cargo of contraband goods which for many years past has appeared upon this coast . . . we are informed that the lugger was commanded by the noted Yawkins and that she was loaded at Ostend'.

According to Athol Forbes (*The Romance of Smuggling*) '. . . popular tradition alleged that Yawkins insured himself against capture by a bargain with the evil one. The vessel, famous for many a day, was the *Black Prince*. She visited to discharge her cargo at Luce, Bekarry and elsewhere along the coast, sometimes running as far down as the Tyne and Tees.'

Wigtown and Creetown, at the north of Wigtown Bay, were both rife with smuggling ventures during the eighteenth century, and a cave known as 'Dirk Hatteraick's cave' is to be found on the northern shore of Wigtown Bay, accessible off the A75 Dumfries to Stranraer trunk road, between Gatehouse-of-Fleet and Creetown. Another cave associated with the smuggler is in Torrs Cove, on the east side of Kirkcudbright Bay.

A few miles to the west of Kirkcudbright Bay, across the Machars peninsula, lies the large expanse of Luce Bay, ideally suited to the landing of smuggled cargoes, due to its gently slopings beaches. According to Richard Platt, Stairhaven, near Glenluce, and the Bay of Auchenmalg were favoured landing spots within Luce Bay.

The area from Luce Bay around the Mull of Galloway, and as far north as Stranraer, was very popular with smugglers bringing goods in from the Isle of Man and Ireland. Irish salt was of much better quality than most Scottish salt, and customs raids on Galloway farms searching for illegally-imported salt were a common sight. Tea, brandy and tobacco were also staple smuggled goods, but strong English beer, much stronger than its native counterparts, was also regularly smuggled.

Early one morning a richly laden lugger from the Isle of Man was surprised off the coast of Galloway by the government cutter under the command of Sir John Reid. The smuggler was running for Cairndoon, on the Glasserton shore of Luce Bay, and disregarding the hail and the order to heave to, set every stitch of canvas, and with a freshening south-western breeze, sped merrily away followed by the cutter also carrying as much sail as she could stagger under. The wind was increasing, but both vessels held on and made no attempt to shorten sail. An eye-witness describes the rate at which they were going as almost incredible. The lugger stood in for the Glasserton shore, closely followed by the cutter, and as the distance between the two vessels was gradually lessening, it was very apparent that unless something turned up in favour of the smuggler he would have to heave to, it being thought impossible that she could get round the Burrow Head, whose iron coast and jagged cliffs were at the time, on account of the high wind, causing an extra rapid tide more than ordinarily dangerous.

But the fearless smugglers' maxim was 'Do or die', and after now being carried to the giddy pinnacle of a gigantic wave and anon plunged into a yawning chasm of the mighty deep, the dangerous head was rounded. At length it seemed that the weary chase was to end in favour of the Revenue cutter, for when the object of its pursuit was off the Isle of Whithorn, it was observed that she was making for the Isle harbour, as if giving up her attempts to elude her pursuer. The cutter, satisfied that her prey was soon to be in her grasp, shortened sail, and followed into the Isle under easy canvas.

But what was her surprise on finding, after she had leisurely moored, that no lugger was in the harbour! At the time this incident took place the Isle harbour could be entered by one route and vessels of small tonnage could clear by another. No one would have thought the smugglers' large craft would have attempted to depart by this narrow channel of egress. But owing to the high tide at the time she made the attempt, she succeeded. The chagrin of Captain Reid was of no moderate nature, when on looking through the port he had the mortification of seeing his imagined prize standing away for the English coast all sail set. When the tide receded a few curious seamen at the Isle examined the hazardous route of the lugger in leaving the harbour, and found a track made by the keel of the vessel in the shingly bottom about 100 yards long. Carrying so much sail and having great way on, she had completely forced her passage through the unlikely channel.

– From *John Maxwell Wood*, Smuggling in the Solway and Around the Galloway Sea-
board (*1908*)

After the Act of Union, lucrative markets in England were opened up to Scottish landowners who therefore wished to enclose land in order to create large areas of pasture in which to fatten cattle and sheep for the English markets. One example was Sir David Dunbar of Baldoon near Wigtown, who proceeded to evict tenant farmers and sacrificed many agricultural jobs as he began the process of enclosure.

Some of the small-scale Scottish farmers resisted as their land was taken over, and in 1723 and 1725 uprisings occurred. In the 'Levellers' Revolt' of 1725 up to 2,000 people took part in a rising in the south-west corner of Scotland, tearing down the 'drystane dykes' which had been erected to form pasture by the large landowners. Troops crushed the revolt, and agricultural 'reform' continued apace.

Some of the displaced agricultural workers turned, inevitably, to smuggling and in this area the trade probably reached its peak in the early years of the nineteenth century, just as it was dying off in some other places. Soldiers and sailors returning from the Napoleonic Wars around the same time, swelled the ranks of smugglers throughout Britain.

One of the most active areas for smuggling was the remote stretch of coast between Port William and Whithorn, at the foot of the Machars peninsula. Here vessels from the Isle of Man discharged cargoes of tea, tobacco and spirits, with trains of pack-horses meeting boats in creeks and inlets to carry off the goods. Local farmers, clergymen, and even substantial landowners acted as 'go-betweens' in the smuggling trade, hiding contraband goods in specially constructed concealed cellars and other artful places.

Government troops were stationed at Auchenmalg and nearby Port William, on the eastern shores of Luce Bay, in order to deter smugglers on this stretch of coast. The waters were also patrolled by revenue boats, but such measures failed to give the forces of law the upper hand. In the *Statistical Account of Scotland*, however, the Reverend John Steven of the parish of Mochrum, near Port William, wrote that 'in 1788 a small barrack-house was erected here for the accommodation of the military, and customs-house officers occasionally sent to prevent the landing of smuggled goods. This measure seems to have been attended with complete success, as neither box, anker, nor bale, though not infrequent before, are now to be seen'.

The Mull of Galloway forms the western shores of Luce Bay, and was a favourite place with smugglers because of its remoteness. Breddock Bay, on the west side of the Mull, was particularly popular. Rock-salt was imported into Scotland illegally, usually from Carrickfergus on the Antrim coast of Ireland. This was just thirty-five miles from the Mull, and salt was often landed at Breddock, as well as at Ardwell Bay, Clanyard Bay and Float Bay, all on the west side of the Mull, south of Portpatrick.

Surviving testimony to the smuggling activities which once took place in the area can be found in a number of smugglers' caves, according to Richard Platt. Breddock Cave is in Clanyard Bay, a remote inlet on the west coast of the Rhinns, just south of Port Logan, while there are a number of caves at the Mull Head. These were used to store goods as they were brought ashore before being moved later for distribution. 'Brandy holes' have also been discovered on a number of local farms.

As one would expect in a social climate where smuggling was widely tolerated and even approved of by members of the 'establishment', customs and excise officers, and in particular troops brought in to support them, were not immune to bribery. Officers were badly paid and had little incentive to make themselves targets for local anger in the communities in which they were based. A blind eye turned to smuggling activities kept the peace, and would usually result in a keg or two on the doorstep as an expression of gratitude.

Richard Platt (in *Smugglers' Britain*) tells how on one occasion a detachment of troops was dispatched to Luce Bay to deal with an imminent landing of smuggled spirits. They found themselves vastly outnumbered by two heavily armed smuggling luggers with more than a hundred men on board, waiting offshore to unload. It was 'suggested' by the smugglers that the troops and accompanying excise officers should retire out of sight until the business was over, rather than take on the superior force in what would undoubtedly be a very bloody conflict. Discretion seemed the better part of valour, and the troops did as advised. When they returned, there was no sign of the smugglers or their vessels, just a line of casks on the beach by way of a 'thank you'.

Platt writes that Clone Farm, close to Port William, was the headquarters of a major smuggling gang during the eighteenth century, and an underground passageway linked the farmhouse to the shore close by. A fireproof trapdoor in the farm's kiln concealed the 'brandy hole', and the smuggler who posed as the farmer to allay suspicion would light a fire in the kiln if a visit from the authorities seemed imminent. Records show that one successful raid on the farm in 1777 yielded 200 bales of tobacco, 140 ankers of brandy, and 80 chests of tea. Even today, Platt notes, water sometimes bubbles up in a hollow area of the farmyard from the old smugglers' tunnels below.

In his 1867 *History of Dumfries* Robert McDowall told a tale that illustrates one of the roles played by women in smuggling during the heyday of the traffic. It was the same sort of role that is documented in many cases regarding whisky smuggling, and went far beyond the sort of passive involvement which is often supposed to have been the extent of female participation. Numerous stories are told of women defying gaugers intent on searching for, or seizing, illicit whisky, perhaps most famously one which is attributed to Pluscarden on Speyside, as well as to Orkney.

On one occasion, an excise officer reputedly spent the night in Pluscarden, near Elgin, waiting and watching by a local croft where illicit distilling was known to be taking place. Early the following morning he approached the house and was confronted by a Mrs Watson, who was a large lady, while the officer in question was of modest build. On entering the house he discovered that equipment from the previous evening's distilling remained in place. 'Did anybody see ye come in here?' asked Mrs Watson. Perhaps naively, the officer replied in the negative. 'And naebody'll ever see ye gang oot,' she said menacingly. The gauger fled from Pluscarden for ever, and was replaced by an officer who always obligingly announced his intended visits well in advance . . .

McDowall's tale took place in 1777 at Ruthwell, a few miles west of Annan. A local tide-waiter and a law officer went to the house of a well-known smuggler, Morrow of Hidwood, having been told that he had just returned from a smuggling trip to the Isle of Man. In his Hidwood House they discovered a sizeable stash of tobacco, and were about to remove it, when a large group of women rushed in, seized the tide-waiter and locked him in, proceeding to dispose of the 'evidence'. He escaped and was sent back by his superiors to the scene with a force of ten men, but the women, armed with pitchforks and cudgels were again present, and all that the officers were able to do was locate and seize one parcel of tobacco which had been abandoned in a ditch. McDowall noted that this was not an atypical occurrence, and indeed a very similar incident took place just a month later at Glenhowan, near Glencaple, a few miles to the west.

According to local legend, an attractive girl called Maggie McConnell, of Dally Bay in the Rhinns of Galloway, once played a major part in liberating a seized smuggled cargo when she seduced the exciseman guarding the haul, finally shaking his hand in an apparent gesture of farewell. Instead, she wrestled him to the ground and blindfolded him with her apron, holding him there until the cargo had been carried away by the smugglers. This is reminiscent of an incident near Inverness, when a pretty girl was caught by an excise officer trying to smuggle illicit whisky into the town in a jar. Pretending to be feeling faint, the girl begged the officer for a sip of the whisky. He obliged, and the girl duly spat the mouthful of raw spirit into his eyes, seizing the jar and making her escape as he staggered around, temporarily blinded.

McDowall (*History of Dumfries*) wrote of the intriguing way in which smugglers' horses had also been trained to play a part. He noted that '. . . one famous troop of these quadrupeds' had been seen on many occasions '. . . heavily laden, at day-dawn, with contraband goods, unattended by any human being, and preceded by a white horse of surpassing sagacity, scouring along the Old Bridge, down the White Sands, and through the streets of Dumfries, without anyone daring to interrupt their progress.'

'On one or two occasions', he wrote, 'when some individual more officious than the rest rashly attempted to intercept the leader of the troop, the wily animal either suddenly reared and struck its opposer to the ground, or by a peculiar motion swung the kegs with which it was loaded with so much violence that no one durst approach within its reach.'

The most famous Scottish excise officer was poet, songwriter and latter-day Scottish legend Robert Burns, who joined the service in October 1789, subsequently being based in Dumfries. He was in its employ until his untimely death in 1796.

As a boy, Burns was clearly exposed to smuggling and smuggling legends, as detailed by the Reverend George Gilfillan in his 1886 volume *The Life of Robert Burns*:

> His mother, originally from Craigeston, in the parish of Kirkoswald, had a brother living at the farm of Ballochneil, about a mile from the village of Kirkoswald – Samuel Brown by name, at one a farm labourer, fisherman, and dealer in wool. Burns resided with his uncle in a farm house which he occupied along with his brother-in-law, Niven, the farmer, his own wife being dead; and walked every morning to the village school at Kirkoswald. The coast of Carrick, near this, is the commencement of a long line of sea margin, extending by various reaches and windings from Ayr to Girvan, and thence to Stranraer, and thence to Wigton, and thence to that romantic region below Creetown, called usually Guy Mannering's country. Carrick, though far away from this, may be said to begin the waving line which, after many bendings, culminates in one of the most interesting spots in all the south of Scotland, both in itself and its associations. One rugged band then united all this tract of sea coast. It was, from Kirkoswald to Kirkcudbright, the haunt of a smuggling population; the Isle of Man forming a midway station between it and

France, Ostend, and Gothenburg. We must not judge, however, of the Kirkoswald smuggler by Vanbeest Brown, senior, or Dick Hatteraick [smugglers in Scott's *Guy Mannering*]. He was half smuggler, half farmer, jolly, kindly, though somewhat rude and riotous. Burns' uncle, Brown, belonged apparently to this type . . . he here got acquainted with wild men and wild usages, saw wild scenery, bathed his young system and his soul, too, in the salt breath of the ocean and met the first rough model of his inimitable 'Tam o'Shanter.' This was one . . . Douglas Graham, whose farm of Shanter . . . lay on a slope near the site of Turnberry Castle, and who was a good decent man to be a habitual smuggler and occasionally a hard drinker, and whose wife, Helen MacTaggart, was as fearful and superstitious as the Kate of the poem.

Burns later wrote of this time in his life, 'I made a great progress in the knowledge of mankind. The contraband trade was at that time very successful, and it sometimes happened to me to fall in with those who carried it on. Scenes of swaggering riot and roaring dissipation were till this time new to me; but I was no enemy to social life.' Gilfillan observed:

We pass now to a curious incident [in 1792], which has much exercised the biographers of Burns. A superintendent, a kind of 'Frank Kennedy,' was stationed in Annan to watch the smuggling trade, then carried on with great activity along the Galloway coast. Burns was one of the party employed to watch a suspicious-looking brig which appeared in the Solway Firth. As it seemed too strong and well-armed to be attacked rashly, Lewars, a brother exciseman, went off for a party of dragoons to Dumfries. Burns and his companions waited impatiently for their return, and one of them expressed a wish that the Devil had Lewars for his slowness in returning, and that Burns might indite a song on the laggard. Burns said nothing, but after a few strides along the wet marsh, came back roaring out the clever ditty, 'The Deil's awa' wi' the Exciseman.' By-and-bye Lewars arrived with his troop, the brig was boarded, Burns being the first man; and the next day, when the vessel was sold in Dumfries, he purchased four carronades (at £3) and presented them to the French Legislative Assembly . . . We were still at peace with France, although possibly, ere these carronades reached, war might have begun. It was a fine erratic impulse on the part of the poet, and showed with what evident sympathy he was watching the rising of the Day-Star of Liberty, soon to be quenched in darkness and blood.

Burns' ambiguity towards the British establishment and his duties as an excise officer surfaces in his writings from time to time. Indeed, he went so far as to declare that the occupation was an '. . . insignificant existence in the meanest of pursuits, and among the vilest of mankind'.

## 2. Ayrshire and The Clyde

According to the *Kilmarnock Standard* in November 1908

> Ayrshire attained pre-eminence as a centre for smuggling. People otherwise
> respectable openly took part in the unlawful traffic, the foundations of
> many present-day fortunes being laid on the profits acquired during those
> times . . . On the coast of Carrick mischievous spirits were supposed
> to guard the places where contraband was concealed and were even
> known to attack too adventurous excisemen. Aged women received and
> concealed stores and passed, by repute, for witches. Coffins carried on
> the backs of demons were often seen during the night near these women's
> houses. About a century ago, Kate Steen, a repute sorceress, flourished at
> Kirk Uswald. She was so popular among the tenant farmers that she was
> sustained by their gifts. In her one-room house was a deep hold in which
> the contents of many a smuggling lugger found a temporary home. Over
> its entrance, covered with grass and rushes, she sat at her spinning wheel,
> the picture of aged innocence and simplicity.

On the Ayrshire coast, the fishing village of Ballantrae was once a great
centre for smuggling, while the distinctive island of Ailsa Craig, out in
the Firth of Clyde, was also a base for 'free-trading'.

In his 1888 book *Ailsa Craig*, the Reverend Roderick Lawson
wrote:

> At the foot of Kennedy's nags (as the rocks above are named), is a cave
> of considerable dimensions called McNall's Cave. The cave is 113 feet in
> length, with a width of 12 feet, and reaching in the loftiest part a height
> of 21 feet. Its entrance is not easily noticed, being about 40 feet above
> sea level, and is reached by climbing an immense bank of debris. Some
> years ago when the floor of this cave was being cleared of a stock of guano
> which in the course of ages had accumulated in it, the labourers came
> upon two stone coffins containing bones. Whether one of these was that
> of McNall himself is not known; but it is not at all unlikely that a bold
> smuggler like him, with every man's hand against him, would like to
> be buried away from gaugers, beside the sounding sea. I have not been
> able to learn anything of McNall except that he was a smuggler who
> lived in this cave. But it is well known that about the end of last century,
> smuggling was very prevalent along our Ayrshire coast, and a safe place
> for receiving the goods would be a desideratum. In these circumstances,
> what would be more natural than to land these goods on Ailsa, and hide
> them in this cave, which would probably be little known, till opportunity
> occurred for taking them quietly ashore in a fishing boat, and disposing
> of them to the best advantage? Such, at any rate, was the plan adopted
> by MacNall; and it is said that one of the tenants of Ailsa, David Bodan,
> who lived in the early part of this century, used to follow MacNall's

example. On one occasion he was beset by six armed men of the Coast Guard, near Dunure, and called on to surrender. Bodan, however, put his back to a rock, and taking his assailants one by one as they approached, forcibly seized their guns, hurled the men back, and after breaking their weapons across his knee, threw the fragments down the cliffs.

Regarding Ayrshire smuggling, Lawson pointed out that 'about a mile from Ballantrae, on the Colmonell Road, there may still be seen in a brae-face called "The Heck," a large hole named "the Brandy Hole," and most of the fishermen of those days had secret trapdoors in their kitchen floors. In later days smuggling was confined to carrying salt from Ireland, and the exploits of the fishermen in "doing" Dowie's [revenue] cutter were fireside stories fifty years ago.'

In his 1847 *History of Ayrshire*, James Paterson wrote that

> Smuggling of tea, tobacco, and brandy was carried on in South Ayrshire formerly. Large vessels, then called Buckers, lugger rigged, carrying twenty and sometimes thirty guns, were in the habit of landing their cargoes in the Bay of Ballantrae; while a hundred Lintowers, some of them armed with cutlass and pistol, might have been seen with their horses and ready to receive them, to convey the goods by unfrequented paths through the country and even to Glasgow and Edinburgh. Many secret holes, receptacles for contraband articles, still exist, in the formation of which much skill and cunning is shewn. The Old Kirk of Ballantrae itself contained one of the best.

The ancient port of Ayr was a popular landing place for contraband from Ireland, while the Carrick shore, including Dunure and Culzean Bay, was frequently used for smuggling whisky across the Irish Sea. Additionally, in excess of 45,000 gallons of rum from the West Indies was imported into Ayr between October 1765 and June the following year, and was then legally shipped to Ireland. Much of it, however, seems to have found its way back onto the coast of Scotland as smuggled goods.

The docks of Ayr and Irvine were also well-used by the tobacco trade, and, additionally, there was also a growing coal trade between Ireland and these two ports during the 1750s and '60s. Irvine came to specialise in trading coal with Dublin, while Ayr had wider maritime trading interests.

Writing in *A Tour Through the Whole Island of Great Britain*, Daniel Defoe noted that 'from Air, keeping still north, we came to Irwin, upon a river of the same name; there is a port, but barr'd and difficult, and not very good, when you are in; and yet, here is more trade by a great deal than at Air; nay, than at all the ports between it and Dumfries, exclusive of the last . . .'

Ayr was one of six outports on the west coast where 'king's boats' were stationed during the latter part of the eighteenth century in order to try to stem the flow of smuggled goods. These king's boats operated under the authority of the Tide-Surveyor and were crewed by up to eight boatmen. Revenue cutters covered wider areas, with half a dozen working the west coast during the late eighteenth and early nineteenth century. They were stationed at the Isle of Whithorn in Galloway, at Ayr, and the isles of Cumbrae, Arran, Islay, and at Stornoway on Lewis.

At Ardrossan, between Troon and Largs, the Castlecraigs – a ridge of basalt rock – provided a safe place to unload cargoes of smuggled brandy and rum, while Prestwick and Monkton were also popular smuggling locations on the Ayrshire coast. Troon Point, a promontory situated midway between Ayr and Irvine, was described by the Ayr Customs Collector in 1767 as '. . . the safest place on all this coast for vessels to land their cargoes'. He referred to it as '. . . the famous smuggling harbour the Troon or Turnpoint'.

According to Richard Platt (*Smugglers' Britain*), 'Troon Bar provided shelter from the wind, and the smuggling ships would be run up the sands at Barassie Burn, on the Barassie shore'. He notes that 'many of the houses in Troon are reputed to have brandy holes, or concealed rooms for the storage of contraband, and others have double gables for the same reason'. Further north, Largs and Inverkip were favoured places at which to land smuggled cargoes from the Isle of Man and Ireland.

In his *History of the County of Ayr*, James Paterson noted that in 1764 in Troon ' . . . about 100 men, mounted on horses, having large sticks in their hands, accompanied with some women' tried to prevent the seizure of recently-landed contraband spirits, and ultimately 'liberated' three cartloads from the clutches of the customs officers.

The Ayr Collector of Customs wrote in April 1775 that '. . . it [landing of contraband] is now more in Carrick than at the Troon', and in December of the following year he was of the opinion that 'by the many large seizures made by the commanders of the sloops and land officers, the smugglers at Troon are so reduced that little or no smuggling prevails there at present'. He added that instead of Troon, 'the places of landing' had become Ladyburn, Turnberry and Heads of Ayr.

Inevitably, smuggling on the west coast threw up its characters. According to the *Weekly Scotsman* in October 1909, 'James Walker of the Clyde had earned a reputation second to none. He had long eluded the police – with spies and informers everywhere, Walker snapped his fingers at the law . . . Powerful and athletic, swift of foot and sure of hand, and never without weapons of reference, he swore he would never be taken alive. From Largs to Ayr his name was familiar to all those interested in the game of "jink the gauger", and there was not a hiding place within a dozen miles of the shore with which he was not acquainted.'

Walker was finally captured by excise officers and a complement of dragoons while trying to swim to a boat in Troon harbour one day in October 1821, having been betrayed by an associate. He was preparing to set out on a smuggling trip to Ireland when apprehended.

~

As is so often the case, the *Statistical Account of Scotland* gives an interesting view of the smuggling scene around the time, and entries for Ayrshire are particularly numerous and illuminating.

The Reverend Dr Dalrymple and the Reverend Dr McGill of the parish of 'Air' wrote that 'the people in general are humane and charitable, live comfortably, and are contented with their circumstances. Their morals, in many instances, have suffered by the practice of smuggling, which is not entirely suppressed in this place.'

In Dundonald, the Reverend Mr Robert Duncan noted that 'the Trome . . . is an arm of rock running near a mile into the sea . . . In its natural condition, it affords safe anchoring ground from every quarter but the north-west'.

He went on

> While the Isle of Man remained a distinct sovereignty, the Trome was found to be a very convenient station for vessels employed in contraband trade. The British government gave the first check to smuggling upon the coast, by purchasing the regal power of that petty state. Happily the commutation act has nearly annihilated the hostile traffic. It must be acknowledged that lessening some duties to a certain degree would not injure the revenue; and yet more effectually cut up the business than a fleet of cutters, or an army of custom and excise officers.

In Girvan, the Reverend Mr James Thomson made the telling observation that 'the practice of smuggling . . . which, for a number of years, was carried on to a considerable extent on this coast, contributed in no small degree to the increase of the town of Girvan . . . habits of regular industry were probably prevented or destroyed by the practice of smuggling, to which the inhabitants were, for a long time, so much addicted.'

The Reverend Mr Thomas Pollock of Kilwinning observed that

> . . . so high are the Irish duties on Scottish muslins, and on every kind of Scotch goods, in which there is so much as a single thread of cotton

yarn, as amounts to a total prohibition of carrying these goods to the Irish market. This gives the greatest encouragement to smuggling, and has also made several very considerable cotton manufacturers leave Glasgow, and other places in its neighbourhood, and settle in Ireland. At the same time, it is not a little surprising, that Irish linens are brought into Scotland duty free. Does this not discover an undue partiality in favour of that kingdom? It is thought, that no less than 100,000L. worth of Scottish muslins, and other Scotch cotton goods, would be annually sold in the Irish market, were it not for these excessively high duties.

Kirkoswald's Reverend Mr Matthew Biggar echoed Robert Duncan's views on the Isle of Man and the Commutation Act, but noted that much smuggling was also carried on from '. . . France, Ostend, and Gottenburgh'.

In addition to the Commutation Act, he believed, smuggling had been reduced by '. . . the greatest attention and vigilance of his Majesty's revenue officers. Little is now done in that way, and it is to be hoped that the time is fast coming, when the illicit trade will be at an end. Though the character and behaviour of those engaged in this business, were, for the most part, in other respects good; yet, without doubt, it produced very bad effects on the industry of the people, and gave them a taste for luxury and finery, that spoiled the simplicity of manners which formerly prevailed in this parish.'

The Reverend Mr Gilbert Lang of Largs noted that 'there is no smuggling worth the mentioning, unless the pitiful and occasional help given to the poor seamen, in their little adventures, can be called such.' Mr William Crawford of Straiton was apparently of much the same opinion regarding his parish: 'Before the late extension of the excise laws, there were in Straiton a considerable number of smugglers. The late regulations, having increased the risk, at the same time that they diminished the profits, have, in this place, almost entirely put an end to this kind of illicit trade.' It is interesting to note that despite his disapproval of the smuggling trade, he added that 'the decay of smuggling had reduced several families, that used to live plentifully, to great poverty, so that the number of poor may be expected to increase.'

Writing of the local saltpan, the Reverend Dr James Wodrow of Stevenston observed that 'a cargo of salt is sometimes shipped from Saltcoats to the coasts of Galloway and Nithsdale, but never to Ireland; on the contrary, over the whole west coast of Scotland, from the Mull to the Solway Firth, the Irish salt is smuggled in such quantities as to be very prejudicial to the salt manufacturers and to the revenue.'

～

In 1634 the first Revenue ship appeared in the Clyde, and in 1647 we have an early record of a customs operation on the west coast when the vessel *Margaret of Cumbray* had her cargo of smuggled Irish cloth and silk stockings impounded.

In 1684 John Boyle of Kelburn and a business partner, Robert Grierson, bought the rights to collect duty for the sum of £38,000 annually, which illustrates the large amount of dutiable goods being imported to the west coast even at that time. Under the terms of the arrangement, Boyle and Grierson were granted the right to '. . . search for, seize and apprehend all Irish victual and cattle, and salt beef made thereof, as shall be imported from Ireland into any harbour, river, etc . . .'

The economic shift from east to west coast midway through the following century was largely brought about because of the tobacco trade, with Glasgow becoming the most important tobacco port in Europe.

In *A Tour in Scotland in 1769,* Thomas Pennant wrote of Aberdeen that 'it once enjoyed a good share of the tobacco trade, but at length was forced to resign it to Glasgow, which was so much more conveniently situated for it.' Pennant observed of Glasgow: 'The great imports of this city are tobacco and sugar: of the former, above 40,000 hogsheads have been annually imported, and most part of it again exported into France and other countries.'

Thousands of vessels arrived each year at the ports of Port Glasgow and Greenock with their cargoes of tobacco, and the following letter extract, dated 8 July 1775, from the Collector of Customs at Port Glasgow to the Board of Customs in Edinburgh hints at the amount of business which the port was dealing with at that time.

> We have to observe on this affair that we sincerely wish a stop could be put to the discharging of these vessels with grain at the Holy Loch and that for obvious reasons. The business of this port is so great that it cannot admit of sending a landwaiter to attend such tedious discharges where they (in a manner) make warehouses of the vessels and sell the [oat]meal out of them as they find purchasers, sometimes not above a few bolls per day of the discharge being intrusted to tidesmen, they are not vigilant and attentive as they should be but not only allow the vessels into which they discharge it to come over the water into this country but that means entirely defeating the intention of the law, but we have good reason to likewise believe they discharge upon the warrant they receive whatever quantities may be on board the vessels.

The Collector concluded:

> This practice may also be productive of further bad consequences by encouraging smuggling, for as they are so distant from the port in a bay

well sheltered and so much concealed from the view of any revenue vessel and have so small a check upon their conduct, it may well be supposed they will not let slip such opportunities of concealing spirits, tea and other prohibited goods among their meal, and running the same into the country to the great prejudice of the revenue and the fair trader.

In 1765 the Collector at the same port had felt obliged to write to the Board to the effect that smugglers '. . . go about with Foreign spirits in gangs or companies armed with large clubs and attended with mastiffs and bid defiance to the officers of the revenue they even threaten the coll, and say that notwithstanding his endeavours to curb them he shall find to no purpose that all they have to fear is their being prosecute as rioters and pay a fine which they do not regard.'

In most cases, the tobacco arriving at ports such as Port Glasgow was legally landed, then ostensibly re-exported, at which point the import duty was refunded. The tobacco would then be landed covertly on British soil again, and sold. Most of the tobacco supposedly exported to Norway, for example, was actually re-imported for smuggling purposes, and the same applied to significant quantities apparently destined for France, Flanders and Holland.

Large amounts of tobacco, and also rum, were legally imported onto the west coast purely to serve the smuggling market. While the Isle of Man was regularly being used for smuggling, rum and tobacco would be shipped from North America to Scotland, then exported to Europe, from where it was sent to the Isle of Man. Along with tea and brandy, the rum and tobacco were then run into Scotland. In most instances, only the final run ashore from the Isle of Man to Scotland was illegal.

Tobacco imports peaked at a value of approximately £490,000 in 1775, three times their worth 20 years previously, and L.M. Cullen notes (*Smuggling and the Ayrshire Economic Boom*) that '. . . the smuggling business followed a corresponding profile. Rum trade peaked also in those years, especially in 1771, and tea activity as well was at a high level'.

The major Glasgow merchants who effectively controlled the tobacco trade, had little interest in tea and rum, so the smaller coastal merchants tended to be significant traders in those commodities. According to Cullen, 'a close cooperation linked interests on the Irish side on the coasts of Louth and Down and in Scotland on the coasts of Ayrshire and Galloway'.

Belfast and Dublin merchants were involved, as rum was the only colonial commodity which could be imported directly into Ireland legally. Due to a quirk of the revenue laws, rum attracted less duty in Ireland if it came in via Britain. Therefore, much of it was hastily turned around in Scottish west-coast ports after being shipped from abroad. This led to the development of close business associations between west-coast and Irish merchants.

Some rum shipped into Ireland was sold there legally, but much was re-exported to Scotland via the Down and Antrim coasts. Central to such operations was the Belfast business syndicate of Galan Thompson & Co.

By the 1760s Scotland had already come to account for more than half the total imports of tobacco into Britain, and, as Cullen puts it, 'that meant that the needs of entrepots which supplied tobacco to smugglers could be satisfied more readily and efficiently from Glasgow than from any other British port'. Daniel Defoe wrote

> Glasgow is a city of business; here is the face of trade, as well foreign as home trade; and, I may say, 'tis the only city in Scotland, at this time, that apparently encreases and improves in both. The Union has answer'd its end to them more than to any other part of Scotland, for their trade is new form'd by it; and, as the Union open'd the door to the Scots in our American colonies, the Glasgow merchants presently fell in with the opportunity; and tho', when the Union was making, the rabble of Glasgow made the most formidable attempt to prevent it, yet, now they know better, for they have the greatest addition to their trade by it imaginable; and I am assur'd, that they send near fifty sail of ships every year to Virginia, New England, and other English colonies in America, and are every year increasing.
>
> Could this city but have a communication with the Firth of Forth, so as to send their tobacco and sugar by water to Alloway, below Sterling, as they might from thence again to London, Holland, Hambrough, and the Baltick, they would, (for ought I know that should hinder it) in a few years double their trade, and send 100 sail, or more.

The development of the Forth–Clyde Canal, which opened in 1790, created that communication, and it provided a valuable and well-used trading link between the west and east coasts. By then, however, Glasgow's tobacco trade had been devastated by the American War of Independence.

William Ferguson (*Scotland 1689 to the Present*) notes that growth in trade between Glasgow and American and West Indian colonies 'stimulated the industries of Scotland as a whole. Such trade was not new, but after 1707 it was free to expand, though at first hampered by lack of capital and of adequate shipping. In the first decade of Union ships had to be chartered from the port of Whitehaven in Cumberland. Up to 1728 the trade fluctuated, but overall there was fairly steady expansion, especially after 1718 when Clyde-owned shipping played the major part in the trade.'

According to Ferguson, 'the route to and from the Clyde was easier for vessels and safer than that used by the English ports; the Scots merchants were accommodating in the matter of debts, and, living frugally, they managed to undercut their rivals'.

L.M. Cullen notes that Robert Arthur was a key west-coast figure in the supply of tobacco to the smuggling trade, dealing with the most important of Glasgow's 'tobacco lords', Alexander Speirs. Arthur was also involved in importing tea from Gothenburg during the early 1760s.

Cullen makes the point that the need to trade with ports such as those in Guernsey, Holland, France, and even the Faroe Islands after the Isle of Man ceased to be a haven for smugglers in 1765, necessitated the use of larger vessels than had plied the short Man to Scotland route, and added considerably to overall costs. Capital and credit were required as never before, and this aspect of the smuggling business, combined with growing legal trade, led to the growth of banking services in the west of Scotland.

Cullen singles out the Ayr Bank as a particularly interesting example relevant to smuggling. According to Cullen, 'the most prominent of the merchant shareholders, in terms of number of shares held, had a large stake in the smuggling business'.

Leading figures included John Christian, David McClure and George McCree, the latter two being partners in a venture which supplied merchandise to the smugglers. Later, Robert Arthur, a merchant from Irvine with smuggling connections, also became involved in the bank as a significant shareholder. Christian was the bank's cashier, but his smuggling antecedents drew criticism from many quarters. His business was originally based in Man, and he only moved to Ayr in 1769, the year in which the bank was founded.

He probably stopped having direct smuggling dealings in 1769, but he continued to be associated with a number of Clyde coast smuggling-related businesses while involved with the bank. Cullen notes that 'the Ayr Bank, with its smuggling interest, was by definition something of an anti-establishment venture'. A recession in 1772 helped bring about the collapse of the Ayr Bank, which was placed in liquidation in August 1773.

Large quantities of spirits were smuggled into the long, remote Kintyre peninsula, an area ideal for the purpose, being sparsely populated and conveniently close to Ireland. Such was the scale of this smuggling during the eighteenth century that legal Scottish distillers complained that their trade was suffering as a result. Salt from Ireland was also regularly smuggled into Kintyre, as illustrated by the following letter, dated 13 May 1776, from the Customs Surveyor in the Kintyre 'capital' of Campbeltown:

> Be pleased to received inclosed a return (No. 62) by Lachlan McNeill surveyor at this port of an open boat belonging to Whiteing Bay in Arran, Archibald McAlester master, which was seized on the 12th instant, off Glenmanuilt in the Mull of Kintyre for having imported a parcel of Irish salt from Glenarm in Ireland, which was landed said day on the shoar of Glenmanuilt. When the people of the seized boat saw the king's boat in chase of them they run immediately for the Mull of Kintyre (the nearest shoar), where they got the salt thrown out on the rocks and beach before the surveyor and his people could come up and by the time our boat got there a mob of men and women had gathered about the salt, who pelted the surveyor and his hands with stones so smartly that they were obliged to go off without the salt. Neither Mr McNeill nor the boatmen knew any of the persons concerned in the mob nor could we since hear what afterwards became of the salt, nor any other certain account of the quantity that had been landed.

Campbeltown and its customs staff also feature in the somewhat farcical story of the smuggling vessel *Nancy and Peggy*. In the autumn of 1792, Campbeltown customs officers seized the boat in Kilbrannan Sound, the stretch of water which separates the east side of the long Kintyre peninsula from the west shore of the Isle of Arran. However, the smuggling crew somehow managed to re-take the *Nancy and Peggy*, forcing three members of the customs cutter involved into a small rowing boat. This subsequently sank, drowning the cutter's mate. The rest of the cutter's crew succeeded in retaking the *Nancy and Peggy* after firing on her, and the three smuggling ringleaders were placed in Campbeltown jail, which already held several debtors.

The leader of the smugglers, John King, managed to escape very quickly, as a result of which the jailer was relieved of his position, the guard increased, and the keys to the jail placed with the local Collector of Customs.

This was no guarantee of security, however, and after a fortnight, one of the debtors escaped, followed a few days later by a second smuggler. It took the last of the three smugglers a further four days to escape, a feat accomplished by cutting a hole in the floor of his cell and getting away via a window in the courtroom below.

By the end of the eighteenth century, the smuggling trade on the west coast was a shadow of its former self, partly due to the general reduction in the level of many duties, and also to the fact that by the late eighteenth century, the market had become 'flooded' with many types of smuggled commodity, thus reducing their value and thereby the attraction of smuggling them.

The collector at Port Glasgow noted in March 1822 that it appeared from comparative records covering the previous three years that '. . . smuggling from foreign parts at this port is now in a great measure at an end upon the whole'.

According to the Customs Collector at Rothesay on the Isle of Bute in 1828, he knew of no smuggling within his jurisdiction taking place at that time, although he did indicate that smuggled goods continued to be carried as far up the Firth of Clyde as 'the Troon point', and that Irish salt was smuggled on small, open boats to various locations on the coast, 'particularly up Loch Fine' – no doubt because of the thriving herring fishery there.

In 1834 the officer in charge of the Largs Revenue Post reported that smuggling principally consisted of whisky from the Highlands and soap from Ireland.

## 3. The North-West and Islands of the West

If remote parts of the mainland were ideal for landing and hiding smuggled goods, then islands were even more suitable. Many small west-coast islands, such as Lunga and Sanda, provided convenient places to store contraband while waiting for weather conditions to improve before landing on the mainland, or until the smugglers were convinced that the coast was clear at the places where they wished to land their goods.

Sanda is just off the southern tip of the Mull of Kintyre, and was popular with Irish smugglers seeking to land items on the Ayrshire coast, while Lunga lies north of Jura and south of Mull. Rathlin, off the north Antrim coast of Ireland, was also noted for its role in the storage of smuggled goods.

In *The Ordnance Survey Guide to Smugglers' Britain*, Richard Platt notes that the Monach Islands, off the west coast of North Uist, were used as a smuggling base and for storage of contraband commodities, but heavy tides and poor weather in this very exposed location meant that the removal of goods to the mainland was always fraught with logistical difficulties. It was reported in 1791 that the swell was so extreme that two boats spent a fortnight unloading 1,500 casks of brandy.

Larger, more populous islands, such as Arran, Skye and Lewis, were in themselves good markets for smuggled goods, though sometimes cargoes were just 'passing through'.

On 16 March 1784 the Stornoway Collector wrote to the Board of Customs, noting that the comptroller, James Robertson, had seized a quantity of tea – which was dispatched to the Board along with the letter – '. . . at the side of Loch Maree a fresh water loch twelve miles in length'. The Collector noted that the tea had been '. . . brought from Gairloch by land and carried across the loch in a boat by William Fraser, Alexander McDonald and Murdoch MacPhail, tenants upon Sir Heston of Machmore's of Gairloch's estate, who only pay about 30s each yearly by rent and have not a subject should they be prosecuted'.

The tea, the Collector continued, '. . . was intended to be carried to the low country of Ross and Inverness-shire, where the comptroller was informed large quantities of tea had been carried about that time . . .'

In a letter of 5 July 1766 the Collector of Customs in Stornoway wrote to the Board stating that he believed '. . . brandy and rum with some quantities of tea are the principal foreign commodities that are run into this island'. They further stated that the majority of the contraband was consumed by the inhabitants of Lewis, '. . . and the remainder furnished by them to the people of the neighbouring islands and continent'.

On 22 October 1807, the Stornoway Collector responded to the Board's request '. . . to procure the best possible information respecting the smuggling trade carried on upon the coast of our own and neighbouring ports and the most effective means of suppressing the same'. He noted that

> . . . the smuggling trade carried on upon the coast of the ports of Stornoway, Isle Martin, Fort William and Tobermory, being the extent to which our information connects, is principally confined to and carried on by three or four cutters or luggers of and from Guernsey, who generally visit the most remote lochs and creeks of the above mentioned ports once and sometimes twice a year. The articles of which their lading chiefly consist are rum, brandy, Geneva and wine in small casks, each of the contents of nine gallons, and unmanufactured tobacco in matts or bales, weighing 120lbs each. These goods are disposed of in small quantities to the gentlemen tacksmen tavern keepers small tenants and fishermen inhabiting the coast and adjacent country of the different lochs and creeks at which they call, landed in small open boats from the shore, manned by the natives and immediately dispersed over a large tract of country, being for the most part carried on mens [sic] shoulders. The quantities so landed in the course of the last twelve months on the coasts of the above specified ports may amount to betwixt 1,200 and 1,500 gallons of spirits and wine and from one to two tons of tobacco. We are much of opinion that on the coast of our own port and probably on the coasts of the other ports mentioned the pernicious trade might be greatly suppressed if the different landed proprietors were to give their hearty concurrence by not

only discouraging their factors tacksmen small tenants and fishermen but by threatening them with their severest displeasure in every instance where they could be detected in purchasing contraband from to anywise aiding or assisting a smuggling vessel or any person having concern therewith. In case this measure may be resorted to we subjoin a list of the proprietors who have property in the district of this port and it is very probable that the numerous volunteer force [sic] along the coast might be found, under proper regulations, very serviceable in checking this illicit trade.

The letter bears the names of John Reid and Jas Robertson, respectively Collector and Comptroller at Stornoway.

Stornoway also features in one of the more obscure episodes of Scottish smuggling history. Writing of Sir James Matheson, noted nineteenth-century Scottish society figure and philanthropist, Jeremy Watson observed in a *Scotland on Sunday* newspaper article (October 2002), ' . . by today's moral standards, Matheson might be better described as a major international drugs baron who enriched himself by smuggling opium into China in one of the darkest chapters of Victorian empire building'.

James Matheson was born in Lairg, Sutherland, in 1796, and became a trader in the Far East, founding Jardine Matheson and Co. during the 1820s, in partnership with William Jardine, a former surgeon from Lochmaben in Dumfriesshire.

Jardine had previously worked for the East India Company, which produced opium in India. The company's most significant market was China, but the respectable East India Company could not be seen to sell opium into China, as it was officially banned by the Chinese government.

The EIC was desperate to obtain Chinese tea and silks to sell in Britain, and so used independent traders such as Matheson and Jardine to smuggle the opium into China, where it was exchanged for the desired commodities.

The venture was a massive success, with the Scots traders working from hulks which were based among the islands of the Pearl River. The trade earned Matheson and Jardine a fortune, and became so important to British interests that the country fought the 'Opium War' from 1839 to 1842 in order to maintain it. The conflict began when the Chinese government refused to pay compensation for opium seized from British traders. William Jardine returned from the Far East in 1839, and acted as an adviser to Lord Palmerston, the Foreign Secretary, on the best ways to fight the Chinese.

Matheson became a taipan in Hong Kong, subsequently returning to Britain in 1842, when his fortune was estimated to have been worth in excess of £1bn in today's terms. He purchased the island of Lewis in 1844 for £190,000, going on to build Lews Castle in Stornoway, which was to be his home for the next three decades. He spent some £200,000 improving the island economy and infrastructure, being awarded a knighthood for his efforts. He died in 1878.

In *A Summer in Skye*, written around 1867, Alexander Smith observed

> The house of my friend Mr M'Ian is set down on the shore of one of the great Lochs that intersect the island; and as it was built in smuggling times, its windows look straight down the Loch towards the open sea. Consequently at night, when lighted up, it served all the purposes of a lighthouse: and the candle in the porch window, I am told, has often been anxiously watched by the rough crew engaged in running a cargo of claret or brandy from Bordeaux. Right opposite, on the other side of the Loch, is the great rugged fringe of the Cuchullin hills; and lying on the dry summer grass you can see it, under the influence of light and shade, change almost as the expression of a human face changes.

When touring the Hebrides, Dr Samuel Johnson soon discovered that the wine which he and his companion James Boswell were drinking had not been the subject of duty. Johnson wrote in *A Journey to the Western Islands of Scotland* (1775), while referring to time spent at the Mackinnons' house of Coriatachan on Skye, and the quality and range of food available, 'if an epicure could remove by a wish, in quest of sensual gratifications, wherever he had supped he would breakfast in Scotland'.

He added 'where many questions are to be asked, some will be omitted. I forgot to inquire how they were supplied with so much exotic luxury. Perhaps the French may bring them wine for wool, and the Dutch give them tea and coffee at the fishing season, in exchange for fresh provision. Their trade is unconstrained; they pay no customs, for there is no officer to demand them; whatever therefore is made dear only by impost, is obtained here at an easy rate.'

In *The Book of Arran*, W.M. Mackenzie wrote at length on the subject of smuggling and the Isle of Arran:

> An occupation, which by the close of the eighteenth century had grown to the proportions of a national industry, was the smuggling of dutiable articles; and in this business Arran, possessing many advantages from its insular character, had a good share. As duties, under the demand for a greater revenue, spread and increased, one thing after another became a profitable speculation for the smuggler. The malt duty of 1725 discouraged the ancient brewing of the home-made ale, and Dutch gin and French brandy became its unfortunate substitutes. We have observed the trade

in French wines to the Ayrshire ports; there was gain now to be made by receiving the spirits from ships passing up the firth, before they reached a custom-house, and retailing at a profit what had not paid duty. A tax on salt had been levied in 1702, which rose to 5s. a bushel in 1798, but was ultimately pushed up to the extravagant figure of 15s., or from thirty to forty times the prime cost. Here was a huge margin of profit, and it is no matter of surprise that enterprising fellows were found eager to tap it and take the risks. Finally, the taste for spirits encouraged the making of whisky, which then was also scooped into a narrower revenue net. Improving agriculture was increasing the yield of barley, and rents rose correspondingly, yet the wretched condition of the roads made it almost impossible to bring the grain to central markets from remote districts, while multiplying legal restrictions made small stills impossible. In fact, over the Highland districts legal distillation was practically prohibited in order to concentrate the industry in the larger distilleries of the south. Yet barley had to be disposed of or rents could not be paid.

There were thus two sides to the smuggling business; introducing stuff which had escaped the duty, and the manufacturing of whisky under illegal conditions, which therefore again had to be sold clandestinely. Both practices flourished in Arran; in time smuggled salt and illicit whisky, and particularly the latter, became the staples of this commingling of industry and adventure.

Mackenzie also made the rarely documented point that in addition to the illegal distillation of whisky from barley 'there was also a distilling of rum from treacle'.

Mackenzie quoted from the *New Statistical Account*, relating to the Arran parish of Kilmorie, in the south-west of the island, a notorious place for illicit whisky distilling and smuggling of various goods:

> . . . [there were] few if any in the parish who at some period of their lives were not engaged in some department of smuggling. To the smuggler no stigma was attached on account of his employment; on the contrary, it was considered rather an honourable occupation, as exhibited an intrepidity and art that acquired for their possessor a distinction in the minds of his companions. It was in the darkest night, and in the most tempestuous weather, when no [revenue] cruiser would stand the gale, that, in his little skiff, the smuggler transported his cargo to the opposite shores of Ayrshire.

To illustrate specific examples of Arran smuggling, Mackenzie drew on the Kirk Session Records for Kilmorie parish and presented a series of extracts relating to one not untypical case, 'final judgment upon which, however, is wanting . . .':

(*Session*) July 16, 1711. – It is reported to the Sess. that John Hamilton Elder having taken on board drawback tobacco in Clyde and deponed in the Custom house of Newport Glasgow that he would export it from Britain and not reland it in any part whatsomever within the S'd Kingdom: notwithstanding of which oath he did put the sd tobacco on shore at Cambray he is therefore appointed to be sum: against next Dyett.

July 29. – John Hamilton Sum: Cited, and compering confesses that he did but put the tobacco on shore in the Isle of Cambray, but denies he gave his oath at the Custom house. The Session Suspends John Hamilton from his office of Eldership till further tryall of the business, and appoints the rest of the shipping to be sum: against next Dyett, viz: William Stirling in Strawhillan, James Fullerton in Brodick, and Patrick Hamilton in Glenshent.

August 19. – William Stirling being absent from the country the appointment is continued.

James Fullerton sum: cit: and compeiring declares that he knows not whether John Hamilton entred skipper and deponed in the Custom house, but that indeed the tobacco was landed in the little Cambray. The Session delays the business till the other witnesses compeir.

October 18. – John Hamilton sum: cit: and compeiring is further examined anent the report given of him and he confesses that about Candlemas 1709 he as Skipper of his own boat was fraughted by severall Merchands to take tobacco on board the which he actually did; and that one of themselves or some other employed by them, ent'red Skipper and Merchand in the Custom house and that the sd tobacco was landed in the manner above confessed by himself and that he thought himself Guiltless upon the account he did not give his oath in the Custom house.

The crew of John Hamilton's boat are all appointed to be sum: against next Dyett.

(Nothing further.)

Taking quotations from the *Glasgow Courant* for 1754, Mackenzie wrote

The next case is of a more serious colour. On July 4, 1754, three Arran men are on trial before the High Court of Justiciary in Edinburgh for obstructing the officers of the Customs at Lamlash. They are James M'Kirdy, Thomas Hamilton, and Alexander Hamilton. The charge is of forcibly attacking, deforcing, and obstructing in October 1753, 'Daniel Campbell, an officer of the Customs, and his assistants in the execution of their duty, in seizing and securing prohibited and uncustomed goods.' Found guilty, they were sentenced 'to be banished during their lives to one or other of His Majesty's Plantations in America, never to return to Scotland under pain of being whipped through the streets of Edinburgh by the hands of the Common Hangman, and to be banished again as aforesaid, and to remain in prison until a fit opportunity shall offer for their transportation – To the great satisfaction of all fair Traders.'

And so a long farewell to the unlucky M'Kirdy and his associates.

This case involved another, in so far as an Arran farmer, Archibald M'Killop, had tried to save M'Kirdy by the simple device of perjury. For this he was brought to trial in November, when he threw himself on the mercy of the court, and for his 'enormous and horrid crime' was banished for one year on the terms of a similar whipping if he returned before that time. Fortunately for M'Killop there was no duty on truth-telling, or he would have gone all the way of his friends.

Sometimes, smuggling in the islands was of the local, opportunistic variety, as demonstrated in the following vivid account from the *Argyllshire Herald* of 27 May 1859:

The brig Mary Ann, of Greenock, now lying a wreck at Kilchoman Bay, Islay, is fast breaking up, and portions of the cargo floating ashore. Up to Saturday there had been about 200 boxes saved, containing bottled brandy, whisky, and gin, and upwards of six puncheons of whisky, brandy, and wine; but the wildest scenes of drunkenness and riot that can be imagined took place. Hundreds of people flocked from all parts of the neighbourhood, especially the Portnahaven fishermen, who turned out to a man. Boxes were seized as soon as landed, broken up, and the contents carried away and drunk. Numbers could be seen here and there lying amongst the rocks, unable to move, while others were fighting like savages. Sergeant Kennedy and constable Chisholm, of the County Police, were in attendance, and used every means in their power to put a stop to the work of pillage. They succeeded in keeping some order during the day of Thursday, but when night came on the natives showed evident symptoms of their disapproval of the police being there at all, and on the latter preventing a fellow from knocking the end out of a puncheon, in order, as he said, to 'treat all hands,' they were immediately seized upon by the mob, and a hand to hand fight ensued, which lasted half an hour, and ended in the defeat of the police, of whom there were only two against from 30 to 40 of the natives. The police beat a retreat to Cuil Farm – about a mile from the scene of action – closely pursued by about 30 of the natives, yelling like savages. Mrs Simpson of Cuil, on seeing the state of matters, took the police into the house and secured the doors, at the same time placing arms at their disposal for their protection. The mob yelled two or three times round the house, but learning that the police had got fire-arms, they left and returned to the beach. Next morning the scene presented was still more frightful to contemplate. In one place there lay stretched the dead body of a large and powerful man. Donald M'Phayden, a fisherman from Portnahaven, who was considered the strongest man in Islay; but the brandy proved to be still stronger. He has left a wife and family. Others apparently in a dying state were being conveyed to the nearest houses, where every means were used to save life. Mrs Simpson, who is a very kind and humane person, supplied every remedy, but there was no medical man within fifteen or sixteen miles of the place. Mr James Simpson got a coffin made for M'Phayden, and had him interred on Friday. At the time when the corpse was being taken away, some groups could be seen fighting, others dancing, and others craving for drink, in order, as they said, to bury the man decently. Up to Saturday there was only one death, but on Monday it was reported that two more had died.

Wreckings were common occurences, but the captains of smuggling vessels tended to run greater risks at sea than captains carrying legal cargoes, as they were often forced to wait off shore for considerable periods of time in inclement weather before landing, when maritime prudence would have dictated taking shelter in harbour.

In January 1805, a Galway-based sloop called the *Rover* went aground at Carrick, on the coast of the Isle of Lewis. She had sailed from Guernsey with a mixed cargo, predominantly consisting of tobacco, along with a little port, brandy, 'geneva' and a keg of sugar, ostensibly bound for Bergen in Norway.

The Collector of Customs in Stornoway noted in one of a series of letters to the Board of Customs – with the names of John Reid (collector) and Jas Robertson (comptroller) appended – his opinion that the *Rover* had actually been bound for the west coast of Ireland, and had almost certainly unloaded part of her cargo there before bad weather forced her back out to sea. The Collector wrote, however, that '. . . the master gives out that he hove what was wanting of it [the cargo] overboard to lighten the vessel. It was undoubted that they were in great distress for want of provisions and intentionally ran the vesel [sic] on shore to save their lives, being almost exhausted to the last pitch. The goods were discharged and scattered for and on behalf of the master and by agents employed by him with the promise of being rewarded in proportion to what they may save from the search of the revenue officers.'

The *Rover* was subsequently sold to local fishermen by the master, and by the time the Comptroller of Customs arrived on the scene, six days after the wreck had occurred, he found only the vessel and forty-eight bales of water-damaged tobacco 'in the custody of servants'. The vessel was seized, but fortunately for the fishermen who had purchased it, the '. . . sale was conditioned by the purchasers to be non-effective in case of seizure by revenue officers'.

It was noted that 'what escaped the pillage of the country people of her sails and rigging was given to honest persons in charge of whom it could be properly secured. Two men were given charge of the hull'.

It all sounds rather reminiscent of a wreck that occurred 130 years later not that far to the south in the Sound of Barra . . . (see *Whisky Smuggling*).

Billy Kay (*Knee Deep in Claret*) tells the story of the barque *Suzanne* which left Limerick in the west of Ireland for St Malo during December 1634 with a valuable cargo of wine and other merchandise. The vessel was forced to take shelter off South Uist in bad weather, and in return for the promise of a barrel of Spanish wine and one of raisins, the islanders agreed to help the *Suzanne* to reach a safe anchorage. Once this was accomplished, the islanders proceeded to plunder the vessel, with the clear support of the Macdonald laird Clan Ranald and Benbecula's Ragnall Mor. Having emptied the vessel of its cargo the locals then offered the captain £8 for his vessel, which was worth closer to £150. They seem to have made it clear that they were not prepared to take no for an answer.

Contributors to The *Statistical Account of Scotland* in the Western Highlands and Islands had some informative observations to make with regard to smuggling, with the Reverend Mr Lachlan McLachlan of the parish of Craignish in mid-Argyll lamenting the scarcity of salt which was essential if the herring industry was to prosper: '. . . under the present system of management, [salt] is an article with which people in the Highlands can never be properly supplied. The want of stores judiciously disposed through the country – the bonds and provisos that stand in the way, render it impossible to make a general provision for a herring fishing which, on many parts of the coast, is transitory and precarious. Thus smuggling is encouraged, nay, made necessary; and thus the fishing in general is discouraged . . .'

The Reverend Mr Dugal Campbell of the parish of Kilfinichen and Kilviceven on the island of Mull echoed his colleague's comments on salt, while another commentator tackled the subject in some detail:

Before the subject of the fishing is dropped, it may be proper to observe the hardship the country people suffer from the salt laws, both as to the herring and white fishing. Every kind of fishing must be partially carried on by them; that is, they can only fish when not throng at their farming. But even this partial fishing, they are restrained from by the salt laws; for it cannot be supposed, that a man will go 40 or 50 miles to a customshouse with the little fish he has cured, or perhaps with his little salt, without any fish at all. Country people also, never will go to a different customhouse for salt, till the herring appear in the lochs, for fear, as often happens, the fishing may fail; and that having no proper place to keep the salt, it may, in different ways be embezzled, and they incur all the penalties of the salt laws. When the herring appear, the weather may be bad, the distance to a customhouse great, the salt damaged in their open boats, and the herring, in a great measure, disappear, or, at least, much valuable time lost before they return home to the fishing. There is a customhouse in Tobermory in Mull; but the Oban customhouse is as near the parish of Ross. The café is nothing better as to smuggled salt. The smugglers will at all times endeavour, by high prices, to indemnify themselves for the risk they run; and in times of scarcity, their prices are very high. The incumbent was told, that, in 1792, it was sold in some parts of the country at a guinea a barrel: but, however low smuggled salt may be in price, no fish cured with it can be sold in open market. If salt were duty free, all these grievances would be done away, and farmers and cottagers would cure fish, not only for their own private use, but also for sale. The incumbent does not pretend to say, what would be best for the herring busses [vessels specifically designed for herring fishing]. In all, he says, he had only in view the country people.

Writing of the parish of Kilfinan, on the Cowal peninsula to the east of Loch Fyne in Argyll, the Reverend Mr Alexander McFarlane attributed the lack of longevity among his parishioners to the fact that '. . . the last generation have been exceedingly addicted to drinking, owing to their having carried on a ruinous contraband trade with the Isle of Man, to an astonishing extent; the bad effects of which are discoverable in the parish to this day. It was only in the southern district of the parish, viz. the Kerry, that this trade was carried on, and consequently they were more wealthy, in general, than their neighbours in the northern division . . .'

He also confirmed the belief of other contributors to the *Statistical Account* that depopulation frequently followed the suppression of smuggling in remote communities. 'The smuggling business being at an end, contributed also to depopulate this parish; the most of those who dealt in it being bankrupt, were obliged to leave the place in order to push their business somewhere else'.

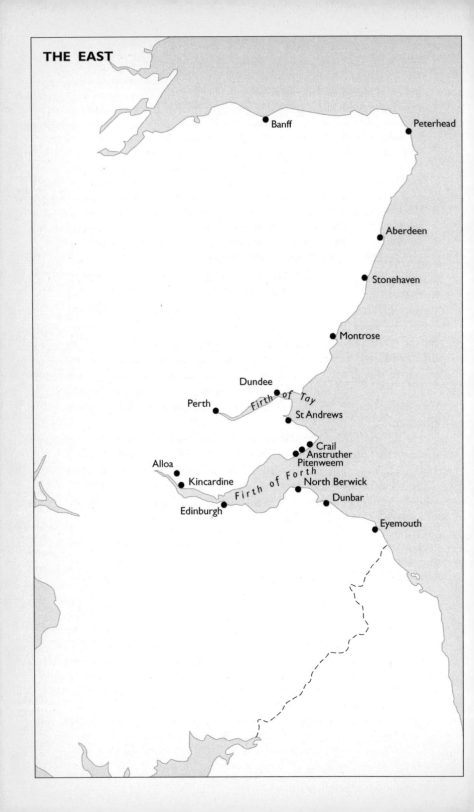

THE EAST

Banff

Peterhead

Aberdeen

Stonehaven

Montrose

Dundee

Perth

*Firth of Tay*

St Andrews

Crail
Anstruther
Pitenweem

Alloa

Kincardine

*Firth of Forth*

North Berwick

Dunbar

Edinburgh

Eyemouth

# 5

# THE EAST COAST

As we have already seen, during the eighteenth century the economy of the west coast, and the Clyde in particular, developed dramatically, while the east coast became less prosperous in terms of legal trading activity. Smuggling onto eastern shores, however, continued to thrive.

Whereas on the west, goods were often smuggled via the Isle of Man and small Scottish islands, the comparative lack of islands off the east coast meant that smugglers tended instead to rely more on fictional destinations, or 'pretended-bound' journeys. A ship would carry documents indicating she was taking a cargo to some plausible port that would necessitate sailing in the North Sea not too far off the Scottish coast. The pretence of bad weather, the requirement of repairs, the need to take on fresh stores or new crew members, would then be used to explain the presence of the vessel in, or close to, an east-coast port, where some of her cargo would then be smuggled onto land.

Smuggling onto the east coast involved vessels from France, Germany, Denmark, Holland, Norway, Poland, Portugal, Russia, Sweden and Spain. It is documented that during the eighteenth century wine and brandy were smuggled from French ports and from Campvere in Holland to St Andrews Bay, while gin and brandy from Germany were landed in Aberlady Bay, near Gullane, on the south shore of the Firth of Forth.

Contraband from Holland, including tea and spirits, often originating in Rotterdam, was regularly smuggled onto the east coast, and Newburgh, on the southern shore of the Firth of Tay, appears to have been a popular landing-place for such cargoes.

There are customs records of wine being smuggled from Spain into Dundee and Leith, and ports on the west coast of Sweden, such as Gothenburg, were inevitably attractive to smugglers bound for Scotland. The nearest Scottish harbour to Gothenburg was Leith, though as we have seen, there was also a significant trade between ports such as Gothenburg and the west coast of Scotland. Bergen in Norway was also ideally located for trading with the Scottish east coast, and was notably popular as a 'pretended-bound' destination, as well as an actual one.

The Isle of Man is inextricably linked with west-coast smuggling, but in 'The Representation and Memorial of the Commissioners of His Majesty's Customs & Excise in Scotland to the Right Honourable the Lords Commissioners of His Majesty's Treasury' (24 December 1764) the role of the Isle of Man in relation to east coast smuggling was examined.

Noting that Man was very convenient for running smuggled goods to the British mainland, the Commissioners also recorded

> . . . another advantage the smugglers draw from its situation. For at present the greatest part of the vessels loaded from Holland, Gothenburg etc. with uncustomed and high-dutied goods, intended for the east and northern ports of Britain, take out clearances and bills of lading for the Isle of Man, then run for the east coast, and if not discovered, unload their cargoes; but if they are found hovering, and are boarded by any of His Majesty's ships, they produce fictitious bills of lading, and consignments, and as they are really and truly but little out of their pretended course, they often save themselves under the pretence of being bound to the Isle of Man.
>
> Formerly vessels loaded in Holland etc and intending to run their cargoes on the east side of Great Britain, took up clearances for some port in Norway. But as nothing but contrary winds, stress of weather or want of provisions could be pleaded in excuse of their being found within the limits of a port, or the forbidden distance of the shore, they have changed their practice, and pretend they are bound for the Isle of Man; which is found by experience to be fatal to the revenue, and more safe and convenient for the illicit practices of the smugglers.

## 1. THE BORDERS, THE FORTH, AND FIFE

Because of the extensive trade in illicit whisky and Irish salt, which was transported through the Cheviot Hills, smuggling stories in the Borders often take place a long way from the sea. Coldstream and Kirk Yetholm – home to the legendary Wull Faa (see p. 157) – were places where salt in transit was stored, and at nearby Town Yetholm smuggling is said to have occupied up to twenty per cent of the population.

Borders smuggling had a long history, and the Reverend Thomas Somerville, Minister of Jedburgh, wrote in the *Statistical Account of Scotland* that 'the inhabitants of the Borders, while the taxes and the commercial regulations of the two kingdoms were different, enjoyed the opportunity of carrying on a very advantageous contraband trade, without danger to their persons or fortune. Into England they imported, salt, skins, and malt, which, till the union, paid no duties in Scotland; and from England they carried back wool, which was exported from the Frith (sic) of Forth to France, with great profit.'

The Roxburghshire town of Hawick is almost equidistant from both the east and west coasts of Scotland, yet it features in a popular story relating to smuggled gin. Hawick merchant and smuggler 'Wat the Candlemaker' had a reputation as a practical joker, and on one occasion he had a cask of smuggled gin in his possession when he learnt that the excise officers were aware of its presence. Lodging the gin with a trusted friend, he filled a cask with water and sank it in the Auld Brig Pool behind his house at Tower Knowe. He then let it be known around Hawick that this was where the gin had been hidden from the officers, and, not surprisingly, they soon mounted a search and located it. They were less than pleased to find when they sampled the contents that they had been fooled, but the joker was hoist with his own petard, as his 'trusted friend' refused to hand back the gin, and there was nothing Wat could do about it.

During smuggling's eighteenth-century heyday, the Berwickshire coast was a favourite area with smugglers, being blessed with steep cliffs, caves, and small, secluded creeks. Its most important port was Eyemouth, described in *The Report by Thomas Tucker upon the Settlement of the Revenues of Excise and Customs in Scotland* (1656) as 'not farre from South Barwick, where the Scots and English both did usually shippe out Skyns, Hides, Wooll, and other prohibited commodityes, and againe bring in such, which were there landed, and afterward carried away for the consumption and expence of the northerne parts of England. The distance of it from the first head-port of Scotland, and the vicinity of it to the last in England, whose officers had noe power there, gave occasion of much deceipt, which hath beene remedyed of late by placeing an officer there constantly to attend at that place, but to have an eye on all the creeks between that and Dunbarre, when any goods passe up by him into the Firth.'

The bay of Eyemouth is one of the few safe places to land vessels on the Berwickshire coast, and there was a harbour there by the thirteenth century. At various times during the sixteenth century, the town was held by the English, and it became known as the 'London docks of the Borders', a major smuggling centre during the eighteenth century.

Brandy, gin, tobacco, tea, and even spectacles were smuggled into Eyemouth bay and illegally traded in the town and beyond. When the poet Robert Burns was inducted into the local Masonic lodge, the event was celebrated with copious glasses of locally-landed illicit claret.

Contraband goods would be stored in town houses, many of which were built with secret cellars and hiding places expressly for this purpose. There were underground passages, vaults and cupboards, not to mention places built into roof thatches where contraband could be hidden. It has been said that more of the town existed below the ground than above! During the eighteenth century the headquarters for local smuggling was a building that is now the public library. A network of passageways linked it to nearby properties, and a secret compartment in which to hide bottles of smuggled spirit was built into a staircase. As smuggling diminished, Eyemouth developed into a significant fishing port, and by the mid-nineteenth century was one of the leading white-fish centres in Scotland.

Central to Eyemouth's smuggling heritage is Gunsgreen House, built in the 1750s to the design of James and John Adam. The mansion overlooks the harbour and was reputedly built for a local man who had made a fortune dealing in contraband. The house was apparently equipped with a number of secret chambers, and it is said that there was an opening in a wall that acted as a slipway straight into the sea. According to local lore, tunnels led as far as the village of Burnmouth, two miles to the south. Massive cellars were excavated under the lawn, and like something out of an Enid Blyton *Famous Five* tale, a fireplace swung open at the touch of a concealed lever to reveal the entrance to a secret passageway into the cellars below. During the 1880s a field on the Gunsgreen estate was being ploughed when the ground gave way and a horse plunged into a vaulted underground chamber, built as a storehouse for contraband.

Gunsgreen House has been described as the finest example of smuggling architecture in Scotland, and it has recently been refurbished, incorporating facilities in the basement for visiting yachtsmen, while the cellars have been converted into a 'smuggling interpretation centre'.

Just to the north of Eyemouth lies St Abb's Head, which provided not only a place to land cargoes, but also useful recesses in the rock of the promontory in which contraband could be concealed. Scootie Cove, between Eyemouth and Burnmouth, was a popular landing spot with smugglers, as was nearby Coollercove, near Killiedraughts.

On the southern shore of the Firth of Forth, Aberlady Bay – between Longniddry and Gullane – was a favoured spot at which to land contraband cargoes during the eighteenth century, and smuggling operations involved most of the villagers of Aberlady. Gullane Point was known as 'Jovey's Neuk' after Jehovah Gray, who lived in a stone cottage west of the Hummel Rock. Barges were beached in the bay and loaded with ironstone hewn from the headland and taken upriver to be smelted at the Carron Ironworks in Falkirk. Gray was a caretaker for William Cadell, owner of the Carron Ironworks, and legend has it that he supplemented his modest earnings by smuggling.

Thomas Tucker's 1656 'Report' consisted of an assessment of

Scotland's ports and coastline, written for Oliver Cromwell. Tucker observed that 'according to the most eminent places of Trade, the Commissioners have erected or established eight severall had ports or offices for Customes and Excise. Those lyeing on the East sea are Leith, Burrostones, Brunt Island, Dundee, Aberdeene and Invernesse; those on the west are only two, Glasgoe, and Ayre.'

Of Leith he wrote 'this place formerly, and soe at this time, is indeed a storehouse not onely for her owne traders, but alsoe for the merchants of the citty of Edinburgh, this being the port thereof . . . This Port being the cheife port of all of Scotland, the Commissoners, out of a willingnesse to have a particular eye upon the transacting of things, have therefore made election of it for theyr particular residence.'

After visiting Leith while preparing his *A Tour Through the Whole Island of Great Britain* (1724–26), Daniel Defoe declared, 'here is a very fine key well wharf'd up with stone, and fenc'd with piles, able to discharge much more business than the place can supply, tho' the trade is far from being inconsiderable too'.

Leith was the centre of the legitimate Scottish wine trade, doing brisk business in claret imported from Bordeaux by the early fifteenth century, though certainly French wine was being shipped to Scotland as early as the mid-thirteenth century. The 'Vaults' in Leith, part of the building now occupied by the Scotch Malt Whisky Society, were in existence by 1439, and the monks of Holyrood Abbey used the Vaults to store wine imported for their own use. Additionally, they had a right to dues on the importation of all wine entering the port of Leith. Such a levy could be quite a money-spinner, as Billy Kay (*Knee Deep in Claret*) has pointed out. Some 250,000 gallons of wine were imported into Leith per annum during the early seventeenth century, and 'with the impost of wine settling at round £32 8s. per tun in 1612, one sees why James [VI] looked after his wine trade – in Leith alone it brought him an annual income of over £32,000'.

During the eighteenth century, before the Nor' Loch was drained in 1787 and Edinburgh's New Town was developed, smugglers would row across the loch with casks of contraband wine and spirits from Leith under cover of darkness, and it would be taken up the closes of what is now the Old Town, to be decanted and distributed.

For many years before the Act of Union, Leith had been a centre for smuggling, and the local glassworks, wool-card factory and soap-works had long laboured under the difficulties of trying to compete with glass, wool and soap smuggled from abroad into the port, without the burden of duty. After the union, these difficulties were magnified once duty levels rose, as was the case throughout Scotland, and smuggling into Leith grew at a dramatic rate.

Edinburgh and Leith had formerly been home to all the business of the Scots parliament, whose noblemen and officials brought large volumes of trade. Post union, all this commerce vanished. There was also no short-term gain in international trade for Edinburgh and Leith, as so many businessmen had expected. Trade with France evaporated, as she was the traditional enemy of England, and the newly-unified Great Britain fought numerous wars with France during the eighteenth century. English manufacturing industries produced better quality items at cheaper prices than those of Edinburgh, and so local markets were soon flooded with their goods. Not surprisingly, these sold well, causing the decline of many local industries, particularly woollen manufacturing, which had developed significantly in and around Leith. The linen trade also went through a long period of depression.

If smuggling in Leith had begun long before union, it went on for many years after the two parliaments united.

A trading vessel put into Leith harbour in December 1821 with a full cargo of apples from Hamburg. Everything seemed fair and square, yet the excisemen insisted on prying into the sweet-smelling contents of the casks. There they found a very large amount of foreign silk, neatly done up in parcels, rolled in lead sheet and snugly stowed in the midst of the luscious fruit. The lead taking the impress of the great weight of apples both above and below it, retained its position immovably and being at the same time, absolutely waterproof, preserved the smuggle as no other wrapping would. On another occasion a casting vessel from the north put into Leith with hundreds of geese ready plucked aboard. Each contained a bottle of whisky!

– *Athol Forbes*, The Romance of Smuggling

Under the headline 'LEITH – ANOTHER EXTENSIVE SMUGGLING CASE', *The Scotsman* newspaper of 11 January 1883 wrote that 'Yesterday a seaman named James Smith was brought before a special Court, and remanded on a charge of concealing 28lb of tobacco on board the screw steamer *Geneva*, from Hamburg. Smith, it appears, paid a fine of £50 about two years ago for a similar offence. He will be tried on Wednesday.'

Another smuggling seaman who had served under Admiral Vernon at the siege of Portobello in Panama, during 1739, built a house near Leith in his retirement and named it Portobello after the South American town. His house was on the site where the town hall was later built, close to Bath Street, and it was a noted rendezvous point for local smugglers.

Vessels used in smuggling would have their appearance changed between runs to try to catch watching customs officers off guard, and in the case of Leith, they would frequently sail ostentatiously past the port during daylight, as though their destination was further up the Forth, then under cover of darkness would double back and deliver their contraband cargoes.

The harbour of Newhaven lies to the west of Leith, and was constructed by monks during the early sixteenth century. Later called Acheson's and Morrison's Haven, Newhaven was the centre for a great deal of smuggling by the late seventeenth century, as well as large-scale legitimate trade. As much as ten per cent of Scottish trade with foreign ships was transacted through the Forth port.

In his entry for the parish of Currie, south-west of Edinburgh, in *The Statistical Account of Scotland* Dr William Nisbet, 'an Edinburgh physician', wrote about the various causes of depopulation in the parish. He noted

> A peculiar one here may be added, viz. the suppression of smuggling. As this part of the country, is the opening to the shire of Ayr, (the chief seat of that trade,) it formed the retreat of those adventurers engaged in it, when bringing their goods to Edinburgh, being at a convenient distance, so that when a fit opportunity offered, they could easily transport them. Hence that clandestine commerce added formerly to the numbers of this parish, especially in the remote parts of it.

West of Edinburgh, as the Firth of Forth narrows, the port of Bo'ness on the southern shore was once of great significance. Defoe called it Boristown Ness, and wrote:

> It has been, and still is, a town of the greatest trade to Holland and France, before the Union, of any in Scotland, except Edinburgh; and, for shipping, it has more ships belong to it than to Edinburgh and Leith put together; yet their trade is declin'd of late by the Dutch trade, being carry'd on so much by way of England: but, as they tell us, the Glasgow merchants are resolving to settle a trade to Holland and Hamburgh in the Firth, by bringing their foreign goods, (viz.) their sugars and tobacco by land to Alloway [Alloa], and from thence export them as they see occasion. I say, in this case, which is very probable, the Borristoun [sic] Ness men will come into business again; for as they have the most shipping, so they are the best seamen in the Firth; and particularly they are not sailors only, but even pilots for the coast of Holland, they are so acquainted with it, and so with the Baltic, and the coast of Norway also.

Bo'ness had gained official recognition as a port in 1601, although it had already been trading as such for at least thirty-five years prior to that date. So much smuggling took place via the harbour that the Scottish Privy Council closed the port in 1602, and it remained out of legal commission for several years.

The first harbour was constructed at Bo'ness in 1707, and in 1733 the Custom House was moved to the town from nearby Blackness. In the same year the harbour was improved, but eleven years later the deteriorating condition of its quays and progressive silting were causing concern. It was decided to raise money to redevelop the harbour by imposing a tax of 2d. Scots per pint on Bo'ness beer, and despite opposition from brewers and publicans, an act of parliament was passed authorising this levy. Inevitably, significant quantities of beer were subsequently smuggled into Bo'ness through the very harbour that the beer duty was designed to improve!

Bo'ness enjoyed a long association with salt manufacture, and although the salt produced was said to be of good quality, production was not exactly efficient. It took around 100 tons of water and 50 tons of coal to produce three tons of salt, but yields were improved by adding rock salt, imported from Liverpool and Carrickfergus in Antrim.

By the late eighteenth century, forty-four officers were employed at Bo'ness Custom House, and salt remained a major local industry, attracting duty of £3,000 at the port in 1796. The harbour was also well used for the export of locally mined coal.

One of the few tangible reminders of the great days of international trading in Bo'ness is an old tobacco warehouse, the ground floor of which now forms the town's public library. Built in 1772, tobacco from North America was stored here in raw-leaf form before being exported to France, as it was from a number of east-coast ports.

On the north bank of the Forth, to the west of Bo'ness, lies the industrial town of Alloa, or 'Alloway', as Daniel Defoe spells it in his *A Tour Through the Whole Island of Britain*. Defoe wrote that 'there is a harbour for shipping, and ships of burthen may come safely up to it: and this is the place where the Glasgow merchants are, as I am told, erecting magazines or warehouses, to which they propose to bring their tobacco and sugars by land, and then to ship them for Holland or Hamburgh, or the Baltick, or England, as they find opportunity, or a market . . .'

In August 1786 the Board of Customs in Edinburgh sent a letter to each Collector of Customs and Customs cruiser captain asking specific questions relating to the amount of smuggled spirits landed within his jurisdiction during the past year. The Board was also keen to know the probable element of profit for the smugglers and the price at which the spirit was sold.

Captain Laurence Brown of the customs sloop *Princess Royal* sent an illuminating reply to the Collector of Customs at Alloa, which gives us a very useful indication of the scale and economics of smuggling at that time:

> I am of the opinion from my observations upon the manner in which smuggling is carried on upon the different parts of the east coast that 10,000 gallons may have been landed in your district in the period above-mentioned and that the difference in price between smuggled spirits and spirits of the same strength and quality or reduced to the same strength legally imported may be 80% or even 90%. It is impossible to be exact as to the receipts the smugglers may make, as that must depend upon their expense, which must vary greatly from circumstances and from the hire of boats, carts, horses, and porters etc differing very much in different parts of the country. But I apprehend they never would carry on a trade of that nature and continue it at such a risk and have so much trouble and anxiety as they must naturally have, if they did not clear a profit of at least 60%. I believe two thirds of the spirits smuggled upon this coast is Geneva.

Despite Brown's apparently authoritative response, and similar evidence from the captain of a second customs sloop, the Alloa Collector submitted that no spirits at all had been smuggled within his jurisdiction during the past year. The only conclusions to be drawn are that *someone* must have been mistaken, the officers at Alloa were either deeply incompetent or lazy, or somehow implicated in the smuggling of spirits themselves.

Having said that, the Collector at Perth also filed a 'nil' return for smuggled spirits in the same manner as his Alloa compatriot, while Brown wrote that some 60,000 gallons had been run within his jurisdiction during the year in question. The mystery endures.

An example of the danger to which customs employees were exposed comes from Kincardine, a few miles south-east of Alloa on the northern shore of the Forth. In October 1748 the salt watchman at Kincardine, one John Paterson, reported the arrival of a vessel likely to contain contraband to the Alloa Collector of Customs. The *Christine & Magdalene* was known to be involved in regular runs between Holland and Scotland, hence Paterson's suspicions.

According to a letter from the Collector to the Board of Customs, it had become known to the smugglers or their supporters that Paterson had reported the vessel, and he was subsequently attacked, the Collector wrote, '. . . by three sailors or persons disguised in sailors' habit, beat, bruised and wounded to the degree that he was rendered incapable of doing duty'.

∽

The famous political economist Adam Smith was born in Kirkcaldy in 1723, shortly after the death of his father, who had been Controller of Customs in the Fife port. Smith attended Glasgow University and Balliol College, Oxford for ten years from the age of fourteen. He then returned to Scotland and made a living lecturing in Edinburgh. In 1751 he was appointed to the Chair of Logic at Glasgow University, and became Professor of Moral Philosophy the following year. In 1764 he relinquished this post and spent two years in Geneva and Paris, tutoring the third Duke of Buccleuch. In 1766 he returned to his native Kirkcaldy, and lived there for a decade, writing *An Inquiry Into the Nature and Causes of the Wealth of Nations*, which was published in 1776. This formed the blueprint for the Victorian free-trade movement, and included his observation that a smuggler was '. . . a person who, though no doubt highly blameable for violating the laws of his country, is frequently incapable of violating those of natural justice, and would have been, in every respect, an excellent citizen, had not the laws of his country made that a crime which nature never meant to be so'.

In 1778 Smith was appointed a Commissioner of the Scottish Customs, and lived in Panmure House, on Edinburgh's Canongate. This position commanded an annual salary in excess of £500, with an additional annuity of £300 per annum. Eleven years later he was appointed Lord Rector of Glasgow University, but it has been suggested that the burdens of his customs office were responsible for the production of less writing than might otherwise than been the case.

Many landowners in Fife were just as pro-smuggling as their peers elsewhere in Scotland, and during the 1730s Lord Elphinstone was one Fife laird notorious for using his role as a Justice of the Peace to ensure smugglers were convicted as rarely as possible.

Another and more blatant example of the attitude to smuggling taken by some members of the aristocracy also comes from Fife. In 1719 the advocate Sir Alexander Anstruther of Newark, a member of one of the leading families in the East Neuk, James Graham (a former baillie of Anstruther East), and a ship's captain were arrested for attempting to smuggle 4,700 gallons of brandy into Scotland.

Once released on bail the trio had two sailors who were potential prosecution witnesses kidnapped until the trial was over. Anstruther's brother, Sir Robert Anstruther of Balcaskie and his nephew, Sir John Anstruther, held the two men captive in their houses. One sailor escaped and the other was freed after legal pressure was applied on the Anstruthers.

Sir Alexander and the ship's captain subsequently faced charges relating to the kidnap, but were found not guilty despite clear and unequivocal evidence of their guilt. Better still, the charges relating to the brandy smuggling were dropped.

This is an interesting example of powerful men not just condoning smuggling but taking an active role in it, and being prepared to go a long way outside the law in order to avoid conviction.

The harbours of the Fife coast had long-established commercial links with northern Europe. Crail, for example, developed into one of Scotland's leading trading ports, and was exporting salt fish to Europe as early as the ninth century.

The prosperity brought to the country by these ports led King James VI (1542–1625) to describe his kingdom as 'a fringe of gold on a beggar's mantle'. The 'fringe of gold' was the coastline of Fife with its numerous harbours, and inevitably legal trading was supported by a significant amount of smuggling. The coast of Fife was ideal for smuggling, in that its coastal towns provided an eager market for the goods brought in, there was an abundance of vessels and experienced sailors, not to mention remote beaches, inlets and caves, particularly in the 'East Neuk'.

Dysart, to the north of Kirkcaldy, was an important port, and it became known as 'Little Holland' because of the major business of wine and gin importation carried on there. The harbour at Elie was built in the sixteenth century and at the time of its construction, Elie was the most important port on the Fife coast, conducting large-scale trade with Europe.

Pittenweem, in the East Neuk, did a great deal of business with the Baltic and Low countries, and also claims a place in smuggling history as the apparent venue for the start of the sequence of events that culminated in the Porteous Riots (see pp. 165–167) in Edinburgh.

The incident involved Andrew Wilson, a baker from Pathhead, near Kirkcaldy. As well as being a baker, Wilson was also a smuggler, and frequently had smuggled goods seized by the local customs officers, to whom he was well known. One day early in 1736 he took part in a robbery in Pittenweem, when he stole saddle-bags containing £200 from the lodgings of the Kirkcaldy Collector of Customs, James Stark. The Collector was staying in the fishing village for the night, returning from business in Anstruther, and the stolen money was the proceeds from the sale of smuggled goods offered for auction. Wilson committed the robbery in company with George Robertson and two other smugglers, no doubt partly as revenge for all the goods which had been seized from him by Stark.

However, as Frances Wilkins has pointed out in *The Smuggling Story of Two Firths*, a customs document dated 22 January 1736 contains details of the theft of £96 12s. 7d. from the Kirkcaldy custom house by a number of people, including one named only as Wilson, with probable 'inside' assistance from local tidesman John William Cosens.

If this is a coincidence then it is a remarkable one, and it may well be that the story of the Pittenweem robbery, uncorroborated by contemporary documentation, is just another example of how 'folk-tales' can develop and be distorted with the passage of time.

Whether the robbery took place in Pittenweem or Kirkcaldy, Wilson and Robertson were soon arrested, partly due to the work of an informer, and the pair were subsequently tried in Edinburgh, found guilty, and sentenced to death. With the assistance of Wilson, Robertson escaped from his confinement during a service in the Tolbooth kirk, and Wilson was hanged alone on 14 April 1736.

In *Edinburgh and the Lothians* (1912) Francis Watt writes of Edinburgh's Grassmarket:

> This was the scene, in 1736, of the Porteous Mob. Scott has told the story so fully, both in the text and notes to the *Heart of Midlothian*, and again in his *Tales of a Grandfather*, that the briefest mention must suffice. Porteous, Captain of the City Guard, presided at the execution of Wilson the smuggler. Wilson had almost become a popular idol. Smuggling to the Edinburgh mob, since it involved cheap brandy and a hit at the hated English Government – in 1736 the union was a very recent sore – was rather a virtue than a crime, and Wilson, moreover, had shown self-devotion in aiding the escape of a comrade, a heroism of a kind affecting to the mass of people. Finally, Porteous had treated him with unnecessary cruelty, and too apprehensive of a riot had caused his soldiers to fire on the people. He was tried for murder and condemned, but was reprieved by order from London. The mob, however, broke into the Tolbooth, and hung him from a dyer's pole at the place of execution. Romance and art have embellished the scene. The street 'crowded with rioters, crimson with torchlight, spectators filling every window of the tall houses, the Castle standing high above the tumult against the night and the stars,' were the decorations of a scene of itself sufficiently impressive.

Just to the north of Pittenweem is the port of Anstruther, from which, during the eighteenth century, ships sailed on legitimate trading expeditions to places such as Danzig in Poland and to the Low Countries. Not all the trading was legal, however, and given high tide and the cover of night, cargoes of contraband brandy and rum were often brought up the Dreel Burn which separates Anstruther Easter from Anstruther Wester.

The leading merchant in Anstruther Easter was one Charles Wightman, a great smuggler, whose home stood next to the site of

Dreel Castle. The house had a rear entrance leading onto the beach, through which smuggled goods were transported. Legend has it that the house was haunted by the 'Black Lady', and David Stevenson (*The Beggar's Benison*) speculates that this might have been useful in deterring anyone from prying into activity around the house during the hours of darkness. Similarly, suspicion of witchcraft or pagan rituals conveniently kept people away from fires lit in remote coastal locations by smugglers to guide ships in to the shore.

The Smugglers' Inn stands next to the Dreel Bridge, and is said to date from the thirteenth century. The four properties that now make up the Smugglers' Inn were formerly divided by a vennel or passage, the 'dreel' in Scots vernacular. This dreel led from the burn below, and was used by smugglers to carry cargoes of spirits into the town, while coal and linen were smuggled out via the dreel. The Smugglers' Inn was a noted tavern during the reign of Queen Anne (1665–1714), and the leading Jacobite Earl of Strathmore made it his headquarters during the 1715 Jacobite rising.

One way in which the authorities attempted to curb smuggling was by the use of 'revenue cruisers', which covered large areas of sea, embracing several ports, and were answerable directly to the Board of Customs rather than to local Collectors of Customs.

Revenue cruisers were considered to be particularly effective by many Collectors, as confirmed by the Anstruther Collector writing in a letter of 26 October 1807 regarding the decline in smuggling in his area. He declared that one reason for this decline was '. . . keeping the cruisers constantly at sea, as far as circumstances permitted, which has certainly had a great effect in the prevention of smuggling. For within these two years we have heard of several instances when the smuggling vessels have been obliged to leave the coast without being able to land a single anker of Geneva, a circumstance which was formerly unknown in the smuggling trade . . .'

Anstruther has a fascinating, smuggling-related link to an extra-ordinary eighteenth-century 'gentlemen's dining club', as one might politely describe it. The port was home to the 'Beggar's Benison', founded partly to celebrate 'rebel' Jacobite politics and opposition to high post-union taxes, and its members therefore tended to have a natural sympathy with the smuggling trade. 'Anstruther seems to have been awash with brandy', notes *The Spectator*'s review of David Stevenson's *The Beggar's Benison: Sex Clubs and their Rituals in Enlightenment Scotland*.

As the title of Professor Stevenson's book suggests, the third activity celebrated by the society was more controversial than the first two mentioned. Essentially, it was sexual freedom, and specifically public masturbation, and part of the regalia of the society consisted of a snuff box which contained the pubic hair of one of King George IV's mistresses. Celebrants drank (smuggled) alcohol from glasses with phallic depictions on them, one of which sold at auction by Sotheby's in 2001 for £16,450. Only two others survive, one in St Andrews University, where the rest of the surviving regalia is housed, and where David Stevenson is an emeritus professor of history.

A 'benison' was a blessing, and the society took its name from a story that King James V was once carried across Anstruther's Dreel Burn by a beggar woman. She later blessed the king's sexual prowess and his purse. It is believed he rewarded her with both money and sex.

Essentially, members of the Beggar's Benison were anti-establishment, though some were officers of the customs and excise services. The Benison was opposed to current thinking on the debilitating effects of masturbation, which was raised during the 1730s. 'Free sex', or sexual liberation, was an extension of the members' belief in what they considered to be free trade.

The Beggar's Benison society spread from its origins in Anstruther in 1732, with 'chapters' being formed as far afield as the East Indies and Russia. The original was formed by a group of some thirty lairds, craftsmen, merchants and customs officers.

One of the founders of the Beggar's Benison society was Highland chieftain and customs officer John McNachtane, and the membership of the Benison consisted of a number of aristocrats, at least one bishop, fellow customs officers and even some smugglers. Stevenson notes that a central role in its early days was to enable customs officers and smugglers to meet and socialise. 'Professional enemies but personal friends', as he puts it.

John McNachtane was 'the most senior of local customs officers', being Collector of Customs at Anstruther. Stevenson suggests that to survive and to work with any degree of effectiveness, customs officers, who were invariably outsiders in the community, and local smugglers, must often have arrived at 'accommodations' to make life bearable for everyone concerned. The Beggar's Benison seems to have embraced just such an accommodation.

McNachtane first arrived in Fife as a Land-Waiter at Anstruther in 1725, having previously served at Montrose and Bo'ness. Three years later he became Collector at Anstruther, and in 1761 moved to Edinburgh as one of the two 'customs inspectors general of outports'.

Second in command to McNachtane in his role as Collector was the Comptroller, David Row. In 1742 he was caught drinking smuggled brandy during a raid by excise officers from Kirkcaldy on Cambo House, owned by Sir Charles Erskine of Cambo.

When the customs and excise services operated as two separate entities there was frequently great rivalry between them, and sometimes even the unedifying spectacle of officers from the two services coming to blows when one thought the other had stepped out of line in order to get the credit for making a seizure. It is not difficult, then, to imagine the excisemen's pleasure at apprehending Row in this situation. Both Row and Erskine were Benison members.

The brandy was seized and locked in the king's warehouse in Anstruther, but Row, who lived next door to the warehouse, had previously made a passage between the cellars of the two adjoining properties, and in due course the brandy disappeared. The passage was discovered during a search for the missing brandy, and the assumption was that Row had helped himself to confiscated contraband from the warehouse on previous occasions. He was dismissed from the service but was not prosecuted, presumably to spare public embarrassment for his employers.

Within sight of the East Neuk harbours, some five miles out to sea, near the mouth of the Firth of Forth, is the Isle of May. May was home to an early monastery, and a noted place of pilgrimage during the later medieval period. By the eighteenth century the island was the base of a fishing community, and was also much frequented by smugglers.

David Stevenson points out that, unlike the west coast, there were very few islands on the east which smugglers could use as 'half-way houses' for their goods. The Isle of May was, therefore, very attractive to free-traders. It even had a coal fire burning in a brazier as a warning to shipping of its presence. The smugglers found this a most useful aid to navigate their vessels to the island! Only a few people lived on May, and in the face of sometimes large and ruthless bands of smugglers they were hardly likely to make vociferous complaints. The island boasted many natural caves, but to supplement those, smugglers constructed an underground timber storage chamber covered in shingle as camouflage.

North of Anstruther on the East Neuk coastline lies St Andrews, formerly one of Scotland's greatest ecclesiastical centres, and home to the country's first university, founded in 1411. During the fifteenth and sixteenth centuries it was also one of the most important ports north of the Forth, conducting trade with all the major centres of northern Europe. Business slumped after the Reformation, however, and by the mid-seventeenth century very little legal trading was taking place from St Andrews.

Smuggling continued though, and even students at the university were not above occasional involvement in it, as Frances Wilkins notes in *The Smuggling Story of Two Firths*. University minutes record that in February 1728

> . . . some few students have been so weak and foolish as to suffer themselves to be enticed and misled into this evil practice, by forcibly detaining some of His Majesty's officers of the customs in a cabin of a ship [William Greig's *The Dorothy*] in this harbour, while the goods therein were carried off. Therefore for preventing the like practice in time coming they do hereby strictly prohibit and discharge all students of this University and everyone of them to give any countenance or assistance unto the running of goods or any manner of way to hinder or disturb any of his Majesty's officers in making seizures of such goods by threatening or opposing or using violence to deforce them in the execution of their office with certification that the contraveners of this statute shall be declared infamous and deprived of all degrees and promotion in this university and extruded therefrom.

Eventually, no criminal action was taken against the ten students involved, on the basis that they co-operated in a prosecution against Greig and a Cupar merchant, David Rutherford.

Surviving customs records sometimes allow us to build up quite a picture of the network of people involved in smuggling. Custom house letter-books relating to St Andrews and its environs during the first decade of the nineteenth century are a good example.

In January 1803, the Anstruther Collector of Customs wrote that a carter, John Hay, was prepared to testify that on the morning of Sunday, 30 January

> . . . he was taking a walk along the shore on the West Sands of St. Andrews where he met with a fisherman of his acquaintance, who had just found several ankers that appeared to have been buried in the sands but washed up by the tide. He and the fisherman carried them up to the bents when immediately Andrew Cochrane and some other men started up from behind a bush and claimed these ankers, informing them they were smuggled gin belonging to John Braid, that they had been hid by him in the sands for fear of the revenue officers and that they were watching them till it was dark, when they might be brought into St. Andrews. One of the persons pierced a cask and gave them a draw of it. This was not far from Cochrane's house at Rabbit Hall and Cochrane and those that were with him appeared to be going and coming between it and the place where the gin was. By desire of Cochrane he took his acquaintance the fisherman, who is both deaf and dumb, away in John Braid's house in St. Andrews and kept him there all the day, lest he should have made signs to some of the revenue officers informing them of the smuggle. When it was

dark he (John Hay) assisted them in digging up and bringing into Braid's house the smuggled gin. He saw both Braid and his wife, who promised him a great deal for his assistance and for concealing the smuggle. But he never got a shilling for Braid became bankrupt shortly after that.

Andrew Cochrane, a weaver by trade, was an associate of John Braid, in whose employ he had formerly been. Braid was one of three men named in a customs document of 1805 as being '. . . well known to be the smugglers in St Andrews'. The other two men were Thomas Mitchell and John Wilson.

From the Union of Scotland with England to the end of the first quarter of the 19th century the Revenue was annually defrauded on a colossal scale by the clandestine importation of foreign spirits and by the unlawful manufacture of spirits at home. All classes of the community participated in the trade: kirk elders, pompous provosts, lairds, baillies and solemn JPs deemed it no sin to 'jink the gauger' or exciseman.

So universal was the infection that the gaugers themselves were often prone to accept bribes on the price of their silence regarding evasions of duty. An illustration of this is found in the story of Sandy Tameson, the St Andrew's gauger, who, meeting a man on Tentsmuir with a keg of brandy on his shoulder, was thus hailed by the smuggler: 'Maister Tameson, I'm thinking if ye had a crown in either hand, ye coudna tak haud o'th 'keg.' 'That's so', quoth Sandy, 'an if I had anither in my mouth, I coudna speak about it!'

– The Weekly Scotsman, *April 1908*

In *The Statistical Account of Scotland* (1791–99) the Reverend Mr Kettle of the Parish of Leuchars, to the north-west of St Andrews, wrote that

in the Tents-moors, smuggling was carried on to a great extent, by those men in the neighbourhood, who were determined to risk their fortune and character on the events of a day; for the inhabitants of this corner, were only assisting in concealing and transporting their unlawful imports. By the wise and vigorous interposition of the directors of our justly admired government, smuggling, that illicit traffic big with many evils to mankind, is now happily unknown over all our coasts. The inhabitants of this remote corner have been blamed for cruelty to ship-wrecked sailors. If the charge be just, it does not belong to them alone; they are but a handful; the place is thinly peopled. In the days of old it might have been so; but I have seen much attention and kindness shown to such unhappy sailors as were cast upon our shore.

The 'Tents-moors' or 'Tentsmuir', an area between the rivers Eden and Tay, features in another episode, reported by the Collector of Customs in Anstruther. This anecdote nicely illustrates the degree of popular support which existed for smugglers.

In January 1805 the Anstruther Collector noted that a smuggling lugger was anchored off the Red Head, by Arbroath, and that fishing boats from Auchmithie, East Haven and West Haven, '. . . but particularly the first, fifteen boats went off and were loaded from her, some part of whom landed their cargoes in that neighbourhood and part went to this district'.

Three of the smugglers' fishing boats were seized by a tidesman at Boarhills, to the south of St Andrews. The Anstruther Collector noted that the 'daring, lawless felons' who crewed these vessels

> . . . pursued an excise officer on the morning of the day of their seizure upwards of an hour at Tentsmuir, with their boat-hooks in their hands, and finding themselves discovered at that place they put off to sea and in making across St Andrews Bay for Boarhills were discovered by Boyack [the St Andrews tidesman] and Mr Brodie, the supervisor of excise. The men belonging to them, assisted no doubt by the people of Boarhills, concealed part of the tacking of the boats. This circumstance along with the daring conduct at Tentsmuir of the crew of the boats induced us to bring them round to Anstruther as a place of security, Boarhills, where they were seized, lying nearly opposite to Arbroath, in which neighbourhood these boats are owned. From all we have been able to learn these are the boats that have usually been employed this winter in bringing smuggled gin from the Angus side to the coast of Fife.

The pages of the *Statistical Account of Scotland* also yield informative material relating to other aspects of smuggling in Fife.

Writing of the parish of Carnbee, the Reverend Mr Alexander Brodie described the character of his parishioners, observing that 'they are in general a sober and industrious people, religiously disposed, and mind their own affairs. In the last age, when smuggling was carried to a great length in this neighbourhood, many of the farmers and others were, by various means, induced to give assistance to the smugglers, and carrying away and disposing of vast quantities of foreign spirits, which had a very bad effect upon their health and morals. Happily, however, that illicit trade is in a great measure abandoned, and the farmers, with their servants, now employ themselves to much better purpose in improving their lands.'

The Reverend Mr James Burn, Minister in the parish of Forgan, near St Andrews, echoed Brodie's comments on the bad effects of smuggling and the extent to which the trade had declined. He did, however, append a little homily.

> One young man, a tenant in the parish, was most unhappily addicted to it [smuggling]; in a few years he hurt many others and ruined himself.

The last time he called at the manse, he expressed his wish that he had followed the advice the minister had often given him. – Had he done this, he would probably have succeeded as a tenant, and escaped the miseries which, by smuggling, he unhappily brought upon himself. He lay in a prison for several months, reduced to great indigence. This is mentioned as a warning to others, who by smuggling hope to be made rich, but are far more likely to become ruined, and to entail misery and mischief on themselves and others.

## 2. Perth, Angus, Kincardine and Aberdeen

The 'Fair City' of Perth is so far inland that it seems surprising to find it retains a working harbour. Situated some twenty miles from the sea, Perth lies at the head of navigation on the River Tay, and its port facilities were first promoted by a Royal Charter of 1137. By the end of the thirteenth century, Perth had links with the Netherlands and towns in the Hanseatic League, and during the eighteenth century traded on a regular basis with Italy, Spain, France, Germany, the Netherlands, Russia and Scandinavia. Flaxseed, linseed and flax were imported for use in the area's expanding textile industry.

Strong Jacobite sentiment in Perth meant that legitimate trading was accompanied by a significant amount of smuggling. There was a great deal of anti-English, anti-union feeling, which meant that customs officers were not popular, and frequently required military support to carry out their duties.

One documented case occurred in 1725, when Perth customs officers intercepted a party of smugglers who refused to stop when challenged. The Comptroller of Customs called for reinforcements and saw one keg of spirits being carried into the Thistle tavern. A guard was put on the door, while a search of the premises took place. One of the sentries on guard somehow became separated from his comrades, and he was grabbed by the smugglers, strangled, and then his body was slashed. Leaving him for dead, the smugglers took flight, abandoning the keg near to the market cross on the High Street.

At the eastern end of the River Tay lies the city of Dundee, described in 1656 by Thomas Tucker as '. . . a pretty considerable place, lyeing by the mouth of the river Tay . . . the trade of this place inwards is, from Norway, the East countrey, Holland, and France; and outwards, with salmon and pladding. Here is a collector, a checque, and five wayters established, three of which wayters constantly reside here, and the rest are bestowed the member ports . . . St Johnstons . . . Arbroth . . . Montrosse . . .'

Dundee was already an important trading port by the twelfth century, and during the eighteenth century formal docks and wharves were put in place. Ships regularly arrived in Dundee from Sweden, Holland, Spain and Norway. Principal cargoes included timber (from Sweden and Norway), brandy (from Norway), salt (from Norway and Spain), and wine (from Spain). Ships from North America also landed cargoes of tobacco in ports such as Dundee and Montrose. As we have seen in the case of Bo'ness, tobacco was then re-exported to continental Europe.

Smuggling in the Tay area was principally conducted with Holland and Scandinavia, though smuggled goods also came in from France. Inevitably, because of the amount of legal trade being conducted there, Dundee was at the hub of smuggling activity around the River Tay.

In December 1724 the *Margaret of Dundee* arrived in her home port from Rotterdam, carrying only half a cargo, raising suspicions that the rest might have been run ashore nearby. A party of customs officers duly set off to search the area, and eight casks of wine were subsequently found in a barn five miles west of the city. The officers left four of their men as guards, but at 9 p.m. a group of some forty people attacked them with pitchforks and staves. The sergeant in charge of the guard was injured, but the wine remained intact.

In 1766 Dundee customs officers searched a French vessel called the *Friendship*, and discovered it to be carrying contraband. The sails, tackle and even provisions were removed from the ship to prevent its crew from escaping with it, but the resourceful Frenchmen managed to get new sails and ancillary equipment made on shore, and escaped at midnight.

As late as 18 July 1806 The *Dundee Advertiser* declared that 'one of the greatest banes to the coast of Angus is the pernicious and increased system of smuggling', and in 1890 David Barrie recalled Dundee's even more recent smuggling past (*The City of Dundee Illustrated*):

> Smuggling was carried on in Dundee and neighbourhood in my young days, and was very common in Forfarshire all along the coast, as well as amongst the hills in the north part of the county. I recollect an old gentleman telling me he has seen a French lugger at Westhaven, near Carnoustie, landing smuggled goods, each man of the crew of the boats landing the goods sitting at his oar, with his loaded musket alongside of him. All the men, women, and boys, even girls, for miles round, were helping, carrying off and securing the goods, consisting of brandy, tea, tobacco, laces, &c., as fast as they possibly could. One day he himself looked out of his office window on the High Street of Dundee, and was not a little astonished and horrified to see a cart with a cask of French brandy (smuggled) going away to his own house, quite openly, not even a cover on the cask to conceal it. Half an hour afterwards a message was delivered to him, wishing to see him for a few minutes at the Excise

Office, he found out, and his presence was wanted in connection with the business. Upon, however, calling at the Excise Office, he found it was on some private business of one of the officials. His mind, as the reader will easily conceive, was much relieved. In this case it would have been doubly awkward for him, as he at the time had something to do with the collection of a certain portion of the government taxes.

When I was a boy, a young cousin of mine was mate of a vessel lying near the west end of King William's dock, a little east of the Royal Arch. On going down to the vessel one afternoon, my cousin asked me to take up and to carry under my arm a small half-anker of gin from Elsinore. I did it at once without thinking much about it. My cousin and the custom-house officer, who had just been relieved from watching the ship, walked out all the way to my aunt's house on the Perth Road, not more than one hundred and fifty yards behind me. We boys did not think smuggling a crime.

I have seen a custom-house officer stationed on a vessel in King William's dock, standing talking with a lot of schoolboys at the bow of the ship, while all the time smuggled goods were being landed at the stern as fast as hands could do it. I do not suppose smuggling can be so prevalent now-a-days, as almost everything comes in free of duty; at least, we hear very seldom of convictions for smuggling.

North of Dundee, on the Angus coast, the fishing settlement of Auchmithie near Arbroath, was a great smuggling centre. During the mid-eighteenth century many fishermen there were said to live comfortably on the proceeds of the smuggling trade. One of Auchmithie's attractions for smugglers was the range of caves in the red-sandstone cliffs around the village, ideal for hiding contraband goods. Auchmithie is reputedly one of the oldest fishing settlements on the Angus coast, and was the model for Musselcrag in Sir Walter Scott's *The Antiquary*, while Arbroath was fictionalised as Fairport. (See pp. 164–5)

Writing in *The Statistical Account of Scotland*, the Reverend Mr George Gleig observed that 'before the year 1736, Arbroath had little or no commerce, unless a little traffic in fish, and a kind of contraband or smuggling trade deserve the name . . . A few years subsequent to that mentioned above, several gentlemen of property jointly undertook to establish the manufacture of Oznaburghs, and other brown linens here, and to import their own materials'.

In *The History of Arbroath* (1876) George Hay wrote that

A curious glimpse into the state of matters in the town [of Arbroath] as regards trade, lawful and unlawful, is obtained in a minute of the council of date 20th July 1744. At that time smuggling was common on the coasts of the island. In Scotland it was stimulated by much political antipathy to the Government, and even those who had no Jacobite leanings nevertheless hated the new excise laws. In a poor country, considerations of gain powerfully reinforced those of politics. Thus it happened that smuggling was not looked upon as a disreputable, though hazardous, business. The following is the deliverance of the Town Council of Arbroath on the subject:

> The Magistrates and other members of the Town Council convened, considering that the practice of smuggling did a few years ago greatly prevail in this place, but that of late, by the diligence of the officers of the Customs and Excise, the same hath been almost totally defeated and suppressed, to the ruin and undoing of almost all the dealers therein, they, the Magistrates and Council, out of a Christian tenderness for the great though just sufferings of their unhappy neighbours, and a firm persuasion that this destructive trade was upon the point of expiring, and that the general inclination of the inhabitants was now turning to the more lawful and commendable business of improving the linen and other manufactures, agreed not to have taken any notice of what was past, and to have followed the general bent of the nation in discouraging smuggling for the future, had they not been called upon by the late Convention of Royal Burghs to manifest their sentiments in a public manner; they therefore hereby declare their abhorrence of the unlawful and pernicious practice of smuggling, and their firm and hearty resolution to discourage and suppress the same by all lawful means for the time to come, and to encourage and support the sober and diligent tradesmen and manufacturer as the only visible means left to restore frugality and industry, and thereby repair the evils that have happened; and they appoint this their unanimous resolution to be recorded in the Council books, and an extract thereof to be transmitted by the clerk of the town's agent, to be inserted in the public newspapers.

As with Perth, the port of Montrose was home to many Jacobite sympathisers, which helped to stimulate the smuggling trade and put the local customs staff under great pressure.

There had been a settlement at Montrose as early as AD 980, and the first harbour was built during the Middle Ages. Trade was principally with Scandinavia, and was sufficient to justify the development of warehouses, shipyards, granaries and a customs house.

By the eighteenth century, Montrose had a major legitimate trade in tobacco, flax, and corn with a variety of European and Scandinavian countries. This gave cover to smuggling operations, and there was no shortage of local fishermen willing to help bring smuggled goods ashore.

North of the town were eight miles of bleak, rocky coast, ideal for landing contraband, and to the south, the shore between Scurdy Ness and Boddin Point was peppered with caves. Wide bays like Lunan and the five miles of beach between Montrose and St Cyrus were also perfect for smuggling purposes. Sometimes, however, smugglers operated quite openly on the main harbour quay, thanks to corrupt officials.

Apart from the fact that customs officers were often open to bribery, there was also the problem at Montrose, as at so many places, that the customs service was perpetually under strength. There were only fifteen officers to patrol twenty-five miles of coastline between Montrose and Johnshaven, as well as undertaking all the harbour-based duties and paperwork that their job demanded.

Salt was among the commodities smuggled into Montrose, being used for the purpose of curing herring caught in local waters. In 1656, Thomas Tucker had noted that a customs 'wayter' was based at Montrose '. . . because there hath usually beene salt brought in . . .'

Brandy was also imported illegally at Montrose, and in 1709 it was noted by the Collector of Customs that this trade was '. . . carry'd on by Dutch and Danish ships to the prejudice of the Revenue and due not in the least doubt that the same is countenanced and encouraged by the merchants, skippers and others'. The Collector wrote that 'brandy is imported in anchors and half anchors to the number of 1,000 or 1,200 at a time'.

On one occasion 2,000 gallons of contraband brandy were seized in the town, and on another, dozens of hogsheads of wine were carried ashore from the ferryboat. Apparently they filled no fewer than 3,000 bottles.

Writing in October 1789, the Collector of Customs at Montrose observed that 'this morning between the hours of 12 and 2 the door of His Majesty's Warehouse was broke open and 107 ankers of brandy . . . carried away. At 2 o'clock in the morning when the guard came to relieve the two centrys that were placed at the warehouse door they found the door open, the centrys gone, their muskets lying near the warehouse and one of the bayonets lying broke before the door.'

A party of soldiers was subsequently dispatched to the town links, '. . . where they found the two centrys lying tied neck and heel. The officer asked them why they had left their posts, they told him that 14 or 15 men had come upon them with clubs and other weapons and had knocked them down and tyed them . . . and afterwards dragged them to the links.'

Richard Platt (*Smugglers' Britain*) notes that in May 1734 a more subtle method of retrieving confiscated contraband cargo had been employed in Montrose, when the smugglers tunnelled under the custom-house from the cellars of neighbouring premises. An official report on the incident noted that although the sixty casks of brandy in question were transported through the house of the neighbour, a shipbuilder by the name of Dunbar, and rolled out of his window and carried away, neither Dunbar nor the sentries outside the custom-house admitted to seeing or hearing anything untoward!

Writing in the *Statistical Account of Scotland*, the Reverend Mr James Paton noted of the parish of Craig, near Montrose, that 'there are 6 houses for vending ale and spirits, in one of which only ale is brewed. The practice of smuggling foreign spirits, from which this coast is not yet free, is productive of much loss to the public, and of many evils to individuals.'

In the same volume the Reverend Mr Alexander Molleson stated of Montrose itself that 'about 50 years ago smuggling was much practiced here, and indeed almost every where on the coast of Scotland, and scarcely any sort of manufacture was carried on. The first manufacture, of any consequence, that of canvas, was erected here by a company in 1745.'

Montrose features in an interesting example of a vessel 'pretended-bound' from Campvere to Bergen. In March 1747 the *Marjorie & Anne* was in Montrose with a cargo of spirits, wine, soap and tobacco, when she was forced to make a run for the open sea to escape from the port's customs officers.

This sort of 'pretended-bound' journey was plausible on the Scottish east coast, and sometimes skippers maintained that their vessels were bound from Ireland to ports such as Danzig in Poland. The route between Rotterdam and Bergen was used on a number of occasions for smuggling into Scotland, and the Faroes islands were another convenient destination for vessels from Campvere and Bordeaux.

Surviving records show that the 'Bervie sloop', as she was known, was purpose-built during the 1760s for smuggling, trading between Montrose, Holland, and Gothenburg in Sweden. The vessel was christened the *Peggie* and was commanded by George Largie of the little port of Johnshaven, twenty-five miles from Montrose, and itself something of a smuggling haunt. Tea, tobacco and spirits were common cargoes carried by the *Peggie*, which was owned by Walter Sime and Robert Napier, local merchants and owners of a tobacco factory close to Gourdon. The pair were described by the Collector of Customs at Montrose as '. . . the greatest smugglers upon this coast', and he added that they '. . . drive little or no other trade whatsoever'.

In *The Statistical Account of Scotland*, Mr Walter Thom of Bervie

[Inverbervie], between Montrose and Stonehaven, wrote that 'Bervie has been long famous, or infamous, for an illicit and illegal trade in teas, spirits, tobacco, &c; but the ruinous and baneful trade of smuggling is now much on the decline, being confined to the running of a few hundred ankers of spirits annually, and by a set of worthless desperadoes, who do not belong to the town, but bring their goods to Bervie beach, for the sake of conveniency, and an easy landing.'

Some twenty years earlier, the Montrose Collector had written in a letter of May 1773 that in Bervie and nearby Gourdon there were three smugglers who '. . . from their long experience and connections in that part of the country are employed as agents and trustees for all the illicit traders in this place and a considerable way to the westward . . . who consume and deal in large quantities of spirits, teas and tobacco, which are all instantly carried off the beach upon their being landed to their respective places of destination . . .'

Stonehaven was noted as the best harbour between Arbroath and Aberdeen, and it developed into a major fishing port during the herring boom of the late nineteenth century, when up to a hundred boats operated from the town. A century earlier it had been a popular smuggling locale, but much of the area's smuggling trade was destroyed by the most effective of all excise officers, Malcolm Gillespie.

Gillespie was born in Dunblane, Perthshire, in 1799, and joined the excise service at the age of twenty. He was first stationed at Prestonpans, on the Firth of Forth, where he was involved in overseeing the manufacture of salt, and earned a reputation for diligence and ability in detecting significant amounts of fraud. After two years, he was transferred, at his own request, to the Aberdeen Collection, where he was stationed at Collieston.

Steve Sillett (*Illicit Scotch*) writes that at Collieston '. . . over 1,000 ankers of foreign spirits were being landed every month. From 1801 until 1807, when he moved to Stonehaven, Gillespie concentrated the whole of his prodigious energies in breaking up this extensive trade in contraband liquor'.

Sometimes, as Gillespie himself put it, spending 'over thirty nights at a time watching the movements of the smuggler, and that too in the middle of winter'. He claimed that while at Collieston he seized some 10,000 gallons of contraband, imported spirit, and destroyed a further 1,000 gallons.

As Sillett notes, 'By the time he left to take up his new appointment at Stonehaven, coastal smuggling had virtually died out in the neighbourhood of Collieston. At Stonehaven, where he remained until 1812, Gillespie pursued his duties with such zeal that he became a 'complete terror' to all smugglers.'

Gillespie was then moved to the Skene Ride, on Deeside, where most of his work involved dealing with whisky smugglers, and he earned a reputation for fearlessness in the face of great odds, often receiving quite serious injuries in the pursuit of his duties.

Malcolm Gillespie faced a problem common to almost all excise officers in that his salary was modest, and much of his income came from the proceeds of seizures. He did, however, have to pay his men, and feed and arm them out of his own pocket, not to mention give them bonuses for seizures made. Considerable sums of money also changed hands between excise officers and informers, and again Gillespie was forced to meet the cost.

The end result was that even such an able and conscientious officer as Gillespie plunged into debt, with a wife and children to support. In his pamphlet *The Memorial and Case of Malcolm Gillespie* (1828) he noted '. . . captures of the greatest magnitude are attended with very great expenses; for in a country where the inhabitants are almost wholly connected with the illicit trade, it is difficult to find a person among them who can be prevailed upon to give information against his neighbour and nothing short of the Officer's Share of the Seizure can induce the informant to divulge his secret. It has principally been in this way that that I have involved myself in debt.'

In 1827 Gillespie was arrested for forging Treasury Bills, a capital crime, and was tried at Aberdeen Circuit Court of Judiciary in September of that year. He was found guilty and was subsequently executed on 16 November 1827.

In his 1656 Report, Thomas Tucker wrote that

The port of Aberdeene lyes next northward, being a very handsome burgh, seated at the mouth of the River Donne and is commonly called the New towne, for distinguishing it from another town hard by, of the same name, but more antiquity, lyeing at the mouth of the River Dee, some a mile distant from the New towne, and is the chiefe academie of Scotland. This being now a place more for study than trade, hath willingly resigned her interest that way, unto the New towne, which is noe despicable burgh, either for building nor largenesse, haveing a very stately mercat place, sundry houses well built, with a safe harbour before it for vessells to ride in. But the widenesse of the place, from the inlett of the sea coming in with a narrowe winding gut, and beateing in store of sand with its waves, hath rendered it somewhat shalowe in a greate part of it, and soe lesse usefull of late than formerly. But the inhabitants are remedyeing this inconveniencye by lengthening theyr key, and bringing it up close to a necke of land which, jutting out eastward towards an headland lyeing before it, makes the coming in soe straight. At the end of which foremost necke of land there is a little village called Footdee, and on the other headland, another called Tocye, and both nigh the harbour's mouth, and lyeing in very neere unto the place where the ships usually ride (being forced to keep some distance from the key, because of the shallowness of the water), have given opportunity of much fraude in landing goods privately, but prevented of late, by appointing the wayters, by turnes, to watch those two places narrowly, when there are any shipping in harbour. The trade of this place (as generally all over Scotland) is, inwards, from Norway, Eastland, Holland, and France; and outwards, with salmon and pladding, commodityes caught and made hereabout in a greater plenty than in any other place of the nation whatsoever.

In this port is a collector, a checque, and three wayters; some of which are still sent into the member ports as often (which is but seldome) as any opportunity is offered, or occasion requires. Those are in number five: Stonehive, a little fisher towne, where formerly goods have been brought in, but not of late, because hindred from doeing soe by the neighbourhood, and priviledges of the burgh of Montrosse; Newburgh, where sometimes a few deales and timber are brought, Peterhead, a small towne, with a convenient harbour, but spoyled of late by stress of weather; Fraserburgh and Bamffe, where, in like manner, something now and then is brought in from Norway, but theyr onely trade is coasting, except that from the latter of them some salmon may happen to be shipped out.

During the eighteenth century, a fleet of whaling vessels was a feature of Aberdeen's harbour, but in 1788 three luggers and two sloops were also said to be engaged in smuggling contraband into the port. The vessels apparently made some six smuggling voyages per year, each bringing in an annual total of around 200 hogsheads of spirits and large quantities of tobacco in the process.

As with Montrose, customs officers in Aberdeen did not really have the manpower to tackle the problem of smuggling effectively, having a coastline of more than seventy miles to cover, as the smugglers were only too well aware.

Wine, brandy, tea and tobacco were the principal cargoes smuggled into Aberdeen and its environs, but less obvious commodities such as prunes, raisins, soap, starch, writing paper and Swedish iron also feature in the port record books relating to seizures during the first half of the eighteenth century. Wool was smuggled *out of* Aberdeen at times when it was illegal to sell wool abroad and was subsequently shipped overseas via other Scottish ports.

Vessels involved in smuggling into the Aberdeen area were frequently on 'pretended-bound' voyages, regularly carrying documentation claiming that they were destined for Bergen. If challenged, the skippers would simply claim to have been blown off course. Rather than landing directly at Aberdeen itself, contraband cargoes were often put ashore at Collieston and Newburgh, between Aberdeen and the port of Peterhead to the north.

One of the most enduring stories in Scottish smuggling heritage has its origins on the stretch of coast around Collieston, where Malcolm Gillespie proved so formidable an adversary to smugglers.

The *Crooked Mary* was a notorious lugger used in the smuggling trade around the Cruden, Peterhead and Slains area, and on the afternoon of 19 December 1798 she was sighted off the coast, ready to land a cargo of contraband Dutch gin. A 'land party' was warned by those co-ordinating the *Crooked Mary's* voyage on shore to prepare for a run. Six local men with two carts were ready just before midnight that night, and went to the small bay just north of Slains Kirk where the run ashore was to take place. One of them was 35-year-old Philip Kennedy, a farmer, whose role was to help land the gin, then hide and store it locally before it was moved inland to be sold.

However, the local exciseman, Anderson, had heard what was due to take place that night, and took two assistants to the road which led from the bay. They proceeded to ambush the laden carts by firing pistols in the dark, but their shots failed to hit anything and the horses pulling the carts bolted. All the smugglers fled into the night except for Philip Kennedy, who stood his ground and fought Anderson and his men, before being cut down by a sword and left where he fell.

According to one version of the tale, in the light of morning Kennedy was discovered in Slains kirkyard, where he had dragged himself during the night. He was fatally wounded. His last words were supposedly, 'If the others had been as true as I, the goods would have got through, and I would not be bleeding to death'. Kennedy was buried in the kirkyard, and his grave can still be seen. Anderson was subsequently tried for murder, and acquitted. The wooden bench in Collieston on which Kennedy reputedly died is now looked after by local resident Rear-Admiral Steve Ritchie, and the story of Kennedy was the basis for a Radio 4 documentary broadcast in 2002.

In his book *From the Brig o' Balgownie to the Bullars o' Buchan* (1897), James Delgarno wrote his version of the events of 19 December 1798:

> Philip had on that night secured sixteen ankers of Holland gin at the shore of 'Cransdale', Collieston, and employed women to carry it off in creels to the hiding-place on his farm at Ward, a distance of three miles, while he and his brother John went off to protect the property from two gaugers and a tide watcher, who were on the way to Collieston

from having made a seizure of gin at Sandend, Cruden. The Kennedys had scarcely gone a mile when they came in contact with the gaugers, two of whom were armed with cutlasses. They had not exchanged many words when a desperate struggle ensued. Philip, with his oak cudgel, in which there was sunk a lump of lead, warded off the cutlass, and tripped up two of them, and held them down in his giant grasp, calling on his brother to secure the other. John was in combat with the other gauger, and in parrying off the cutlass with the stick got a severe cut on the forehead, piercing through his thick bonnet, the blood flowing over his face and eyes rendering him helpless. After wounding the brother, the gauger roared out to Philip to let go his grasp or he would sever his head from his body, but he still kept his hold. Anderson then, uttering an oath, brandished his weapon, and with one stroke laid open the head of poor Kennedy. He immediately started to his feet and shouted out 'Murder!'

Although severely wounded he walked the distance of three quarters of a mile to the farm of Kirkton, and seating himself heavily on a chair in the kitchen said, 'If a' had been as true as me the prize wid a' been safe, an' I widna' a' been bleedin' to death!' After which he expired with a groan. It was said a finer, broad-shouldered, stalwart fellow never entered the Kirk of Slains, and that he was always known among his fellows on the Kirk road by his uniform home-spun blue suit, staff in hand, and broad blue bonnet with red tap. He might have been useful in the sphere in which he moved for other fifty years, but for the wiles and deceit of two informers under pay, who betrayed him into the clutches of the gaugers. The skull of Philip Kennedy has been repeatedly turned up in excavating the graves of others of the name buried in the same spot. His brother John, who died in 1842, bore the marks of the cutlass as long as he lived.

Anderson, the exciseman, who inflicted the fatal blow, was tried on the 28th September following, on charge of murder, but was acquitted by the jury on a verdict of 'Not Guilty!'

Customs records relating to this event provide another perspective. 'Foreign Geneva without a permit' was the Kennedys' smuggled commodity, and in addition to three ankers seized during the skirmish in which Kennedy received his fatal wound, a further nine ankers were recovered close to Ellon later that night. Fifteen more ankers were subsequently recovered. Tidesman Gilbert Leighton described being attacked in a 'cruel and ferocious manner' by a member of the Kennedy party. 'I suppose their intention was to murder us all', he added. 'On the evening of 20th December we heard that one of the men who attacked us was wounded and since dead, which we were sorry to hear.'

In his *Bygone Days in Aberdeenshire* (1913), John Allardyce wrote that at a dance at a farm near Slains Castle, close to Collieston, the earth gave way one night, tumbling the dancers into a chamber below that had been used by smugglers. The network of caves in the area was vast, and the smugglers put them to good use. Additionally, pits were sometimes dug into the beach, occasionally large enough to conceal up to 300 casks of gin.

In the *Statistical Account of Scotland*, the Reverend Mr George Morison of the Parish of Banchory Davinick wrote that '. . . the people might enjoy good health, did they not drink too freely, particularly of ardent spirits. Besides the quantities of gin smuggled in upon the coast, which by the way is not so great as formerly, we have two whisky distilleries in the parish, and 10 or 12 public houses.'

The Reverend Mr James Scott, minister of the parish of Benholme noted that 'smuggling, which formerly tended to debauch the morals of the sea-faring people, is no longer carried on within the bounds of this parish'. Interestingly, he added that 'About 50 years ago, the Excise officer's family was the only one in Johnshaven that made use of tea; when the tea kettle was carried to the well, to bring in water, numbers both of children and grown people followed it, expressing their wonder, and supposing it to be *"a beast with a horn"*. Now the tea kettle has lost the power of astonishing, having become a necessary piece of furniture among the meanest.'

Echoing the Reverend James Scott on the reduction of smuggling in the area, the Reverend Mr Patrick Stewart of the parish of Kinneff, near Inverbervie, observed that 'as this part of the coast lies at some distance from any station of excise or custom-house officers, it has long been famous, or infamous, for smuggling . . . This illicit traffic has, however, considerably declined on this coast of late, owing to the successful vigilance of the cruisers appointed for that purpose.'

Writing of the parish of Foveran, the Reverend Mr William Duff stated that 'in Newburgh are 6 or 7 ale-houses; chiefly frequented by sailors, smugglers, and fishermen . . . Smuggling . . . is frequently carried on, and tends in no considerable degree to corrupt the morals of the people: but this contraband trade seems, through the salutary measures adopted by government, to be at present on the decline; and its total annihilation is devoutly to be wished for by every friend to virtue and industry.'

According to Alexander Simpson, AM, schoolmaster of the parish of King-Edward, in the presbytery of Turriff, 'Banff, and the small licenced whisky stills in the neighbourhood, afford a good market for barley: These last, besides increasing the consumption and price of barley, and supplying us with whisky, of a quality greatly superior to what we have from the large stills in the southern districts, as well as cheaper, and no less wholesome than foreign spirits, have given a great check to smuggling; and in every point of view, are a reciprocal advantage to the farmers, and the country at large.'

This rare approval of alcohol in the pages of the ecclesiastically-biased *Statistical Account* is notable, perhaps reflecting its author's occupation as a schoolmaster rather then a minister!

The Reverend Dr Moir, minister in the Parish of Peterhead, observed that 'it is only of late that the trade of this town has been in a proper channel, and any attention bestowed on fishings and manufactures. Much remains still to be done, but from the exertions that have been made, and still continue with increasing ardour, it is hoped that this will soon be the most thriving town in the north of Scotland . . . Formerly there was too much connexion with an illicit trade from Gottenburgh and Holland, that has now almost ceased.'

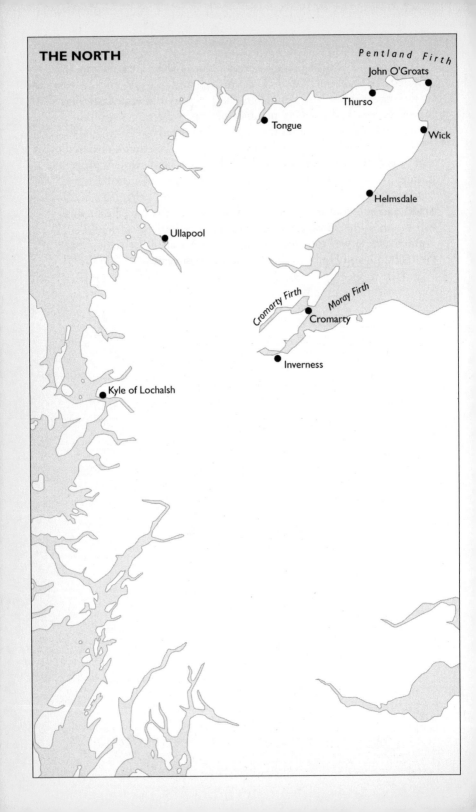

# 6

# THE NORTH AND NORTHERN ISLES

Tea, tobacco, sugar, salt, and spirits of all kinds were smuggled into the north and northern isles, and the variety of ports serving the area is wider than might be expected, considering its remoteness from some of the European trading centres commonly associated with smuggling.

Surviving documentation shows tobacco being shipped from Rotterdam, wine from Bordeaux, and tea from Danzig and Gothenburg, while Kirkwall merchants and those in Shetland were also supplied from Bergen.

Thanks to the records of one of the greatest of Scotland's merchant-smugglers, John Steuart of Inverness, we are able gain a real insight into the merchandise being smuggled and the modus operandi employed, as well as the ports from which contraband originated. Steuart regularly dealt with fellow merchants in Amsterdam, Bilbao, Bordeaux, Boulogne, Campvere, Copenhagen, Gothenburg, Hamburg, Rotterdam, Rouen and Stockholm.

Gin from Holland was a staple of both Orcadian and Shetland smuggling, while France also supplied a significant amount of the islands' contraband. Additionally, timber from Norway was important to the 'free trade' in Shetland. More randomly, Orkney and Shetland ports were often visited by large ships, calling there to take on supplies. In return for food and clothing, tobacco and brandy inevitably found their way ashore instead of cash.

## 1. THE NORTHERN MAINLAND

On the southern shores of the Moray Firth, inlets and bays around Banff and Macduff, were regularly used for smuggling, with Elgin-based merchants directing and financing much of the activity in the area.

Banff was first granted a charter in 1163 by Malcolm IV, and Robert the Bruce made it a royal burgh in 1324. Banff's customs accounts date back to 1390, and they detail a thriving trade during the Middle Ages in hides, wool, sheepskins and salted salmon with the Low Countries.

Until the early nineteenth century, a fleet of ships traded between

Banff and the Baltic and the Mediterranean. As Charles MacLean notes (*The Fringe of Gold*), '. . . the smuggling associated with the town's foreign connection was so successful that the Council minutes of 1744 record that many "fatal consequences attended this pernicious and unlawful trade".'

Banff was also a very successful fishing port, and by 1845 some 30,000 barrels of herring were being cured there annually and exported to Germany, the West Indies and Ireland.

The fertile farm lands of the Black Isle separate the Moray Firth from its narrower northern neighbour, the Cromarty Firth, and the ancient settlement of Cromarty is located at the north-east point of the Black Isle promontory.

Herring fishing was a major local industry, and Charles MacLean writes that '. . . in the 17th century there was no busier port in the entire country, and it was one of only 16 ports in the entire United Kingdom which required a customs clearance certificate'.

Cromarty's most famous son was Hugh Miller, born in 1802. His father was a ship's captain, and Hugh was apprenticed as a stonemason, but he found fame as a pioneering geologist and writer.

In *My Schools and Schoolmasters* Miller wrote about a smuggling event local to Cromarty:

> On the northern side of the burying-ground there is low stone, sculptured like most of the others, but broken by some accident into three pieces. A few stinted shrubs of broom spread their tiny branches and bright blossoms over the figures; they are obscured, besides, by rank tufts of moss and patches of lichens; but despite of neglect and accident, enough of the inscription remains legible to tell us that we stand on the burial-place of one John Macleod, a merchant of Cromarty. He kept, besides, the principal inn of the place. He had an only son, a tall, and very powerful man, who was engaged, as he himself had been in his earlier days, in the free trade, and who, for a series of years, had set the officers of the revenue at defiance. Some time late in the reign of Queen Anne, he had succeeded in landing part of a cargo among the rocks of the hill of Cromarty, and in transporting it, after night, from the cavern in which he had first secreted it, to a vault in his father's house, which opened into the cellar. After concealing the entrance, he had seated himself beside the old man at the kitchen fire, when two revenue-officers entered the apartment, and taking their places beside a table, called for liquor. Macleod drew his bonnet hastily over his brow, and edging away from the small iron lamp which lighted the kitchen, muffled himself up in the folds of his dreadnought greatcoat. His father supplied the officers. 'Where is Walter, your son!' inquired the better-dressed of the two, a tall,

thin, man, equipped with a three-cornered hat, and a blue coat seamed with gold lace; 'I trust he does not still sail the Swacker.' 'Maybe no,' said the old man dryly. 'For I have just had intelligence,' continued the officer, 'that she was captured this morning by Captain Manton, after firing on her Majesty's flag; and it will go pretty hard, I can tell you, with some of the crew.' A third revenue-officer now entered the kitchen, and going up to the table whispered something to the others. 'Please, Mr Macleod,' said the former speaker to the innkeeper, 'bring us a light, and the key of your cellar.' 'And wherefore that?' inquired the old man; 'show me your warrant. What would ye do wi' the key?' 'Nay, sir, no trifling; you brought here last night three cart-loads of Geneva, and stored them up in a vault below your cellar; the key and a light.' There was no sign, however, of procuring either. 'Away!' he continued, turning to the officer who had last entered; 'away for a candle and a sledge hammer!' He was just quitting the room when the younger Macleod rose from his seat, and took his stand right between him and the door. 'Look ye, gentlemen,' he said in a tone of portentous coolness, 'I shall take it upon me to settle this affair; you and I have met before now, and are a little acquainted. The man who first moves out of his place in the direction of the cellar, shall never move afterwards in any direction at all.' He thrust his hand, as he spoke, beneath the folds of his greatcoat, and seemed extricating some weapon from his belt. 'In upon him, lads!' shouted out the tall officer, 'devil though he be, he is but one; the rest are all captured.' In a moment, two of the officers had thrown themselves upon him; the third laid hold of his father. A tremendous struggle ensued; the lamp was overturned and extinguished. The smuggler, with a Herculean effort, shook off both his assailants, and as they rushed in again to close with him, he dealt one of them so terrible a blow that he rolled, stunned and senseless, on the floor. The elder Macleod, a hale old man, had extricated himself at the same moment, and mistaking, in the imperfect light, his son for one of the officers, and the fallen officer for his son, he seized on the kitchen poker, and just as the champion had succeeded in mastering his other opponent, he struck at him from behind, and felled him in an instant. In less than half an hour after he was dead. The unfortunate old man did not long survive him; for after enduring, for a few days, the horrors of mingled grief and remorse, his anguish of mind terminated in insanity, and he died in the course of the month.

Inverness has long been distinguished as the 'capital of the Highlands', and in 1656 Thomas Tucker wrote that

the last port northerly is Invernesse, lyeing at the head of the Firth of Murray, not farre from Loch Ness, where the town is a small one, though the chiefe of the whole North, and would bee yet worse, were it not for the large citadell built there of late yeares. This port hath for its district all the harbours and creekes of the shires of Murray, Rosse, Southerland and Caithnes, with the Isles of Orkney; in which, although there bee many large rivers which, rising in the hills, runne downe into the sea, and the oceane hath indented many more creekes and inlets, with its stormy waves still beateing on the shoare, yet few of them are serviceable, and those few much too bigge for any trade that is, or may be expected in these parts, for as the roughnesse of the sea and weather lye constantly on the east of them, soe on the west they have the hills for theyr portion. The inhabitants beyond Murray (except in the Orkneys) speake generally Ober garlickh, or Highlands, and the mixture of both in the towne of Invernesse is such that one half of the people understand not one another. The trade of this port is onely a coast trade, there being noe more than one single merchant in the whole towne, who brings home sometimes a little timber, salt, or wine. Here is a collector, a checque, and one wayter, who attends here, and lookes (as occasion serves) to Garmouth and Findhorne in Murrayland, two small places, from whence some 60 lasts of salmon in a yeare are sent out, for which salt is brought in from France, and sometimes a small vessel comes from Holland or Norway.

Inverness had enjoyed a degree of trade with Belgium and Holland from the thirteenth century onwards, with wool, cloth, hides, fur and fish being exported. Half a century after Tucker noted 'noe more than one single merchant in the whole towne', Inverness was trading on a much broader basis, and one of its twenty or more merchants was the aforementioned John Steuart.

In 1915 the Scottish Historical Society published *The Letter-Book of Bailie John Steuart of Inverness 1715-1752*, edited by William Mackay, and this bulky volume, covering thirty-two years, serves as a fascinating record of Steuart's trading ventures, both legal and illegal.

John Steuart was born in September 1676, the son of an Inverness merchant who was a Highland gentleman by birth. Steuart began in business on his own account in 1700, and served on Inverness Town Council from 1703 to 1716. He was a magistrate from 1713 to 1715, from which time he was invariably known as 'Bailie Steuart'.

Steuart developed wide-ranging legitimate trading and non-trading business interests, dealing in meal and fish and many other commodities besides. He owned or part-owned around a dozen ships, including the *Christian*.

Despite being a staunch Jacobite, Steuart was enough of a pragmatist to supply meal to the Hanoverian garrisons at Fort William, Bernera in Glenelg, and Duart on Mull. According to William Mackay, 'He was of a speculative disposition and of a sanguine temperament, and he ventured and trusted too much. The result was that, while other Inverness merchants of his class made money and became landed proprietors, he, who excelled them all in industry and enterprise, died in poverty.'

In addition to his civic and legal duties, and his own extensive trading operations, Steuart also found time to act as factor to the Earl of Moray, whose home was Castle Stuart, a few miles from Inverness.

Mackay observed that 'the Highland gentlemen and Hanoverian officers who purchased their wine from the Bailie did so in the knowledge that no duty had been paid. Of the Bailie's wine customers one of the best was John Forbes of Culloden – Bumper John; and we may take it as certain that his brother, Duncan Forbes, who was fond of his wine . . . winked at the traffic, and, even after he became Lord Advocate, enjoyed his brother's famous claret none the less for the knowledge that the king whom he served had not received his own.'

A good example of the sort of ventures chronicled in the letter-book relates to Steuart's vessel the *Margaret*. In April 1722 the *Margaret* sailed to Rotterdam, with Steuart's son-in-law, David Stevenson, as her master. The ship was to be loaded with 'Lisbon salt and wine', according to a letter written by Steuart to Stevenson:

> From Rotterdam you are to proceed for this place [ie Inverness], and bring letters and bills of loading as from Lisbon. But befor you come directly up here you are to make a signall with your ensign off Helmsdeall, if the wind serve, where my orders will waite you either there or Tarbetness. You are to take care that no goods be found in the ship that may endanger her, especially that can be easily seen or diserned. Such goods as may be seen are as follows, vizt., salt, wine in hogsheads, chests with leamons and oranges, barrels with reasins and feggs, or brandie in hogsheads. Except these non other goods can be seen without great danger. You are to be verry cautious that if there be any other you stow it under the salt, or put it in hogsheads and stow it among the wine'.

When merchants sent vessels to collect goods abroad which were destined to be smuggled into Scotland they often loaded them with legitimate cargoes of salmon and herring on the outward trips to help finance the deals. Steuart sent the *Margaret* to Havre in September 1722, with his son in charge of the voyage. One hundred and fifty barrels of salmon were sold there, before the ship sailed for Bordeaux to collect a cargo of wine and brandy.

In June 1726, another of Steuart's vessels, the *Katherine* sailed from Leith to France, and on 22 June, Steuart wrote to the ship's master, Alexander Todd:

> Sir, – You are to proceed without loss of time to St. Martins [in France], and you are yr. to address yourself to Mr. Alexr, Gordon, Mercht. There,

and deliver him ye letter herewith given you, who will furnish you in
what quantity of salt your ship can take in, with ye Liquor which Mr.
Robert Gordon of Bordeaux is to ship for our accot., which will be about
12 tunns. And sd' Mr Gordon is to provoide you in foreign Clearances.
Yule endeavour to gett as much as possible, and notice yt. When, please
God, you return, in case you meet or is taken up by any Coustome houses
yatches, to declare yourself bound for Riga in ye Baltick; and be shure
you be well furnished with Clearances accordingly. If you gett safe to ye
firth yule endeavour to calle off Causea [Covesea in Moray] where orders
will attend you. We beg your outmost care and Dilligence.'

In early 1730 Steuart's vessel the *Christian* left Bordeaux with brandy
and wine and headed for the north-west coast of Scotland. Some of the
brandy was destined for the laird Stewart of Ardshiel, five hogsheads of
claret were for the governor of Fort William, one Captain Campbell,
and the remainder, Steuart instructed, was to be offered for sale to
another leading laird, MacDonald of Kinlochmoidart. Anything left
after this sale was to be sold if possible in South Uist, Dunvegan and
Portree on Skye, and Kyle of Lochalsh on the mainland.

Steuart subsequently wrote to the skipper of the *Christian* when
the vessel was in the Sound of Mull, warning that the customs service
might be aware of the venture. Urging caution, Steuart declared 'I am
apprehensive there may be great danger in your laying any time in the
Sound of Mull, and therefore I hope my friends will order matters so
that no time be lost. Let all you are to unload there be put to shoar
together, so that your lying make no great noice. And I think fitt
yourself and sloop take borrowed names, and that it not be known the
shipe belongs this place'.

Steuart's worst fears were confirmed, however, and customs officers
from Fort William, under the command of the Fort William collector
MacNeill, set out to intercept the vessel, which was forced to jettison
its cargo in the Kyle of Shuna, where it lies to this day.

As William Mackay noted, 'the voyage of the *Christian* appears to
have been the Bailie's last serious smuggling venture. He was often
suspected, and on more than one occasion got Lord Lovat, General
Wade, Colonel Guest, and other men of weight to use their influence
with the authorities in his favour'.

However, a letter written by Steuart on 20 August 1730 to his
brother-in-law John McLeod in Glenelg would suggest that the Bailie
continued to have the 'free trade' on his mind. He observed that

> . . . there is such strong resolutions and endeavours to crush the
> importation of Br---y that it is disparaging to a mans caracter at this
> juncture to be known to medle that way; besides the Duke of Argyle

and Marquis of Seaforth have engadged in the strongest manner to allow no Br---y to be bought or drunk in the severall counties. And, besides Culloden and the Advocate [Forbes of Culloden and his brother, Duncan, Lord Advocate] except [expect] McLeod and Sr. Alexr. Mcdonald to come to the same resolution. So, if such ane project be undertaken, it must be done in the most clandestin manner possible, and the ship can only touch at one remott port, and only ly while the goods can be unloaded, and immediatly thereafter to come of without letting any bodie know the ship or master name, or where she belongs to.

In December 1821 *The Courier* reported a strange trial which took place in Inverness. The Inverness shoremaster had buried eighteen kegs of gin in his garden, and proceeded to plant cabbages in the fresh earth on top in order to conceal them. He had done this for a local skipper whose smack had picked up the kegs at sea. It was assumed that they must have been part of a smuggled cargo that had met with some misfortune or been jettisoned by its smugglers during a pursuit. The kegs were discovered not long after their interment, and the shoremaster and skipper were prosecuted. They insisted, however, that the kegs were 'flotsam', and that by law they were therefore allowed twenty-four hours to report their salvage to the excise service. The officers of the excise, they claimed, had seized the kegs before twenty-four hours had passed, and so it could not be proved that the defendants were not going to hand them in. Amazingly, the court accepted this, and the two men were freed.

Inverness was quite a hotbed of smuggling activity, and the smugglers and their supporters were clearly none too gentle in their methods. On 18 May 1733 the Collector of Customs in Inverness wrote to the Board of Customs in indignant terms, relating that the customs boat stationed in his port had been stolen and destroyed by '. . . some ill-disposed villains'. "Tis hard to tell where this will end. The warehouse has been twice broken open, the boat destroyed, the expresses from the outports stopped and the letters taken away, a person under suspicion of being an informer dragged across the Firth and his ears cut out, and hints every day given to myself to take care of my life; in short no part of the face of the earth is peopled by such abandoned villains as this country.'

Sometimes the authorities made their mark in return, however. An example survives in customs records relating to the death of Inverness merchant Hugh Fraser, '. . . who was killed by one of the soldiers when out in the boat to protect the king's officers'. A number of customs officers and three soldiers were subsequently imprisoned for their roles in the killing of Fraser, but received royal pardons. 'The soldier who fired the fatal shot was called McAdam.'

According to Billy Kay (*Knee Deep in Claret*), Petty Bay, four miles east of Inverness, was a very popular place for unloading illicit wine cargoes, and an Inverness merchant developed a clever communications system for use in relation to Petty Bay landings. When a ship full of contraband wine arrived there, a runner was dispatched to the merchant in Inverness with an empty snuff-box. If the box was filled before being handed back to the runner, this was a signal that all was well for the unloading process to proceed, and the runner returned to the ship with the box. If the box was only half-filled, this meant that there was a risk of detection – perhaps the customs officers were particularly active – and the vessel was to remain offshore for a while until the situation was safer.

On one occasion the runner apparently arrived with the snuff box while the merchant was talking to a customs officer. The merchant half-filled the box – probably quite unnecessarily in the circumstances – gave the runner 6d. 'change', and continued his conversation with the officer without any suspicion being aroused.

The northernmost mainland county of Caithness was ideal for smuggling purposes, being sparsely populated and with many miles of quiet coastline where smuggled goods could be landed with minimal chance of detection.

'Smuggling was rife along the Caithness and Orkney coastline,' writes James Miller (*A Wide and Open Sea*). In March 1837 a new preventive boat was based at Lybster, on the east coast of Caithness. According to the authorities, foreign vessels had for months been trading goods in an '. . . open and mischievous manner'. Tobacco, brandy, gin and rum had all been changing hands for money and also for herring, which was a staple of the Caithness economy, and local traders were aggrieved at this duty-free competition. The *Northern Star* newspaper noted in March 1837 that '. . . theft, drunkenness, and an open violation of the Lord's Day were the baneful consequences'. In 1656 Thomas Tucker wrote that

> in Caithnes there is a wayter constantly resident for looking after Thurso and Weeke, two small ports, from whence good store of beefe, hides, and tallow are usually sent to the coast; his work is rather preventive, for hindering those commodities from being sent into forraigne parts, than profitable by anything hee is likely to receive there. The like also is practiced at Kirkwaile, in the Isles of Orkney, where there is another

officer for looking after those Isles, whence they send corne, fish, butter, tallowe, hides, and sometimes some timber is brought in from Norway, or els a Dutch vessell may happen to touch there in her passing out.

In May 1740, the Reverend Alexander Bryce journeyed north to Caithness, principally to construct a map of the northern coast due to the incidence of so many shipwrecks there. According to the *Biographical Dictionary of Eminent Scotsmen*, 'during a residence of three years, and in defiance of many threats from the peasantry, which made it necessary for him to go always armed, who did not relish so accurate an examination of their coast, from motives of disloyalty, or because they were afraid, it would deprive them of two principal sources of income – smuggling and plunder from the shipwrecks, he accomplished *at his own expense*, the geometrical survey, and furnished "A Map of the North Coast of Britain, from Raw Stoir of Assynt, to Wick in Caithness, with the harbours and rocks, and an account of the tides in the Pentland Firth".'

It would be wrong to assume, however, that smuggling in Caithness was just a disorganised, opportunistic affair. Local merchants orchestrated much of the illegal trade, with Wick-based Thomas Baikie and Alexander Bain junior being among the most prominent during the eighteenth century. Bain operated a number of vessels which were responsible for conveying contraband cargoes from Ostend, Gothenburg and the Faroe Islands to Caithness. Bain also dealt with the Dunkirk merchant Alexander Hunter, who supplied him with gin.

## THE ORKNEYS

In *Around the Orkney Peat-Fires* (1898) W.R. Mackintosh told the tale of a party of revenue officers in Stromness on Orkney getting word that a cargo of contraband goods had been landed on the little island of Stroma, which lies in the Pentland Firth between the Caithness coast and the southernmost Orkney islands. Keen to keep their true destination secret, the officers hired a boat at Scapa and told the skipper to take them to St Margaret's Hope, on South Ronaldsay, hoping to avoid suspicion. Once at sea they ordered him to go to Stroma instead, but he refused, even threatening violence if they tried to interfere with his sailing. They were duly landed at St Margaret's Hope, and then hired a second boat to ferry them to their ultimate destination. However, the first boatman managed to inform the second skipper of what was happening, and he set off as slowly as he could for Stroma, while riders carried news of the officers' imminent arrival along South Ronaldsay to Burwick, where a short sea voyage took the news to the

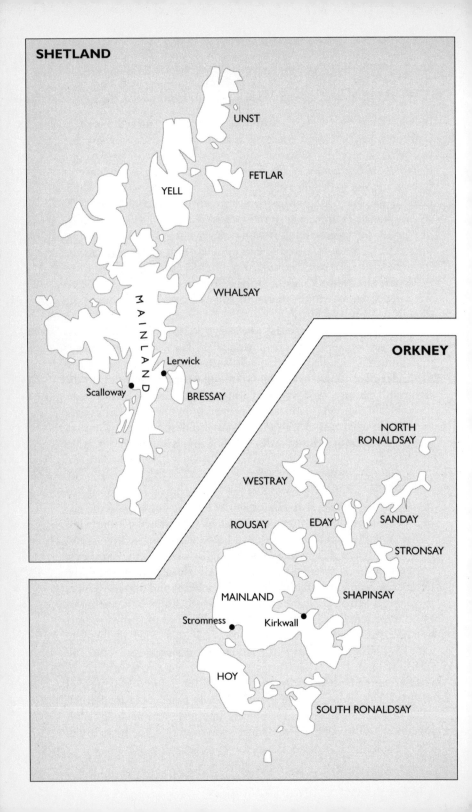

smugglers on Stroma ahead of the officers. By the time they arrived, all the contraband was hidden well out of sight.

Writing of smuggling on Orkney itself, Mackintosh stated that

> Shortly after the Scottish Excise Act [1823] came into force, smuggling was carried on very extensively in Orkney. The illicit traffic was not confined to the lower and middle classes. In fact these may be said to have merely done the drudgery work of the trade, whilst the profits went into the pockets of the gentry.
>
> Kirkwall was the headquarters of the smugglers in the county and the wealthy merchants secured most of the profits. The Magistrates and Town Councillors took a leading part in the traffic, and it must be confessed that they carried on their operations with great success.
>
> It is not more than thirty years [ie the late 1860s] since smuggled gin is said to have been disposed of quite publicly in a bank in town; and eighteen or nineteen years ago some heavy cargoes were landed in Kirkwall, which were disposed of to hotel-keepers and others.
>
> Smuggling, however, is now a thing of the past . . . sometimes a Dutch lugger may dispose of a small cask of gin, or a parcel of tobacco to the crew of a local fishing boat, but the quality of these goods is generally so bad that they would be dear at any money.

'In the early part of this century', according to Mackintosh, '. . . boats were fitted up, and regularly manned, to carry on the illicit traffic between Orkney and Shetland and other places.' Orkney boats would sail to a Shetland voe on the north-west side of Northmavine in order to load up with the contraband.

Mackintosh wrote of an occasion on which a boat from Shetland laden with unspecified smuggled goods was unloading near Banks on Rousay when news came that the customs officers in Kirkwall had somehow got wind of the enterprise.

A classic decoy operation was mounted, with Rousay's finest fishermen persuaded, no doubt with an incentive from the cargo in return, to row out at great speed, with their fishing gear in evidence, when the customs vessel approached. This they duly did, and a vigorous pursuit ensued, with the Rousay boatmen rowing well out into the Westray Firth. There they laid up their oars and began to fish until the customs vessel caught up. The fishing boat's conduct could not have looked more suspicious, and the customs officers obviously anticipated a good haul of smuggled goods, but a cursory examination of the boat was enough to show them that they had been duped, and they set off back to Rousay. However, a strong ebb tide prevented them from landing at Sourin for some five to six hours. As Mackintosh concluded, 'by that time the people on shore had managed to stow away the contraband goods, so that the officers had to return to Kirkwall defeated and discouraged'.

Gin was one of the principal commodities smuggled in Orkney and Shetland, and one day a man from Swannay in Birsay was carrying a keg of smuggled gin on his back, concealed in an old case, when an exciseman began to pursue him. He dodged between several peat banks before making straight for the sea cliffs, where he swung the case off his back and hurled it into the sea.

The exciseman, with no evidence at his disposal, was forced to let the Swannay man go free, but he contended himself with the knowledge that at least the smuggled goods had been destroyed. Not so, for the smuggler had managed to drop the keg out of the case into one of the peat banks, from where he later retrieved it intact.

According to Mackintosh, officials in Orkney were just as liable to succumb to bribes as they were in any other part of the country. 'There is a tradition in the West Mainland to the effect that the Customs officials were in the habit of giving a quiet word of warning to the country people before the raid of rangers [excise officers' assistants] commenced, so that the malt and smuggled spirits could be put in a place of safety. It is also stated that these Government officials received yearly a nice keg of gin, stowed away in a sack of "scrubs", as an acknowledgement of their kindly help in time of need.'

Mackintosh told the story of a notable Orcadian smuggler, George Eunson, who worked as a cooper before going to sea. 'He was very clever, but was of a restless, roving disposition . . . He was a daring character, and just the sort of man that would make a successful smuggler. This was acknowledged on all hands, so that a company which had been formed to purchase a vessel for the illicit trade, approached Eunson, and got him persuaded to take command of the ship. Eunson, though clever in landing his cargoes, was not a success for his employers. He embezzled their goods, and made such exorbitant charges that they were glad to get rid of him.'

Many maritime adventures later, Eunson returned to Orkney and to smuggling, but in 1785 he was dismissed for succumbing once more to his previous failings. As part of a bizarre local political plot he became an officer of excise, but was subsequently imprisoned for several weeks in Kirkwall for assaulting a shoemaker.

'In later years Eunson divided his time between smuggling and performing the duties of a north-sea pilot,' wrote Mackintosh. 'When acting in the latter capacity on a man-of-war vessel, it went down with all hands.'

A second well-known Orcadian smuggling character was Magnus 'Mansie' Eunson, no relation to George. According to Mackintosh, 'He was a flesher [butcher], beadle, and a successful smuggler. In addition to this he was a born character, brimful of pawky humour and resource, which extricated him from many a scrape.'

'. . . Mansie did a big smuggling business, but he was so clever in carrying the goods after they were landed that he could never be caught, though he had many narrow escapes.'

Gin and brandy were the principal commodities smuggled by Mansie. However, the best-known, oft-quoted Mansie Eunson story relates to the origins of Highland Park whisky distillery near Kirkwall, as recounted by Alfred Barnard in his *Whisky Distilleries of the United Kingdom*.

> . . . the site whereon the Distillery now stands, was the place where the famous Magnus Eunson, carried on his operations. This man was the greatest and most accomplished smuggler in Orkney. By profession he was a U. P. Church Officer, and kept a stock of illicit whisky under the pulpit, but in reality he was a 'non-Professing' distiller. This godly person was accustomed to give out the psalms in a more unctuous manner than usual if the excise officers were in church, as he knew that he was suspected, and that a party of the revenue officers, taking advantage of his absence, might at that moment be searching his house. A singular story is told of this man. Hearing that the Church was about to be searched for whisky by a new party of excisemen, Eunson had the kegs all removed to his house, placed in the middle of an empty room, and covered with a clean white cloth. As the officers approached after their unsuccessful search in the church, Eunson gathered all his people, including the maidservants, round the whisky, which, with its covering of white, under which a coffin lid had been placed, looked like a bier. Eunson knelt at the head with the Bible in his hand and the others with their psalm books. As the door opened they set up a wail for the dead, and Eunson made a sign to the officers that it was a death, and one of the attendants whispered 'smallpox.' Immediately the officer and his men made off as fast as they could, and left the smuggler for some time in peace.

Mackintosh's version of the Mansie Eunson story differs substantially from Barnard's, however. Eunson was the church beadle, and did not preach, and there is nothing in Mackenzie's account to suggest that he was, himself, a distiller of illicit whisky.

Mackintosh wrote that 'smuggling was carried on to such an extent, and with such bad effects upon the people, that the Seceding clergymen began to denounce the traffic. One Sunday Mansie's minister held forth on the iniquity of the trade, and declared that no Christian would take any part in it. When the service was over, some person asked Mansie what he thought of the sermon.

"I think," answered Mansie, "that oor minister is no' very consistent, for at the very time he was preaching, he had six kegs o' as guid brandy under his pulpit as ever was smuggled!"

The joke was much appreciated, for Mansie, being church officer, often hid his smuggled spirits under the floor of the pulpit, pretty confident that would be one of the last places that the excisemen would think of searching.'

In *Travels in Scotland* (1807), the Reverend James Hall wrote about his sadness that the clergy of Orkney and Shetland should '. . . so often wink at their churches being repositories of smuggled goods'.

On one occasion, Mansie Eunson needed to bring some casks of illicit whisky from Deerness into Kirkwall, so he purposely told a local worthy of his plan to cross the Bridge of Wideford on the Kirkwall road between midnight and 1 a.m. with the casks loaded on three horses. He was certain that the worthy would tell the excise officers of this plan, as he was a well-known informant. Sure enough, the officers were informed, and proceeded to stake out the bridge at the appointed time, hiding underneath its parapet to shelter from the cold of the night. They duly heard the sound of horses, and sprang out to confront Eunson, only to find that he was heading in the wrong direction, with what turned out to be empty casks. He told the officers that he had taken the full casks into Kirkwall somewhat earlier than he had mentioned to the informant, but that he had not had the heart to keep the officers waiting in the cold for him until morning.

On another occasion Mansie employed his quick wits to engage a party of gaugers in banter and humour after they caught him with kegs of smuggled spirit in a cart and insisted he accompany them to Kirkwall to deal with the matter. So entertaining was Mansie, that the gaugers failed to notice a number of his accomplices creep up behind the cart and remove the kegs one by one as the party made its way towards town. By the time they reached Kirkwall, there was no evidence left, so no charges could be brought against the smuggler.

Mackintosh noted, 'At length Mansie was taken before the Session for smuggling, and he lost his situation as beadle. He took this so much to heart that he gave up attending church.' When Mansie was tackled about his absense by the minister, he had, as usual, a ready answer. Indeed, he insisted that he did still attend church. The minister said that this was not true, but Mansie replied 'My wife is there every Sunday'. He pointed out that when he got married the minister who conducted the service said that he and his wife were now one. 'Either you or the other minister has tellt us a lee,' retorted Mansie!

Mackintosh wrote that 'Captain Askham was a noted smuggler in Orkney about twenty years ago [i.e. in the late 1870s]. He was a native of Hull, but he formed a connection in Orkney, where he did a big trade in contraband goods. The plan he adopted was to take a cargo of spirits out of bond at Leith, carry it to Faroe, discharge it there and then bring it back to Orkney with dried fish and Faroe cattle and ponies.'

Askham's audacious custom was not to land his smuggled cargo in some remote spot, but to sail into Kirkwall at midnight, discharge the smuggled spirits, go out to sea, and sail back in the morning to unload his legitimate cargo, as if he had just arrived from the Faroes.

On one occasion he docked in Orkney's second principal port of Stromness, and went overland to look for potential customers in Kirkwall. The Kirkwall customs house officers heard of this, and Askham was duly advised by a well-wisher that they planned to set off for Stromness early next morning. 'Let them go, they will be welcome to all they find,' he declared loudly. He ordered a bed for the night, but then crept out of his lodgings, hired a horse and travelled to Stromness, where he spent the night unloading and hiding his smuggled cargo.

After breakfast he set out for Kirkwall again, and met the customs officers at Finstown, as they headed for Stromness. They were, not surprisingly, far from pleased to see Askham travelling in the 'wrong' direction.

Mackintosh concluded that eventually Askham became disillusioned with smuggling, its risks and its bad payers. '. . . he went to Australia, where he is said to have got an appointment in the Customs, and his former experience in this country will no doubt be of value to him in his new home in the detection of smugglers.'

Another Orcadian involved in smuggling was John Esson, a merchant from Deerness. On occasion he would buy a cask of rum from Longhope, where he went to sell goods and to buy eggs. Smuggling did not always prove profitable for him, however. Mackintosh recalled that 'a French vessel having landed some contraband goods and hidden them from the coastguard, some persons found them and appropriated them for their own use. The Frenchmen retaliated by poisoning the cattle nearest to the place. The beasts happened to belong to Mr Esson.'

In his 1931 book *A Peculiar People and Other Orkney Tales*, J.T. Smith-Leask told of a particularly strong smuggler from the island of Hoy, who was observed by a number of excise officers when he arrived in his boat at Stromness harbour, ready to unload four casks of illegal spirits. Unable to think how else to avoid detection, he jammed one cask under each arm and picked up the others by the rims, using his strength to such good effect that the watching officers were convinced that the casks must be empty.

The School of Scottish Studies' archive contains details of an interesting, and comparatively late, example of Orcadian smuggling, told by James Bain of Westray to Alan Bruford in 1973.

Bain recalled how, on a trip to buy pit ponies in North Faroe, his father also carried contraband back to Shetland. On another occasion, contraband from Faroe was transported via Orkney to Leith. Once a load of smuggled gin was taken to Broughton on Westray, 'hidden in a pile of tangles', as Bain put it. The gin was subsequently carted to the West Side pier and shipped to Kirkwall on 'mainland' Orkney. The gin was only seized by the excise officers after the carter carrying it tapped into one of the casks and arrived in Kirkwall roaring drunk.

A number of substantial Orcadian merchants were involved in the contraband trade during the late eighteenth and early nineteenth centuries, most notably Thomas Traill, provost of Kirkwall from 1792 to 1812, and his son, William. During a clamp-down in 1805, many illicit whisky stills were seized on outlying Orkney islands, though the activities of the local excise officer were not helped by the involvement in smuggling of the resident Naval Commander Captain, William Richan.

Richan was an Orcadian by birth, and built the impressive house that is now Kirkwall's West End Hotel, in 1824. In his role as captain of the convoy escort ship *Norfolk*, Richan regularly sailed to Scandinavia, escorting convoys of merchant vessels to protect them from privateers. He developed a habit of loading the *Norfolk* with contraband goods before returning to Scotland, and it is believed that he became involved in making money from smuggling tobacco and alcohol, partly on account of the ruinous extravagance of his wife, Esther. In July 1807, excise officers boarded his vessel and discovered 560 gallons of rum, as well as other liquor. Richan was forced to resign his commission.

With Richan removed from his post, William Traill found his supply of illicit whiskies and foreign spirits drying up. He therefore opened a legal brewery and distillery in Mill Street, Papdale, Kirkwall, using smuggling friends such as Mansie Eunson to distribute his whisky.

At the village of Stromness, on the mainland of the Orkney group, lived a witch called Bessie Millie who, for well on into the nineteenth century, gained a living by selling favourable winds to mariners, and providing luck charms for the whalers. Her power and influence were paramount in that part of the Northern Islands.

At that time the captain of the Revenue cutter HMS *Widgeon* – my grandfather – was ordered to hunt out the smugglers and put down their traffic with a firm hand. He was chosen for this post for his intelligence and his signal gallantry.

From the first he found himself thwarted and baffled by the witch Bessie Millie. Soon after his arrival my grandfather was surprised to find her standing before him in his cabin. He sternly demanded from the sentry why the woman had been allowed to invade his sanctum unannounced. The man, a brave and splendid seaman, said she had threatened to blind him and he believed she could do it. He ordered the man under arrest and the woman to leave the ship.

'Not before I have had my say,' she said. 'George Phillips, you come from a proud, wilful race, and most of yer brood have met death by sword, bullet, and violence; beware how ye defy Bessie Millie.'

My grandfather had all the old-world notions of chivalry in regard to a woman, even if she were a witch. He hesitated about laying hands on her. She stood before him habited in a loose hand-woven gown, a plaid shawl of some tartan about her shoulders, and a handkerchief round her head. Her face presented all the appearance of discoloured parchment, her dark eyes were deep set, and flashing with fire. A massive masculine brow and a firm jaw completed her description. 'Say what you have to say and be gone,' said he, not knowing what else to do under the circumstances.

With an utterance of astonishing rapidity and a wonderful choice of words she enumerated certain events in our family history, particularly in connection with the disastrous uprising in favour of the Stewarts in 1745. That my grandfather always maintained she must have learnt from local history, but what did astonish him was her knowledge of certain facts which he did not know then, and which eventually turned out to be true. The object of her visit was no doubt to frighten him, and intimidate the crew so that their vigilance on behalf of her smuggling friends might be interrupted by fears of her vengeance.

When she directed my grandfather to take his ship back to the cursed government that had sent him he laughed. With the crew she was more successful.

A report was brought that a cargo was to be landed in one of the numerous creeks on the main island. A couple of pinnaces were sent off to watch the inlet, while the cutter stood out to sea to cut off any escape that way, should the men get away from the preventive guard. To the amazement of my grandfather the two pinnaces returned to the ship within a couple of hours and the officer in charge reported a mutiny.

While proceeding up the inlet Bessie Millie had appeared on the headland and ordered the men back to the ship, threatening them with curses when they hesitated. What is more, several of the men took to their hammocks and declared they had been bewitched, and discipline was for a time at an end. Calling together what men he could rely on, my grandfather sought the witch. Her house was situated on the brow of the hill overlooking Stromness. She was on the threshold awaiting them, a look of triumph on her face. 'George Phillips, I told ye that ye would come to me before I would come to you.'

'Well, I have come,' was his reply, 'and unless you come down to the Widgeon and remove your spell, I will burn down this haunt of yours.'

He had to proceed to put this threat into execution before she consented.
The men who said they were sick quickly recovered, and something like
an armed truce prevailed between the Government ship and Bessie Millie.
But she always seemed able to divine the plans of my grandfather, and on
more than one occasion she was the means of frustrating them'.

– *Athol Forbes*, The Romance of Smuggling (1909)

The *Statistical Account of Scotland* is informative on the subject of
Orkney smuggling, with the Reverend Mr George Barry of the United
Parishes of Kirkwall and St Ola attributing some of the increase in
population in the parish to ' . . . the partial suppression of smuggling,
which has forced the monied men to lay out their capitals in more
useful as well as in more honest industry'. Later, he wrote:

> To form the minds, mark the characters of the inferior ranks of people
> here, the illicit trade which until lately has been carried on to no small
> extent, has, without doubt, contributed very considerably. Formerly, the
> money they had, which indeed was but little, ran almost all of it in the
> channel of smuggling. This species of business, which has always been the
> disgrace, and at last proved the ruin of almost every place where it has
> been practiced to a great extent, enriched indeed a few merchants, who
> circulated their profits in the place. But it also contributed to introduce,
> among the farmers, sailors, and even tradesmen, a sort of low cunning, to
> give them such a taste for drinking spirits, as not only hurt their health,
> but stints their growth, to draw off their attention from sober, honest
> industry, to a kind of gambling for gain, and what is worst of all, to
> weaken in their hearts that sacred regard for truth and fair dealing, which
> are the principal ingredients in every respectable character. Though this
> shameful trade be now much discouraged by some of the proprietors
> of land, who long saw with regret its pernicious tendency, and indeed
> almost suppressed by the vigorous exertions of the revenue officers;
> yet, though the cause be in a great measure removed, the effects, still
> unhappily indeed, are visible in Kirkwall.

The Reverend Mr Liddell, Minister in the parish of Orphir, noted that

> A low spirit for smuggling . . . has been the bane of Orkney for half a
> century past . . . The writer of the present report, when a very young
> man, inspired with the love of his country, and fired with indignation at
> the unhallowed trade, in which, as in a vortex, truth, honour, integrity,
> and every virtue, was swallowed up, resolved, with the spirit of an ancient
> Roman, to attack the hideous monster; and accordingly, despising the
> misapplied appellation of Informer, in so glorious as well as hazardous
> an attempt, gave in the collector of the customs, on the public street, an
> accusation against a noted smuggler, had his vessel seized, condemned,

and burnt; demanded and received the informer's share, as an inducement
to others to follow the example, and immediately bestowed the same in
erecting a charity school in the parish, whereby they have been since
greatly benefited.

Although it must be confessed, that, in this business, he was
privately supported by some of the first gentlemen in Orkney; whose
representatives, much to their honour, and for the good of their country,
have since completed the business; and it is to be hoped, less from
political motives, than from moral and patriotic principles.

## 3. SHETLAND

In 1656 Thomas Tucker wrote that

> as for Shetland (thought to be the Ultima Thule, soe much spoken of
> and reputed by the ancients to be the furtherest part of the world) it
> lyes over against Bergen in Norway, and very difficult to gett thither but
> in some certaine moneths of the summer. There was never yet officer
> either sent or that would adventure thither till of late, when the farmer
> of the inland commodityes of those parts having prevailed with one to
> undertake his affaires there, the Commissioners did commission the
> same party likewise as to Custome and foraigne excise alsoe, but what
> successe this enterprise may have, must bee left to the discovery of some
> further time. Report speakes the place to be frequented about May with
> some Dutch, who come to fish there, bringing beere, strong waters, and
> tobaccoes with them.

A century and a half later, Dutch fishing vessels were still bringing
'strong waters', in the shape of gin, into Shetland, and during the eighteenth century significant quantities of tobacco and gin were smuggled
into the islands at the behest of landowners and local merchants.

During the 1760s, gin was first smuggled into the islands on a large
scale, frequently using the 'pretended-bound' excuse that inclement
weather had blown the offending Dutch vessels off their intended
course to the Faroe Islands.

In *Shetland Life and Trade*, Hance D. Smith has noted that there
were two distinct phases in the Shetland smuggling business. Initially,
it was carried on alongside legitimate trading, and was concerned
with evading duty on what Smith describes as '. . . goods required for
everyday use that were liable to high duties, principally tobacco, tea
and spirits (mainly corn brandy)'.

He gives a neat example of this, regarding the *Sibella*, which left
Hamburg in October 1752 with a cargo bound for Shetland. The
customs returns for the vessel listed salt, lines, iron and tar – all liable
to low levels of duty or to no duty at all. However, the vessel was also

carrying Cognac and corn brandy, French claret and a selection of other wines. These smuggled items made up roughly half the value of the entire cargo, worth in excess of £5,000 Scots [£500 sterling].

Then, from the 1760s, this kind of venture was accompanied by what Smith calls 'a "true" smuggling trade' in Dutch gin, and he notes that one of the earliest references to a Shetland merchant stocking gin occurs in 1765.

In 1764 and 1765 the customs service, seeing Shetland gin smuggling beginning to burgeon, attempted to make it compulsory for all ships arriving in the islands to unload at Lerwick, in order to be able to control the situation much more effectively.

The local landowners, often with a vested interest in making life difficult for the customs officers, insisted that this was not feasible, though the extent and remote nature of so much of the Shetland coastline made them a smugglers' paradise. It was not difficult to see why the customs service would have liked Lerwick to be designated the only lawful landing place for ships in the islands.

Back in 1723, when 'Customs Creeks' were being established, it was decided that it would be unfeasible to nominate Lerwick as the only such creek, for, in the words of Smith, '. . . a fair wind on one side of the islands almost certainly spelled a contrary one on the other side'. Any serious delays in getting in or out of a port were expensive for traders, and in respect of the Shetland fish export trade, a potential disaster, with catches being totally ruined by delays.

So the notion of having Lerwick as the only designated port in the islands was never implemented, but the idea surfaced again during the 1760s, and landowners one more advanced the same objections. In a petition of October 1769 they pointed out that if 'spirits and other fishing materials', as Smith rather nicely puts it, could be imported duty-free, then smuggling would end.

During the 1770s, merchants from outwith Shetland came to be involved in the lucrative gin smuggling trade. In 1770, there is the first record of a 'professional' smuggler being apprehended, and another was caught in 1776. Smith writes that, 'the following year a smuggler came from Gothenburg with tea, but the Customs were afraid to touch him, as there had been violence in earlier seizure attempts in 1774 and 1775'.

Most of Shetland's gin was transported from the international 'gin capital' of Rotterdam, and on 24 April 1792 the Shetland sheriff-substitute, Walter Scott of Scottshall wrote 'so to your Rotterdam gentry, they deserve punishment, for their trade will ruin this country compleatly'.

Around this time the local landowners largely abandoned the gin trade, leaving it to the merchants, with the landowners concentrating on smuggling timber from Norway thereafter. Such was the scale of gin smuggling in Shetland by the 'Rotterdam Gentry' that in a letter of 24 March 1798, the Collector of Customs in Lerwick reported a shortage of currency in the islands, as so much ready cash had been spent by merchants purchasing supplies of gin.

Some of the Shetland merchants who had previously been actively involved in smuggling, using their own ships, went on to act as agents for smuggling rings based in London, Holland and Norway. They ran rum, brandy and wine into Shetland, sometimes on vessels 'pretended-bound' for Norwegian ports from London, Rotterdam or Amsterdam. This trade carried on until around 1820.

In 1871 Robert Cowie (*Shetland: descriptive and historical*) wrote that 'the ordinary practice was for a vessel (probably not larger than a sloop), after clearing the Custom-house at Lerwick, for Norway, to proceed directly to Holland, where she loaded gin and tobacco, which were quietly landed at Unst, or some remote part of Shetland. The smuggler then made all haste for his acknowledged destination, loaded timber, and returning to Lerwick, reported himself as having been at Norway all the time.'

Wood goods were also smuggled by local merchants during the 1820s on ships bound for Ireland, the Faroes, or Iceland. Timber duty was high at the time, which was why this particular type of smuggling was, for a few years at least, viable. Spirits and tobacco were sometimes smuggled on the same routes.

During the last years of Shetland smuggling, fishing vessels were frequently used to bring in contraband, along with fish, and the Shetland cod fishery was partially established as 'cover' for the illegal importation of goods into the islands. Ostensibly fishing for cod, Shetland vessels would sail to Norway and collect timber or gin, which they then smuggled into their home ports. Customs records for 1822 state that there were around forty 'cod sloops' engaged in smuggling.

Writing of Shetland smuggling and fishing during the 1790s, the Reverend Mr John Morison, of the parish of Delting, in north-east mainland Shetland, showed a pragmatic approach to alcohol rarely to be found in the pious pages of the *Statistical Account of Scotland*.

He declared that 'a total suppression of smuggling would greatly contribute to the prosperity, and preservation of the morals, of the people; provided, at the same time, the excise was taken off such spirits as are consumed by the fishermen during the fishing season. They cannot prosecute the fishing without a little, and they cannot afford to use duty paid spirits.'

Between 1816 and 1823, Dutch vessels carried an estimated 10,000 to 12,000 gallons of illicit gin per year into Shetland, according to customs figures, landing at remote spots like Skerries, Foula and Fair Isle, either in the spring or the autumn. Despite the quantities involved, the quality of the gin was generally poor – a criticism also levelled at tea and tobacco transported by the same vessels. This view echoes William Mackintosh's observations (p. 144) regarding the poor quality of Dutch contraband goods latterly offered for sale in Orkney.

Gin smuggling became so serious that it was considered by the customs service to be detrimental to the Shetland economy, and in a letter of 13 April 1822 the collector at Lerwick wrote that the smugglers had '. . . already drained the poor of this country, who we believe have been the only buyers, of every shilling they could afford or raise'. This reference to only 'the poor' purchasing it supports the view that the merchandise was cheap and not of the highest quality.

The year 1823 saw an end to the smuggling of gin in Shetland, partly due to the increased activity of naval vessels in suppressing it, but also because of the apparent saturation of the market, which left little or no money with which to buy spirits. Merchants were increasingly turning their attention to lucrative fishing activities, and the reduction of duty which came about as a result of the 1823 Excise Act, designed to stimulate legal whisky distilling in Scotland, made good-quality spirit imports from mainland Scotland relatively cheap.

James Hay of Laxfirth had been Shetland's leading merchant-smuggler during the early nineteenth century, and in 1825, his son, William, arranged to buy 1,700 gallons of whisky from the mainland, which shows how times had changed in respect of spirits provision in Shetland. On 10 May of that year, the Collector of Customs in Lerwick was able to write that '. . . regular smuggling is at an end in this country'.

The following anecdote was recorded in 1975 for the School of Scottish Studies, and was subsequently published in Issue 19 of the School's magazine *Tocher*. It is titled 'William Donaldson and the Cat'.

> Weel as everybody knows smuggling in the old days wi the Shetlanders was a graet business. There'd be a lot of smuggling from the Dutchies that would com in, bartering an so on, an of course they were a lot of smuggling wi the men South wi the Merchant Service, mostly tobaaco 'at they would try to get ashoer . . . An among the Fetlar men . . . they were wan fellow was rather notorious for smuggling – his name was William Donaldson. So much so . . . did he carry on the smuggling, that on Salvesen's vessels they put up a noatice on the shippin office: 'Nobody by the name of Donaldson need apply'. (That is correct. There

other Fetlar seamen that could verify the fact.) And it became known that the smuggling was carried on to such an extent that the police and the coastguard tightened up their observations on the short ports, and . . . wan of the worst places 'at they could attempt to land in was . . . Grangemouth . . .

An Will'am arrived hom with a goodly consignment of good Dutch plugs. When he heard about this extry restrictions when he came across to this side he was very downcast 'at he wisna goin to succeed this time. He wondered, an aal his friends said that he didna think 'at he would need try it, 'coz they were a double watch set on the . . . dock gaets an it . . .'d only land him into trouble. An as he's lyin in the bunk meditatin on how he's goin to . . . he had this plugs . . . hoisted down wi a piece of rop down the ventilator . . . how he's goin to get this good plugs ashore – they had a tom cat, for keeping away the rats. It was goin to an fro on the fo'c'sle floor. An he just thinks for a minute, as he's looking at the cat – 'By Jove, yes, I have a braen wave, it might work, but anyway it's worth a try. I'll see what I can do tomorrow an I'll sleep on it.

So tomorrow he went to the steward an he said, 'Could you gi me a good-sized big carrying basket in the hand?'

'What to do with?'

'Well,' he says, 'never you mind what to do with; I'll tell you after A've used it . . . but I'll guarantee to put it back to you.' All right, he gev him the big basket, just a square old-fashioned carrying basket. Took this cat, tied a piece o cloth on the top o the – put in the cat, tied a piece o cloth round this – the basket, went up to the dock gaets. So the police – 'Stop, me lad: what ha' you got in the basket?'

'Oh, it's a cat A'm takin ashoer to a friend.'

'Ha, ha. We're heard that old game – storeis before fae you. Open the basket!'

'Well,' he says, 'if I oapen the basket you know what'll happen . . . I'll lose the cat.'

'Get cracking, oapen your basket.'

'Well, well, aa right, I've toald you.' So he oapen't the basket, out jumped the cat, down for the ship. 'Well, there you are, you see. Now I got to go an get that aal over again.' Wi that he quickly turned and . . . went aboard. But . . . he moved quhick. He filled the basket with Dutch plugs, tied on his cover.

'Now, you're surely not goin to let the cat out o the bag this time then?'

'No, off you go then ashoer; off you go with your cat.'

And that's how Will'am did them again. And that night i the pub in Grangemouth he gathered . . . his shipmates around him, an they drank to the health of Will'am who never was beat yet.'

# 7

# SMUGGLING IN SCOTTISH LITERATURE

Considering the significant role that smuggling has played in Scottish life, both actual and mythological, it is hardly surprising that the activity has found its way into Scottish literature. There is also the bonus for authors, of course, that smuggling can be portrayed as dramatic and exciting, and may therefore be used to counterpoint more pedestrian parts of their novels.

Sir Walter Scott incorporated smuggling characters and episodes into a number of his novels. In *Guy Mannering* (1815), Scott took the real-life smuggler Jack Yawkins (see pp. 21 and 71) and recast him as dastardly Dirk Hatteraick, a significant minor character in the novel which is largely set on the coast of south-west Scotland. It is worth remembering that at the time Scott was writing, smuggling was still a recent phenomenon, and that the author would have had no shortage of personal experience of the trade, having been called to the bar in 1792, subsequently acting as Sheriff-Depute of Selkirkshire and Clerk of the Court of Session.

In the notes that accompany *Guy Mannering*, Scott wrote:

> The prototype of Dick Hatteraick is considered as having been a Dutch skipper called Yawkins. This man was well known on the coast of Galloway and Dumfriesshire, as sole proprietor and master of a *Buckkar*, or smuggling lugger, called the *Black Prince*. Being distinguished by his nautical skill and intrepidity, his vessel was frequently freighted, and his own services employed, by French, Dutch, Manx, and Scottish smuggling companies.
>
> A person well known by the name of Buckkar-tea, from having been a noted smuggler of that article, and also by that of Bogle-Bush, the place of his residence, assured my kind informant, Mr. Train, that he had frequently seen upwards of two hundred Lingtow-men assemble at one time, and go off into the interior of the country, fully laden with contraband goods.
>
> In those halcyon days of the free trade, the fixed price for carrying a box of tea, or bale of tobacco, from the coast of Galloway to Edinburgh, was fifteen shillings, and a man with two horses carried four such packages. The trade was entirely destroyed by Mr. Pitt's celebrated commutation law, which, by reducing the duties upon excisable articles,

enabled the lawful dealer to compete with the smuggler. The statute was called in Galloway and Dumfriesshire, by those who had thriven upon the contraband trade, 'the burning and starving act'.

Sure of such active assistance on shore, Yawkins demeaned himself so boldly, that his mere name was a terror to the officers of the revenue. He availed himself of the fears which his presence inspired on one particular night, when, happening to be ashore with a considerable quantity of goods in his sole custody, a strong party of excisemen came down on him. Far from shunning the attack, Yawkins sprung forward, shouting, 'Come on my lads; Yawkins is before you.' The revenue officers were intimidated, and relinquished their prize, though defended only by the courage and address of a single man. On his proper element, Yawkins was equally successful. On one occasion, he was landing his cargo at the Manxman's Lake, near Kirkcudbright, when two revenue cutters (the *Pigmy* and the *Dwarf*) hove in sight at once on different tacks, the one coming round by the Isles of Fleet, the other between the point of Rueberry and the Muckle Ron. The dauntless free-trader instantly weighed anchor, and bore down right between the luggers, so close that he tossed his hat on the deck of the one, and his wig on that of the other, hoisted a cask to his maintop, to show his occupation, and bore away under an extraordinary pressure of canvas, without receiving injury. To account for these and other hair-breadth escapes, popular superstition alleged that Yawkins insured his celebrated Buckkar by compounding with the devil for one-tenth of his crew on every voyage. How they arranged the separation of the stock and tithes is left to our conjecture. The Buckkar was perhaps called the *Black Prince* in honour of the formidable insurer.

The *Black Prince* used to discharge her cargo at Luce, Balcarry, and elsewhere on the coast; but her owner's favourite landing-places were at the entrance to the Dee and the Cree, near the old Castle of Rueberry, about six miles below Kirkcudbright. There is a cave of large dimensions in the vicinity of Rueberry, which, from its being frequently used by Yawkins, and his supposed connection with the smugglers on the shore, is now called Dick Hatteraick's Cave. Strangers who visit this place, the scenery of which is highly romantic, are also shown, under the name of the Gauger's Loup, a tremendous precipice, being the same, it is asserted, from which Kennedy was precipitated.

The 'Kennedy' referred to is 'riding officer' Francis Kennedy, who, early in Scott's novel, meets an untimely end at the hands of the band of smugglers.

Hatteraick at one point declares 'I'm all in the way of fair trade – Just loaded yonder at Douglas, in the Isle of Man – neat cogniac – real hyson and souchong – Mechln lace, if you want any – Right cogniac – We bumped ashore a hundred kegs last night.'

'The Laird', Godfrey Bertram of Ellangowan, exemplifies the stance of many gentlemen who 'should have known better'. The Laird describes Hatteraick as a '. . . gude sort of blackguard fellow enough naebody cares to trouble him – smuggler, when his guns are in ballast – privateer, or pirate faith, when he gets them mounted. He has done more mischief to the revenue folk than ony rogue that ever came out of Ramsay.'

When Guy Mannering responds 'but my good sir, such being his character, I wonder he has any protection and encouragement on this coast', the Laird replies 'Why, Mr Mannering, people must have brandy and tea, and there's none in the country but comes this way – and then there's short accounts, and maybe a keg or two, or a dozen pounds left at your stable door, instead of a d——d lang account at Christmas from Duncan Robb, the grocer at Kippletringan, who has aye a sum to make up, and either wants ready money, or a short-dated bill. Now, Hatteraick will take wood, or he'll take bark, or he'll take barley, or he'll take just what's convenient at the time.'

The Laird subsequently takes Mannering home to have breakfast, where the tea that they drink has been provided by Dick Hatteraick . . .

Later, Scott gives us an interesting description of a smuggler's cave. 'The opening, not larger than that of a fox-earth, lay in the face of the cliff directly behind a large black rock, or rather upright stone, which served at once to conceal it from strangers, and as a mark to point out its situation to those who used it as a place of retreat. The space between the stone and the cliff was exceedingly narrow, and being heaped with sand and other rubbish, the most minute search would not have discovered the mouth of the cavern, without removing those substances which the tide had drifted before it. For the purpose of further concealment, it was usual with the contraband traders who frequented this haunt, after they had entered, to stuff the mouth with withered seaweed loosely piled together as if carried there by the waves.'

Yawkins finds another fictional incarnation in S.R. Crockett's *The Raiders*, though in this instance his real name is retained. The novel, published in 1894, was written by Galloway-born novelist Samuel Rutherford Crockett (1859-1914), a Kirkcudbrightshire farmer's son. He was responsible for more than forty novels, many with Gallovidian themes, all of which were well-received at the time, though most have dated rather badly. *The Raiders* has weathered the passage of time better than many, and remains a readable adventure yarn.

*The Raiders* is set in the eighteenth century, and in it the Maxwell family of Craigdarroch farm on the shores of the Solway Firth are involved in smuggling activities between Holland and the Isle of Man. They, however, are the acceptable face of smuggling, while the Dutch smuggler Yawkins and his ilk are what Crockett referred to as 'black smugglers'. They were more organised in their methods and more ruthless. In *The Raiders*, Yawkins worked in conjunction with bands of gypsies and outlaws, one of which had its base on an island on Loch Enoch, and Crockett's novel is based on true local history as well as folklore.

Bands of gypsies did collect smuggled goods landed on the Solway shores and spirit them away to their camps for later distribution, and there was almost certainly a gypsy encampment on Loch Enoch in real life. The gypsies also handled stolen goods and stole cattle in addition to their smuggling activities. Principal local gypsy clans included the Marshalls and Faas, and it is interesting to note that the Kirk Yetholm 'gypsy king' and smuggler from the eastern borders was one Wull Faa. Crockett described the Faas as '. . . outcast . . . from sweet Yetholm'.

Wull Faa and Wull Balmer of Jedburgh, a dozen miles south-west of Kirk Yetholm, were high-profile Scottish smugglers who were regular habitués of the Northumberland port of Boulmer, once the smuggling capital of Northumberland. Smugglers came to the port from all over Northumberland and the Scottish Borders to deal in illicit goods there during the eighteenth and early nineteenth centuries.

> Blind Wull Bawmer o'Jethart [Jedburgh],
> His grips are no guid to come in;
> He felled all the gaugers i'Jethart
> Hen comin' frae Boomer wi' gin.

In late nineteenth century, according to Victorian historians, smuggled silks and casks of spirit were still occasionally dug up around Boulmer.

The landscape of Galloway is itself a major 'character' in *The Raiders*, and many of Crockett's place names – such as Rathan Island, Glen Trool and Loch Dee – are real, though Crockett did take some liberties with the location of places in relation to each other.

Yawkins plays a more significant part in this novel than he does as Dick Hatteraick in *Guy Mannering*. We are given quite detailed descriptions of him, of his ruthlessness and his 'derring-do' spirit. Crockett noted '. . . there are two things that no one could ever lay to his charge – that Yawkins was either coward or bad sailor'.

He was not just a smuggler, if this fictional account is to be believed. Crockett has Ebie Hook, one of Yawkins' crew say '. . . it wasna only smuggling, it was black piracy they had against us had we been ta'en, wi' the plunder of a sunken Greenock barkanteen in oor hold. Man, I tell ye I was feared.'

In the very first chapter of the novel the reader is introduced to a band of smugglers who use a churchyard to store their contraband:

> A dozen or more men came swarming over the broken wall. They carried a long, black coffin among them – the coffin, as it seemed, of an extraordinarily large man. Straight across the moon-whitened grass they strode, stumbling on the flat tombs and cursing one another as they went. There was no solemnity as at a funeral, for the jest and laughter ran light and free.
>
> 'We are the lads,' cried one. 'We can lay the spirits and we can raise the dead!'
>
> They went into the great tomb of the MacLurgs with the long, black coffin, and in a trice came out jovially, abusing one another still more loudly for useless dogs of peculiar pedigrees, and dealing great claps on each other's backs. It was a wonder to me to see these outlaws at once so cruel and so merry.
>
> . . . from Ben Rathan . . . looking to the westward, just over the cliffs of our isle, you saw White Horse Bay, much frequented of late years for convenience of debarkation by the Freetraders of Captain Yawkins' band, with whom, as my father used to say quaintly, no honest smuggler hath company.

Yawkins was described by Crockett as '. . . a thick-set dark man, with his head very low between his shoulders. He had a black beard on his breast, and there was a cast in his eye. He swore many strange oaths.'

> For there were, as everyone knows, in this land of Galloway, two kinds of the lads who bring over the dutiless gear from Holland and the Isle of Man. There be the decent lads who run it for something honest to do in the winter and for the spice of danger, and without a thought of hurt to King George, worthy gentleman; and there are also the 'Associated Illdoers', as my father would often call them in his queer, daffing way – the Holland rogues who got this isle its by-name of Rogues' Island by running their cargoes into our little land-locked cove which looks towards White Horse Bay. These last were fellows who would stick at nothing, and quite as often as not they would trepan a lass from the Cumberland shore, or slit the throat of a Dumfries burgher to see the colour of his blood.

Writing of the gypsies who aided Yawkins and his ilk, Crockett noted, 'When a vessel came in these openly marched down to the shore with guns, swords, and other weapons – Marshalls, Macatericks, and Millers, often under the leadership of Hector Faa – and escorted to their fastnesses the smuggled stuff and the stolen goods, for there was as much by wicked hands reived and robbed, as of the stuff which was only honestly smuggled'.

The spoils of one run made onto the Galloway coast by the Maxwells are described as '. . . a tidy cargo of French brandy, German perfumes, and Vallenceens lace . . .' The Maxwells landed this cargo from the *Spindrift*, '. . . the little lugger of fourteen tons, which had run many cargoes and brought much joy and sorrow to the adventurous house of the Maxwells of Craigdarroch . . .' in order to avoid detection by the preventive boat *The Seahorse*. '. . . by the time that the second king's ship, which proved to be the preventive schooner *Ariel*, sent a boat aboard, the Maxwells were once more peaceful, coast-wise traders, with a cargo of salt, alum, barites for the men of Mona, and hides and sheep-skins to take back in exchange to the tanneries of Dumfries.'

> No raid for fifty years had reached so far south as the shores of the Solway, though the smugglers and the gypsies had a regular route by which they conveyed their smuggled stuff to Edinburgh on the east, and Glasgow or Paisley on the west. So complete was their system, and so great their daring, that it is safe to say that there was not a farmer's greybeard between the Lothians and the Solway filled with spirit that had done obeisance to King George, and not a burgher's wife that had duty-paid lace on her Sabbath mutch. The gaugers were few and harmless, contenting themselves for the most part with lingering round public-houses in towns, and bearing a measure cup and gauging-stick about the markets – occupations for which they were entirely suited.

Sir Walter Scott's *Redgauntlet* was published in 1824, nine years after *Guy Mannering*, and the author returned once again to the coast of Dumfries and Galloway, and particularly to the Solway Firth. Some of the events take place in Edinburgh, but the novel also features the area around Cummertrees, along with northern Cumberland, on the English side of the Solway.

As in *Guy Mannering*, smuggling is an activity which goes on alongside the main action, and again there is an element of interaction between the smugglers and the other characters in the novel.

*Redgauntlet* centres on a fictitious attempt at another Jacobite rising featuring Charles Edward Stuart, following on from the failure of the 1745–46 campaign, and there is a clear link between smuggling and Jacobites.

The bibulous skipper of the 'little smuggling rig' *Jumping Jenny*, Nanty Ewart, is involved not only in ordinary smuggling but also in Jacobite-related activity, about which he frequently complains, being himself being a Protestant with 'a hatred of popery'. Thomas Trumbull is a merchant in Annan whose goods are smuggled across the Solway by Ewart for sale in England.

One of Nanty's crew is thus described by Scott: 'Nanty Ewart had now given the helm to one of his people, a bald-pated, grizzled old fellow, whose whole life had been spent in evading the revenue laws, with now and then the relaxation of a few months' imprisonment, for deforcing officers, resisting seizures, and the like offences.'

One of the occasions on which the main action of the novel interacts with the smuggling world is when Ewart transports Alan Fairford across the Solway into England, along with a cargo of contraband dispatched by Trumbull.

On reaching the Wampool River

> The vessel accordingly lay to, and presently showed a weft in her ensign, which was hastily answered by signals from on shore. Men and horses were seen to come down the broken path which leads to the shore; the latter all properly tackled for carrying their loading. Twenty fishing barks were pushed afloat at once, and crowded round the brig with much clamour, laughter, cursing, and jesting. Amidst all this confusion there was the essential regularity. Nanty Ewart again walked his quarter-deck as if he had never touched spirits in his life, issued the necessary orders with precision, and saw them executed with punctuality. In half an hour the loading of the brig was in a great measure disposed in the boats; in a quarter of an hour more, it was landed on the beach, and another interval of about the same duration was sufficient to distribute it on the various strings of packhorses which waited for that purpose, and which instantly dispersed, each on its own proper adventure.

Here we have a detailed fictional account of a smugglers' landing operation, right down to a timetable of how much time was taken up by the various activities.

According to Nanty Ewart, the smugglers were 'a few honest fellows that bring the old women of England a drop of brandy', but ammunition to aid the Jacobite cause was also carried on this trip.

Ewart notes that his vessel's correct name is the *Sainte Genevieve*. 'They call the brig so at Dunkirk . . . but along shore here they call her the *Jumping Jenny*.' Not only did Ewart smuggle brandy and other goods from France to Scotland, but he also smuggled exiled Jacobite sympathisers and activists.

In his notes to the text, Scott wrote that Trumbull's elaborate premises in Annan with their 'subterranean place of concealment for contraband and stolen goods' were based on those of a real-life carpenter Richard Mendham, who ran '. . . an organized gang of coiners, forgers, smugglers, and other malefactors' in a '. . . suburb of Berwick called Spittal'. Medham had been tried and executed at

Jedburgh '. . . when the author was present a Sheriff of Selkirkshire', some twenty years before the novel was written.

Even at the time of writing (1824), Scott noted that 'the neighbourhood of two nations having different laws, though united in government, still lends to a multitude of transgressions on the order, and extreme difficulty in apprehending delinquents.'

Another novel which links smuggling and Jacobitism is James C. Dibdin's 1896 *The Cleekim Inn*. Subtitled 'A tale of smuggling in the '45', this is a romantic novel based around the 1745–46 Jacobite rising, featuring as its hero Will Scott – leader of a pro-Jacobite gang of smugglers '. . . whose headquarters were in Jedburgh, a town then, and for years afterwards, of supreme notoriety for its contraband trade' (see p. 100).

Scott is '. . . a young, resolute and broad-shouldered man of thirty or thereby, who, despite his comparatively few years, had already acquired much reputation as being a daring and successful runner of contraband goods.'

Along with Sir Walter Scott, another of the leading Scottish novelists to utilise smuggling in his work was Robert Louis Stevenson, whose 1889 *The Master of Ballantrae* is located, like *Guy Mannering* and much of *Redgauntlet*, on the west coast of Scotland.

When the Master of the title returns to his estates from exile in France, following the abortive Jacobite Rising of 1745–46, he is transported in a smuggling vessel. Stevenson's narrator is Ephraim Mackellar, who writes of the circumstances of the Master's return:

> . . . I had a spy-glass in my room, began to drop questions to the tenant folk, and as there was no great secrecy observed, and the freetrade (in our part) went by force as much as stealth, I had soon got together a knowledge of the signals in use, and knew pretty well to an hour when any messenger might be expected. I say, I questioned the tenants; for with the traders themselves, desperate blades that went habitually armed, I could never bring myself to meddle willingly. Indeed, by what proved in the sequel an unhappy chance, I was an object of scorn to some of those braggadocios; who had not only gratified me with a nickname, but catching me one night upon a by-path, and being all (as they would have said) somewhat merry, had caused me to dance for their diversion. The method employed was that of cruelly chipping at my toes with naked cutlasses, shouting at the same time 'Square Toes'; and though they did me no bodily mischief, I was none the less deplorably affected, and was

indeed for several days confined to my bed: a scandal on the state of Scotland on which no comment is required.

It happened in the afternoon on November 7th in this same unfortunate year, that I espied, during my walk, the smoke of a beacon fire upon the Muckleross. It was drawing near time for my return; but uneasiness upon my spirits was that day so great that I burst through the thicket to the edge of what they call the Craig Head. The sun was already down, but there was still a broad light in the west, which showed me some of the smugglers treading out their signal fire upon the Ross, and in the bay the lugger lying with her sails brailed up. He was plainly but newly come to anchor, and yet the skiff was already lowered and pulling for the landing-place at the end of the long shrubbery.

The smuggling vessel, commanded by Captain Crail, usually traded with France, and in addition to taking the Master of Ballantrae from France to Durrisdeer, later smuggled him back to France once again.

In John Galt's *Annals of the Parish*, the action moves some fifty miles further north on the Ayrshire coast from the port of Ballantrae to the fictional village of Dalmailing, usually identified as Dreghorn, near Irvine.

Published in 1821, *Annals of the Parish* is essentially a series of scenes from Scottish rural life masquerading as a novel, and its narrator is the Reverend Micah Balwhidder, who records happenings in Dalmailing between 1760 and 1810.

Galt was the son of a sea captain, and was apprenticed to the Greenock Custom House before embarking on a commercial and literary career, so when he wrote of smuggling in *Annals of the Parish* – his best-known and best-received novel – the details he provides are almost certainly quite accurate.

Tea-drinking and smuggling feature large in the novels, with Balwhidder noting for 1761 that '. . . before this year, the drinking of tea was little known in this parish, saving among a few of the heritors' houses on a Sabbath evening, but now it becomes very rife'. However, even his attitude softens. '. . . Although I never could abide the smuggling, both on its own account, and the evils that grew therefrom to the countryside, I lost some of my dislike to the tea . . . and we then had it for our breakfast in the morning at the Manse, as well as in the afternoon.'

> It was in this year [1761] that the great smuggling trade corrupted all the west coast, especially the Laigh Lands about the Troon and the Loans. The tea was going like the chaff, the brandy like well water, and the wastrie of all things was terrible. There was nothing minded but the

riding of cadgers by day, and excisemen by night – and battles between the smugglers and the King's men, both by sea and land. There was a continual drunkenness and debauchery; and our Session, that was but on the lip of this whirlpool of iniquity, had an awful time o't.

Our chief misfortune in this year [1778] was a revival of that wicked mother of many mischiefs, the smuggling trade, which concerned me greatly; but it was not allowed to it to make any thing like a permanent stay among us, though in some of the neighbouring parishes, its ravages, both in morals and property, were very distressing, and many a mailing was sold to pay for the triumphs of the cutters and gaugers; for the government was by this time grown more eager, and the war caused the king's ships to be out and about, which increased the trouble of the smugglers, whose wits in their turn were thereby much sharpened.

After Mrs Malcolm, by the settlement on Captain Macadam, had given up her dealing, two maiden women, that were sisters, Betty and Janet Pawkie, came in among us from Ayr, where they had friends in league with the laigh land folk, that carried on the contraband with the Isle of Man, which was the very eye of the smuggling. They took up the tea-selling, which Mrs Malcolm had dropped, and did business on a larger scale, having a general huxtry, with parliament-cakes, and candles, and pincushions, as well as other groceries, in their window. Whether they had any contraband dealings, or were only back-bitten, I cannot take it upon me to say; but it was jealoused in the parish that the meal in the sacks, that came to their door at night, and was sent to the Glasgow market in the morning, was not made of corn. They were, however, decent women, both sedate and orderly; the eldest, Betty Pawkie, was of a manly stature, and had a long beard, which made her have a coarse look; but she was, nevertheless, a worthy, well-doing creature, and at her death she left ten pounds to the poor of the parish, as may be seen in the mortification board that the session put up in the kirk as a testification and an example.

Shortly after the revival of the smuggling, an exciseman was put among us, and the first was Robin Bicker, a very civil lad that had been a flunky with Sir Hugh Montgomerie, when he was a residenter in Edinburgh, before the old Sir Hugh's death. He was a queer fellow, and had a coothy way of getting in about folk, the which was very serviceable to him in his vocation; nor was he overly gleg: but when a job was ill done, and he was obliged to notice it, he would often break out on the smugglers for being so stupid, so that for an exciseman he was wonderful well liked, and did not object to a waught of brandy at a time; when the auld wives ca'd it well-water. It happened, however, that some unneighbourly person sent him notice of a clecking of tea chests, or brandy kegs, at which both Jenny and Betty Pawkie were the howdies. Robin could not but therefore enter their house; however, before going in, he just cried at the door to somebody on the road, so as to let the twa industrious lassies hear he was at hand. They were not slack in closing the trance-door, and putting stoups and stools behind it, so as to cause trouble, and give time before any body could get in. They then emptied their chaff-bed, and filled the tikeing with tea, and Betty went in on the top, covering herself with the blanket, and graining like a woman in labour. It is thought that Robin Bicker himself would not have been overly particular in searching the house, considering there was a woman seemingly in the death-thraws; but a sorner, and incomer from the east country, and that hung about the change-house as a divor hostler, that would rather gang a day's journey in the dark than turn a spade in day-light, came to him as he stood at the door, and went in with him to see the sport. Robin, for some reason, could not bid him go away, and both Betty and Janet were sure he was in the plot against them; indeed, it was always thought he was an informer, and no doubt he was something not canny, for he had a down look.

It was some time before the doorway was cleared of the stoups and stools, and Jenny was in great concern, and flustered, as she said, for her poor sister, who was taken with a heart-colic. 'I'm sorry for her,' said Robin, 'but I'll be as quiet as possible;' and so he searched all the house, but found nothing; at the which his companion, the divor east country hostler, swore an oath that could not be misunderstood; so, without more ado, but as all thought against the grain, Robin went up to sympathize with Betty in the bed, whose groans were loud and vehement. 'Let me feel your pulse,' said Robin, and he looked down as she put forth her arm from aneath the clothes, and laying his hand on the bed, cried, 'Hey! What's this? this is a costly filling.' Upon which Betty jumpet up quite recovered, and Jenny fell to the wailing and railing, while the hostler from the east country took the bed of tea on his back, to carry it to the change-house till a cart was gotten to take it into the custom-house at Irville.

Robin Bicker was soon after this affair removed to another district, and we got in his place one Mungo Argyle, who was as proud as a provost, being come of Highland parentage. Black was the hour he came among my people; for he was needy and greedy, and rode on the top of his commission. Of all the manifold ills in the train of smuggling, surely the excisemen are the worst, and the setting of this rabiator over us was a severe judgment for our sins. But he suffered for't, and peace be with him in the grave, where the wicked cease from troubling!

*The Antiquary* was the third of Sir Walter Scott's Waverley novels, published in 1816. While *Guy Mannering* was set on the south-west coast, the action of *The Antiquary* – which shares with its predecessor the 'lost heir' theme – centres on the Angus coast of north-east Scotland. Scott's fictional 'Fairport' is Arbroath, which he visited on three occasions prior to writing the book, while 'Musselcrag' is based on Auchmithie. The Mucklebackit family inhabit Musselcrag, and the patriarch Saunders Musselbackit is described by Scott as being 'an old fisherman and smuggler'.

Describing the origins of a capacious local cave, 'as narrow in its entrance as a fox-earth' the beggar, Edie Ochiltree, notes that 'here . . . is a bit turnpike-stair that gaes up to the auld kirk above. Some folks say this place was howkit out by the monks lang syne to hide their treasure in, and some said that they used to bring things into the abbey this gate by night, that they durstna sae weel hae brought in by the main port and in open day . . .'

Just as he had taken the real-life character of Jack Yawkins and fictionalised him as Dick Hatteraick, so Scott featured the Porteous Riots (see pp. 109–10) in *The Heart of Midlothian*. The 'Heart of Midlothian' of the title is the Edinburgh Tolbooth, or gaol, originally built around 1466, and demolished in 1817, the year before the publication of Scott's novel.

The book opens with the events leading up to the Porteous Riots, but a large part of the story is concerned with other matters. Only the first seven chapters of this fifty-two-chapter novel concern the riots. By the end of chapter seven, Porteous is dead, hanged by the mob from a 'dyester' pole' on the spot where Wilson had been hanged. 'The scene of his crime, and the destined spot of his sufferings'.

Regarding the character of Captain Porteous, Scott wrote '. . . he is said to have been a man of profligate habits, an unnatural son, and a brutal husband. He was, however, useful in his station, and his harsh and fierce manners rendered him formidable to rioters or other disturbers of the public peace . . . a character void of principle; and a disposition to regard the rabble, who seldom failed to regale him and his soldiers with some marks of their displeasure, as declared enemies, upon whom it was natural and justifiable that he should seek opportunities of vengeance.'

In the novel, Robertson's real name is George Staunton, the well-born but wild lover of Scott's heroine Effie Deans. The attack on the Tolbooth which was mounted in order to capture Porteous was also, in *The Heart of Midlothian*, partly designed to free Effie, who was being held there.

Although most of Scott's details concerning the Porteous Riots are quite accurate, he did invent Effie, and made her central to the episode. He also altered the timescale of the riot, and glossed over the worst brutalities inflicted on the body of Porteous by the Edinburgh mob. Additionally, he introduced a fictional drunken dinner-party, hosted by Porteous after his reprieve, on the night the mob captured him, which does nothing to give the character sympathy.

In the notes which accompany his novel, Scott wrote that

contraband trade, though it strikes at the root of legitimate government, by encroaching on its revenues, – though it injures the fair trader, and debauches the minds of those engaged in it, – is not usually looked upon, either by the vulgar or by their betters, in a very heinous point of view. On the contrary, in those counties where it prevails, the cleverest, boldest, and most intelligent of the peasantry are uniformly engaged in illicit transactions, and very often with the sanction of the farmers and inferior gentry. Smuggling was almost universal in Scotland in the reigns of George I. and II., [1714–27 and 1727–60] for the people, unaccustomed to imposts, and regarding them as an unjust aggression upon their ancient liberties, made no scruple to elude them whenever it was possible to do so.

The county of Fife, bounded by two firths on the south and north, and by the sea on the east, and having a number of small sea-ports, was long famed for maintaining successfully a contraband trade; and, as there were many seafaring men residing there, who had been pirates and buccaneers in their youth, there were not wanting a sufficient number of daring men to carry it on. Among these, a fellow called Andrew Wilson, originally a baker in the village of Pathhead, was particularly obnoxious to the revenue officers. He was possessed of great personal strength, courage, and cunning, – was perfectly acquainted with the coast, and capable of conducting the most desperate enterprizes. On several occasions he succeeded in baffling the pursuit and researches of the king's officers; but he became so much the object of their suspicious and watchful attention, that at length he was totally ruined by repeated seizures. The man became desperate. He considered himself as robbed and plundered; and took it into his head, that he had a right to make reprisals, as he could find opportunity.

According to Scott, Wilson, his associate Robertson, and two other young men, robbed the Kirkcaldy Collector of Customs as he lodged in Pittenweem. This is the usual 'folk tale' version of the episode, and one questioned by authorities such as Frances Wilkins, who notes surviving records of a robbery in 1736 at the Kirkcaldy Custom House, in which one of the perpetrators was named Wilson (see p. 110).

Another fictional treatment of the Porteous Riots occurs in Mollie Hunter's 1971 novel *The Lothian Run*. The book takes its title from the name given by the customs service to the various smuggling routes which terminated in the ports of the north and south shores of the Firth of Forth.

Much of the novel's action focuses on the smuggling activities associated with the fishing village of Prestonpans, and the climax of the story comes with the Porteous Riots. In the novel, lawyer's clerk Sandy Maxwell works undercover for customs Special Investigations Officer Deryck Gilmour, helping him to track escaped smuggler George Robertson.

~

The most famous fictional treatment of smuggling in Scottish literature occurs in Sir Compton Mackenzie's 1947 novel *Whisky Galore*. The factual episode that inspired the book has already been explored (see pp. 56–57), but Mackenzie turned the saga of the SS *Politician* into a best-selling book that introduced the Hebrides to readers all over the world.

Mackenzie was living on the island of Barra at the time of the incident, and was the grateful recipient of six-dozen bottles of 'Polly' whisky, courtesy of his driver Kenny MacCormack. Many of his friends and acquaintances were involved in smuggling whisky from the stricken vessel, and so his subsequent account of the affair had more than a whiff of accuracy about it. Mackenzie kept his touch light, however, omitting the real-life activities of Customs and Excise officers during the events, and any mention of the jailing of some of the smugglers.

His publisher had been pressing him for another Scottish-based novel, following the success of his *The Monarch of the Glen* and *Keep the Home Guard Turning*, and Mackenzie, now living in the south of England, proceeded to fictionalise the SS *Politician* as the SS *Cabinet Minister*, creating marvellous comic characters such as the officious Captain Paul Waggett of the Home Guard, The Biffer and Dr Maclaren, in the process. Many of the characters in the novel were based on recognisable, living Barra residents.

By the end of 1949, *Whisky Galore* had sold 33,500 hardback copies, and in that year it was made into one of the most enduringly successful of the 'Ealing Comedy' films, starring Joan Greenwood, Basil Radford and Gordon Jackson.

As Roger Hutchinson wrote in *Polly – The True Story Behind Whisky Galore*, '*Whisky Galore* was Compton Mackenzie's legacy to the southern isles, and unlike many another literary offering it was welcomed by the legatees. The story which he loosely based on some occasionally grim incidents is free from malice and condescension. Unlike other comic writers on the Highlands and Islands Mackenzie attempted no cheap laughs at the expense of the native people.'

*Whisky Galore* made Mackenzie '. . . rich, famous, and a Knight', wrote Hutchinson. Not bad for a book which its author always felt was of far less importance than his now rarely read 'serious' novels, such as *Sinister Street* and *The Four Winds of Love*.

As the character Norman Macleod says in *Whisky Galore*, 'Love makes the world go round? Not at all. Whisky makes it go round twice as fast.'

# 8

# SCOTTISH SMUGGLING TODAY

We tend to think of Scottish smuggling as something that only happened in the past, and in the long distant past at that. We think of sailing vessels and cutlass fights, casks of brandy on remote beaches and caches of tobacco in secret cellars.

However, smuggling in various guises is still very much a part of life in Scotland. The techniques used by smugglers may have become more sophisticated, the commodities being conveyed may be less innocent, but the same elemental battle between smugglers and authorities goes on.

In order to maintain and encourage positive public relations, the Customs and Excise service in Scotland operates a converted trailer with a cut-out floor, seized from smugglers at Dover. Attending shows and fairs, the trailer is used to display old spirit stills, ivory chess pieces and a leopardskin coat, along with other items seized for illegal importation. The aim is to give the public a sense of the work done by the service, its breadth and scope, and also to make them more aware of what commodities are being smuggled all around them.

Ron Barrie is Public Relations Officer for Customs and Excise in Scotland, and he notes that there are between 100 and 120 'frontline officers' as he calls them, working from bases in Edinburgh and Paisley. Routinely, Edinburgh staff provide customs cover for Edinburgh airport and the Zeebrugge–Rosyth ferry service, while Paisley staff cover the port of Stranraer, with its Irish ferry traffic, and Glasgow and Prestwick airports.

Barrie stresses that flexibility is at the heart of the operation, with staff from both bases working together on many incidents and investigations. They work closely with police forces, airlines, and the Scottish Drugs Enforcement Agency, liaising, sharing intelligence, and acting in concert when occasion demands. As in days gone by, there is still a customs 'cutter fleet', with one dedicated vessel serving Scotland, while more can be brought in from other areas as required.

The three most commonly-smuggled commodities today are drugs, tobacco and alcohol, so at least some of the suspects are old ones.

As we have seen, tobacco smuggling was a major part of the Scottish 'black economy' for many years, particularly during the eighteenth century, and just as the old custom house letter-books chart its fortunes, so today regular Customs and Excise press releases highlight successes in the continuing battle against contraband of all kinds.

In the 2000 budget the government provided £209m to tackle tobacco smuggling, with the intention ultimately of recruiting 1,000 more Customs officers, as well as providing new and more sophisticated detection equipment for deployment at airports and ferry ports. In 2001 an estimated 17 billion cigarettes were smuggled into the UK, accounting for 20 per cent of the total tobacco market, and costing the Treasury £3.5 billion in lost taxes.

Three men were jailed today for a total of two years after Customs caught them trafficking half a million duty free cigarettes.

In a joint operation with Lothian and Borders Police, Customs officers intercepted a Transit van delivering to premises in Haddington on 25 August 1999. The vehicle and over 359,000 Regal cigarettes were seized and the driver James Sheriff detained. Jamie and Lukas McGowan, who were waiting for the delivery at the yard, were also detained.

A further search that day at a property in Leith revealed a further 150,000 cigarettes. 722 litres of spirits and over 30kg of hand-rolling tobacco. These goods had been delivered by similar means – by Transit from Washington Service Station in north-east England on 11 August 1999.

. . . The potential loss in sales to legitimate businesses was between £100,000 and £200,000.

– Customs and Excise press release, 17 July 2001

Ron Barrie points out that a favourite route of entry for many commodities being smuggled into Scotland is via the M6 motorway through north-west England, and the M74 across the border into the west of Scotland. 'Certainly, the bulk of hard drugs come into the country that way rather than directly from abroad.'

In June 2001 Zahid Ali Khan and Mahraj Din, both of Glasgow, were jailed, having appeared at Dumfries Sheriff Court on charges of trafficking in over £120,000 of duty-free tobacco.

According to a press release of 11 June, 'Din admitted travelling to the Birmingham area with Khan to pick up the Golden Virginia, Old Holborn and Drum tobacco and carrying it to Scotland on 2 February 2000. With assistance from Dumfries and Galloway Constabulary, Customs officers seized the goods at Gretna as the men headed north.'

In March 2001 Dumfries lorry driver Robert William Jardine was jailed for twelve months at Maidstone Crown Court for attempting to smuggle 50,000 cigarettes and 59kg of hand-rolling tobacco through the Channel Tunnel. Again, Scotland, via the M6 and M74, was the planned destination had the smuggler escaped detection.

In April of the same year seven million smuggled cigarettes were seized in a joint operation between Customs and Dumfries and Galloway Constabulary, when a container lorry was stopped at Lockerbie on the M74. 'We have a particularly good relationship with Dumfries and Galloway police,' notes Ron Barrie.

In January 2002 Customs officers made two large seizures of smuggled tobacco in Dundee and Peterhead. Hand-rolling tobacco worth in excess of £30,000 was seized as it was delivered to a house in the Hilltown area of Dundee. The 186kg haul of tobacco was estimated to be sufficient to roll up to 300,000 cigarettes.

In Peterhead, 68,000 smuggled cigarettes were seized from an Estonian fishing vessel. The £14,000-worth of cigarettes had been concealed in tanks in the ship's engine room. A further 5,000 cigarettes and two vehicles were subsequently seized by officers on follow-up raids in the port.

Peterhead was again the scene of a major cigarette seizure in January 2003, when the skipper of a Polish cargo boat was arrested for smuggling 280,000 cigarettes. Polish authorities had tipped off Customs and Excise that a large number of cigarette cartons were being loaded onto Roman Koczab's boat before it set sail for Scotland.

In May 2002 Customs officers targeted markets in Ayr and the 'Barras' in Glasgow one weekend, seizing 4.4 kilos of duty-free tobacco in Ayr and thirty-two kilos in Glasgow. The latter also yielded 38,000 smuggled cigarettes.

Ice cream vans being used to sell illegal cigarettes were seized in a major Customs and Excise operation yesterday.

71,683 smuggled cigarettes and 18.5 kilos of hand-rolling tobacco worth over £18,000, as well as four ice cream vans, one mobile shop, a van and four cars worth around £27,000 were seized after Customs officers mounted a number of raids throughout Ayrshire, Lanarkshire and Glasgow.

Two ice cream vans with illegal cigarettes were parked outside secondary schools, one in Coatbridge and one in Wishaw. One of these vans had 1,308 cigarettes on board, the odd number rather than full packets indicating that individual cigarettes may have been sold to children.

– Customs and Excise press release, 3 May 2001

Mafia connections with cigarette smuggling into Scotland have also surfaced from time to time. Michelle Ianetta was jailed in March 2000 at Falkirk Sheriff Court for two years for smuggling more than two million cigarettes into Scotland, evading customs duty of £250,000. Ianetta's defence was that he believed he was importing cardboard to make pizza boxes.

In fact, an eight-month-long customs operation proved that the cigarette smuggling operation was linked to the Camorra Mafia clan of Naples, who have long been associated with drugs and tobacco smuggling, and were keen to become involved in smuggling cigarettes into Central Scotland.

The cigarettes began their journey in Montenegro, and were subsequently transported to Naples. They were then picked up near Rotterdam, finally being carried via Hull to Falkirk. Ianetta ran a used furniture business close to Falkirk town centre, and hid the contraband cigarettes in a nearby container depot. At the time of the case, Fiona Barrett of the Tobacco Alliance noted that 'one in four cigarettes is smuggled'.

The following month Russian Mafia links to Scottish cigarette smuggling emerged when Glasgow's James McCaffrey was jailed for three and a half years for his involvement in smuggling cigarettes from the former Soviet Union.

McCaffrey had set up a fake Lada car dealership as cover, and customs officers found six million cigarettes hidden in scrap-metal cargoes at Felixstowe docks in Suffolk. A raid on his Glasgow home netted £115,000 in cash, though he claimed all but £23,000 of that belonged to his Russian Mafia associates. All of the money was subsequently confiscated by the Crown.

A major surveillance operation by Scottish customs investigators led to the seizure and a number of arrests, and after McCaffrey's conviction customs operation leader Alan Dryden noted that 'this is not just the seizure of six million cigarettes but the destruction of a much wider sophisticated international smuggling gang'.

According to Ron Barrie, 'Many people in the drugs trade have moved into tobacco smuggling now. There's a quicker turnaround of profit and less severe penalties if caught. They then use the profits made from the tobacco to fund drugs deals.'

If the smugglers of two centuries ago were often viewed as providing a service for all sections of the community, with friends – and customers – in high places, then the same cannot be said of today's drug smugglers.

It is difficult to equate a bag of French lace with a bag of heroin . . .

Four Scots have appeared in court in Airdrie in connection with what Customs believe is the biggest ever cocaine haul destined for Scotland.

Following the seizure at Felixstowe of half a tonne of the Class A drug – with an estimated street value of £50 million – Customs mounted a major joint operation with the Scottish Drug Enforcement Agency.

The following four men have appeared today at Airdrie Sheriff Court, charged with being knowingly concerned in the importation of the Class A drugs. David Frew, age 55, Kilwinning, William McAdam, age 41, Kilwinning, James Mair, age 37, Cumnock, and Sean McAdam, age 35, of Kilwinning.

Customs Minister John Healey, the Economic Secretary to the Treasury, said 'The removal of £50 million worth of cocaine from the criminal supply chain demonstrates how Customs, working with the SDEA and other agencies across the UK, are making a real impact on the Class A drugs problem. We want to make sure that dangerous drugs do not reach our streets.'

*Customs and Excise press release, 2 October 2002*

Herbal cannabis, with an estimated street value of more than £230,000 has been seized from an address in East Lothian, following a ten-day operation concluded yesterday involving HM Customs and Excise and Lothian and Borders Police.

A total of 74.8 kg of the drug has been recovered. Two men were detained by police yesterday, but were later released without charge. Enquiries by Customs investigators are continuing.

The drugs were found amongst the personal effects of a couple returning to Scotland from South Africa. The drugs were found in the interior of furniture not belonging to the couple. Having made the find, the couple contacted the local police who contacted Customs.

A joint operation by Customs and police to recover the drugs and try to establish those behind the importation was commenced.

*Customs and Excise press release, 30 November 2002*

On 8 June 2001 lorry driver Vincent Peter Rostron of Girvan in Ayrshire was jailed for thirteen years at Canterbury Crown Court for smuggling ecstasy and cannabis resin. Rostron was transporting chemicals from Germany via Zeebrugge, and was intercepted by Customs officers at Dover. Again, the M6/M74 route into Scotland was to have been utilised had Rostron not been caught.

A press release of 2 October 2002 stated that drugs with a street value in excess of £18m had been seized during a raid on a lorry near Abington in South Lanarkshire on the M74 the previous day. 40 kg of heroin, 100 kg of cocaine and 64 kg of ecstasy were seized in the operation which was co-ordinated by Merseyside Police.

According to Pete McGee, Customs and Excise head of investigations in Scotland, 'Through joint working with the police, we have prevented a significant amount of class A drugs hitting the streets in Scotland. Excellent multi-agency co-operation throughout the UK has helped us dismantle a prolific trafficking organisation that was feeding the Scottish drugs market.'

Strathclyde Police declared the seizure to be the largest in the region during the year.

In May 2002, two men were jailed for a total of nineteen years having been caught at Glasgow airport with £1m worth of cocaine. The two men, 19-year-old Jason Michael Muzio and his 33-year-old uncle, Paul James Murray, both of Croydon, were found guilty at Glasgow High Court of smuggling 8.1 kg of the drug the previous year, and were sentenced to nine and ten years in jail respectively. Their route had been from San José in Costa Rica via Newark, New Jersey, to Glasgow.

According to a Customs press release at the time of the seizure in September 2001, 'This is the second cocaine seizure at Scotland's airports in the last two months following on from a seizure worth £32,000 at Edinburgh airport in August'.

That case came to court in November 2001, and on 27 November Customs issued a press release.

> A smuggler who taped packages of cocaine around his waist was jailed today for four years.
>
> 42-year-old Scott Currie, originally from Leith, but now living in Portugal, pled guilty at Edinburgh High court today to attempting to import nearly 400 grammes of cocaine.
>
> Customs officers seized the drugs – with an estimated street value of £32,000 – at Edinburgh Airport when Currie arrived from Faro, Portugal on 10 August 2001. The cocaine was concealed in packages taped around his waist.
>
> This follows the jailing for three years yesterday of a South African for trying to import around 20 kilos of herbal cannabis through Edinburgh Airport. 47-year-old Henry Steenkamp had travelled from Johannesburg via Zurich and Brussels, arriving in Edinburgh on 3 August 2001.
>
> Customs officers found cannabis with an estimated street value of £100,000 in his luggage and a false British passport in his shoe. He pled guilty yesterday at Edinburgh High court.

Edinburgh airport has frequently been the destination in recent years for consignments of cannabis smuggled from South Africa. According to Ron Barrie, Nigerian drugs dealers commonly supply cannabis through Johannesburg, often via Brussels. In the three years to April 2002 no less than seventeen individuals on flights from South Africa were caught in possession and given custodial sentences in excess of fifty-five years for trying to smuggle drugs through Edinburgh airport.

On 29 May 2001 three South African nationals were arrested at Edinburgh Airport, and each charged with smuggling separate 30 kg amounts of cannabis into the country.

A press release for 27 September 2001 details the sentencing:

> Today three South African cannabis smugglers were sentenced to eleven and a half years for attempting to smuggle a total of 87.5 kilos of herbal cannabis, worth around £250k, through Edinburgh airport in May this year.
>
> Johannes Christian Schoeman . . . was caught with 28.8 kilos arriving on a flight from Johannesburg via Frankfurt on 28/5/01 and was sentenced to 4 years with a recommendation of deportation after custodial sentence completed.
>
> Brenda Esther Erasmus . . . was caught with 29.5 kilos arriving from Johannesburg via Frankfurt on 29/05/01 and was jailed for three and a half years. Stella Young . . . was caught with 29.3 kilos arriving on a flight from Johannesburg via Paris on 29/5/01 and was sentenced to 4 years.
>
> The smuggled Herbal Cannabis was found concealed in the travellers' suitcases when each of them arrived at Edinburgh Airport.

> A further seizure of cannabis – with an estimated street value of £135,000 – was made at Glasgow Airport this morning. Around 27kg of herbal cannabis was seized by Customs from a Johannesburg flight via Amsterdam. A South African male has been detained.
>
> Customs and Excise press release, 19 June 2001

Commenting on this case, Ron Barrie noted that is was unusual for cannabis to be smuggled into Glasgow rather than Edinburgh airport. As a generalisation, cannabis is usually smuggled into the east of the country, and cocaine, via transatlantic flights, into the west. Again, Barrie pointed to the South African connection that is so often a feature of such seizures. Presumably, having seen several recent seizures made at Edinburgh, the South African smuggling gang decided to switch their operation to Glasgow. The switch did not last, however.

> A man is expected to appear in court today charged with attempting to smuggle cannabis worth £140,000 through Edinburgh airport.

... 31kg of herbal cannabis – with an estimated street value of £140,000 – was seized by Customs on Friday from a Johannesburg flight via Amsterdam. This is the 17th seizure at Edinburgh from a South African arrival in the past two years.

A 40-year-old Glasgow-born male resident of Durban, South Africa has been detained ...

Customs and Excise press release, 3 July 2001

In addition to aeroplanes, smugglers still use the 'high seas' as in the days of sloops and pinnaces, and a number of yachts with stashes of drugs on board have been seized by Scottish customs officers in recent years. Sometimes these seizures have come about as a result of sophisticated surveillance operations, even involving tracking vessels from their home ports into Scottish waters.

In December 2000, three Dutchmen pleaded guilty to a charge of drug trafficking at Edinburgh High Court, after their yacht – the 45 ft *Red Scorpion* – was found to be carrying eight tons of cannabis resin, with a potential street value of £43m. This was one of the biggest hauls of drugs ever seized by Scottish customs officers.

After five weeks of evidence, the three men, led by skipper Albert Hulst, 43, pleaded guilty to the charge of drug trafficking, when the crown dropped its allegation that the cannabis resin was being smuggled into the UK.

The drugs had been loaded onto the vessel off the Moroccan coast, and the *Red Scorpion* was due to rendezvous with a smaller boat in the North Sea. According to a BBC News report, 'it began the long voyage with the intention of keeping out of UK waters because of the more frequent customs patrols. However, the "home run" involved passing through the Fair Isle gap to the north of Scotland. That is when the Aberdeen-based customs cutter *Searcher* came across the *Red Scorpion*.'

The *Searcher*'s commander David Hargreaves said that his suspicions were aroused because the yacht looked 'scruffy' and although registered in Malta it had a German flag wrapped around its flagpole. Also a towel had been hung over the vessel's name in an attempt to prevent identification. The *Searcher* shadowed the *Red Scorpion* for twenty-four hours until Maltese authorities gave permission to board, when the vast seizure was made.

～

The Irish police service, the Garda, shares drugs-related information with its counterpart in Northern Ireland and with the Strathclyde and Dumfries & Galloway forces in Scotland. An obvious smuggling route from Ireland into Scotland is via the Dumfriesshire ferry port of Stranraer, and this has become more of a concern as the west of Ireland has been the landing point for large quantities of drugs in recent years. Yachts, fishing boats and cargo vessels have been running significant amounts of cocaine and hashish into remote areas of the west coast, which are almost impossible to police. Moroccan, Pakistani, Venezualan and Panamanian vessels, or vessels that started their voyages in those countries, land drugs in places such as the Bere peninsula of County Cork.

Writing in 2000, the US Drug Enforcement Administration in an intelligence report noted that the Irish west coast was wide open to the importation of drugs destined for the UK and mainland Europe, stating 'the ministry of justice is proposing legislation that would give naval authorities limited drug enforcement powers. At present, the Irish navy may detain suspect vessels for safety reasons or for fishery protection, but they are not allowed to make arrests.' The report suggested that ships targeted Ireland because of the comparatively low-key anti-smuggling role adopted by the Irish authorities.

The problem was first highlighted in 1995 when the Garda seized over 15,000 kg of hashish with a street value of some £16m in a container at Urlingford in Co. Kilkenny. It later transpired that the container had been brought ashore on the Bere peninsula.

During 2000, three significant hauls of drugs were intercepted at Stranraer harbour, but all involved smugglers trying to transport hashish and ecstasy tablets from Scotland across the Irish Sea to Belfast, rather than in the opposite direction.

Cocaine, cannabis, heroin and ecstasy may be the most common smuggled drugs, but two comparatively recent Customs' seizures have involved opium.

> Customs investigators last night arrested three Iranian nationals at Glasgow Central Station in connection with the illegal importation of approximately 4kg of opium.
>
> The men are believed to have collected the consignment – with an estimated street value of 40,000 – at Glasgow Airport where it had arrived from Iran.
>
> A report has been submitted to the Procurator Fiscal, Paisley.
>
> No further details can be released at this stage, as enquiries are ongoing.
>
> Customs and Excise press release, 13 September 2002

In November 2000, a British national and an Estonian were arrested in the Estonian capital of Talinn following an operation involving customs officials and officers from Scotland's then newly-formed Drugs Enforcement Agency.

A consignment of 20 kg of opium – used for making heroin – was recovered by Estonian police after a raid on a car being driven by a British man as it was boarding a Finnish-bound ferry. Estonian police spokesman Hannes Kont said that 'Estonia was used in this operation as a transit country, and as far as we know, the destination was Scotland'. The Estonian street value of the drugs was around 1.1m dollars, but would be much higher if sold in Scotland.

Opium smuggling links with Scotland go back a long way, with Sutherland-born James Matheson making a vast fortune smuggling opium into China during the nineteenth century (see p. 90–91).

One community which has made a high-profile fight back against drugs is the Shetland Islands. Shetland's 'Dogs against Drugs' initiative was sparked by the death in 2001 of 21-year-old local, John Farquhar, from an overdose of methadone.

According to local businessman and DAD organiser Ian Davidge, 'John's death highlighted the growing problem with hard drugs like heroin and cocaine on Shetland . . . We have seen the number of Customs officers fall from fifteen to just three in fifteen years. We know there are a lot of drugs coming in off our ferries and other boats and through the mail.

'We have young people working mainly in the fishing and oil industries who have both money and time on their hands. Subsequently there is a lot of hard drugs coming in, mainly from Aberdeen, but also from elsewhere.'

The Shetland initiative raised in excess of £20,000 in a matter of weeks during the spring of 2002 to fund the purchase and training of a 17-months-old Labrador. The 'drugs dog', called Breia, is handled by a local police constable.

Later the same year a second dog was purchased, to search for drugs in the main Lerwick postal sorting office and at the islands' various ports. This time, his handler was Michael Coutts, a Shetland-based customs officer who left his job with the service in order to take up his new, community-funded, post.

HM Customs and Excise was offered the sniffer dog, but declined to accept, describing the drugs problem in Shetland as minimal, and pointing out that unless such dogs receive regular detection work, they become less effective. At present Customs and Excise has no snifferdogs permanently located in Scotland, working with a large pool of dogs based at Manchester airport.

Shetland Islands' Lib Dem MP Alastair Carmichael was dismissive of the Customs' attitude, saying in July 2002 that 'Shetland has a growing hard drugs problem and is also a corridor for international traffic. We are a soft target.

'The only people laughing over this ridiculous attitude by customs are the drug traffickers. Here is a community that has fought back and has found that the bureaucrats are effectively on the side of the traffickers.'

He also noted on a later occasion that 'customs posts in ports throughout the Highlands and Islands would be well placed to check smuggling activity. They seem more interested in catching people smuggling cigarettes, because that costs them lost revenue, than in halting drugs which are a danger to our young people.'

Ron Barrie's response is that 'we are certainly pleased the dogs are there. If they help deter drugs than that's obviously great.' He makes the point that the bulk of the transport into Shetland consists of ferries and flights from Aberdeen, Edinburgh and Wick. It is *internal*, and therefore not within the remit of Customs and Excise. Any smuggling which takes place within the country is a police matter, though Barrie is at pains to stress that the customs service and Scottish police forces work closely together to combat drugs' smuggling throughout Scotland.

He notes that the Shetland dogs are being used to search for drugs in pubs and clubs too, which would be outwith Customs' jurisdiction, and observes that the Customs and Excise dog team has 'specialists' within it: 'We have a currency dog, a tobacco dog, a drugs dog in a team – they can work through one flight, say, checking for everything.'

In November 2002 Economic Secretary John Healey responded to a report from the House of Commons Scottish Affairs Committee, which voiced concerns about the lack of Customs' presence in the north and north-east of Scotland. Claiming that the real threat of drugs in Scotland came from substances smuggled via airports and sea ports in south-east England, Healey said, 'There is little to indicate that landings on remote Scottish or Shetland beaches is a favoured method of getting drugs into Scotland or into Shetland.'

The committee demanded that Customs 'increase the number of occasions on which staff are on duty at strategic points', but the deployment of more customs officers in the area was ruled out by the government.

Opposing Healey's claim was Caithness, Sutherland and Easter Ross MP John Thurso, who said, 'The minister should do his homework. One of the biggest drug hauls was at sea, off Wick, six years ago, when a customs officer tragically died in an incident during the seizure of £10m worth of drugs.

'Such occurrences have happened and it is reasonable to assume the lonely shores of the northern Highlands are a preferred location for smugglers to land. Until the minister accepts we need more officers we simply won't know.'

The Scottish Affairs Committee was also critical, early in 2002, of the Customs and Excise service's plans to cover the newly-established ferry link between Rosyth on the Fife coast and Zeebrugge in Belgium with 'mobile inspectors'.

The Committee, chaired by Paisley North MP Irene Adams, raised concerns that no additional customs officers were being taken on to counter smuggling on the new route, suggesting that Scotland had become a 'soft option' for smugglers because too few customs officers were attempting to provide cover at too many ports.

The committee noted that the current level of 287 Scottish-based customs staff was fifty short of what it felt was required. Echoing sentiments of two centuries earlier, the committee pointed out that with so few officers to patrol the vast Scottish coastline, there was no deterrent to smugglers, and that Orkney now has no dedicated customs officers at all.

The committee's concerns focused on drugs, tobacco and alcohol smuggling, but it was also remarked upon that illegal meat imports posed a threat, particularly in the wake of the 2001 foot-and-mouth outbreak.

Ron Barrie replied to the committee's concerns about Rosyth by stressing that 'there is a Customs and Excise presence at Rosyth every day, and they have a scanner to use on all the containers passing through. There's only one ferry in and one out every day, so it's quite easy to service the operation from Edinburgh. Staff tend to be at Rosyth for the arrival of the morning ferry and then probably cover a couple of flights at Edinburgh airport after that. Scottish staff were trained at Hull where there is a roll on-roll off ferry to Zeebrugge. They shadowed colleagues there to learn what to look out for in that type of operation.'

In April 2003 staff training paid off at Rosyth, when 240 kg of cannabis resin, with a street value in excess of £1m, was seized in an unaccompanied freight consignment at the Fife port. The cannabis was discovered when a trailer unit was examined using the Customs and Excise mobile scanner.

Not all Scottish drugs smuggling involves importation. In January 2001, James Crosbie from Springburn in Glasgow was jailed for eight years for attempting to smuggle 4.5kg of cannabis resin into Iceland.

He was stopped by customs officers when boarding the cruise liner *Albatros* [sic] at Invergordon harbour in Easter Ross in August 2000.

The cannabis, with a street value of £22,500, was concealed in two pairs of cut-off thermal trousers, held in place by the cut-off trousers of a wet-suit, which he was wearing under his normal clothes. The modern drugs equivalent of a concealed illicit 'whisky bladder' perhaps?

According to Scottish customs anti-smuggling chief Andy Barr, 'this case shows that there is no hiding place for the Scottish smuggler, whether importing or exporting drugs. Using rapid, mobile units, customs officers can be where the drug runner least expects them.

'Working with our partners in the police and Scottish Drugs Enforcement Agency, Customs will continue to put pressure on drug traffickers and target the profits of their crimes. By keeping the criminals guessing, we will make a major impact on the supply of drugs.'

The press dubbed Crosbie, who had served two previous prison sentences for the importation of cannabis – the 'Long John smuggler'.

Another story concerning an attempt to smuggle drugs out of Scotland involved a spectacular amount of ineptitude. The police and customs officers must wish it was always as simple as this . . .

In May 2000 Colin Malcolmson of Limavady in Northern Ireland was found guilty of supplying ecstasy tablets, during a smuggling run to Scotland. Having got off the ferry in Stranraer he went on a lengthy pub-crawl with drugs dealer Norman Lendrum, later sentenced to eight years' imprisonment for his part in the operation, leaving a rucksack filled with £500,000 of ecstasy tablets in his guest-house bedroom.

During the tour of nine pubs, Malcolmson drew attention to himself by becoming very drunk, and was heard to say that he had a bag of ecstasy in his possession. He and Lendrum were thrown out of their guest house when the landlady found Malcolmson climbing on the roof at 3 a.m., and an hour later a police sergeant on patrol in the town stopped to examine a badly parked Ford Escort, left on double yellow lines and without a tax disk.

The car's boot was not locked, and contained a heavy rucksack. Suspecting a possible terrorist attack, the sergeant called for back-up, and a specialist team with sniffer dogs was brought in. Failing to find any trace of explosives, the rucksack was duly opened, to reveal the ecstasy tablets which Malcolmson was going to take on the ferry next morning to sell back home in Northern Ireland.

At that point Malcolmson approached the car, before turning and hurrying away. When he was caught and detained he was found to have the Escort's keys in his possession and an ecstasy tablet concealed in a shoe.

The route from Scotland to Northern Ireland also features in another attempt to smuggle a commodity *out* of Scotland. The establishment of a Troon–Belfast ferry route during the 1990s in addition to the long-standing Stranraer–Northern Ireland crossings has provided another potential channel for terrorist smuggling in both directions.

In September 2002, two men were jailed for eleven years each at the High Court in Glasgow for attempting to smuggle explosives to Northern Ireland from Scotland for the Ulster Volunteer Force. Donald Reid, from Kilsyth, near Glasgow, and Robert Baird, from Kirkintilloch, admitted conspiring to further the purposes of the UVF by carrying five kilos of explosives on the Troon to Belfast ferry.

Following a two-week-long surveillance operation involving a hundred police officers, Reid was stopped while driving to the Ayrshire port. His vehicle contained enough explosives to make up to ten car bombs. The seizure was the second-largest haul of explosives made in Scotland during the last thirty years.

Tobacco and drugs may be the most obvious examples of items smuggled into Scotland today, but endangered species, and even people, may be less high-profile contraband 'cargoes' too.

Sometimes live items are discovered at ferry ports and airports, including a consignment of rare turtles from Hong Kong which arrived at a Scottish airport and are now in the Skye Serpentarium Reptile World. Ron Barrie recalls that 'four or five years ago a cargo of illegal tortoises was discovered by a customs cutter in Aberdeen on board a Polish ship which had sailed from Morocco. One of the airlines flew them down to Edinburgh airport free of charge, and they subsequently bred at Edinburgh Zoo.'

Coral and conch shells were seized at Lerwick harbour and Edinburgh airport in July 2001, while at Glasgow airport coral from Egypt was seized on a flight via Amsterdam, along with a cobra snake pickled in alcohol from Vietnam. In certain parts of the world, pickled cobras are widely believed to have aphrodisiac properties.

According to Customs Minister Paul Boateng, speaking in the summer of 2001,

> Every year millions of tourists flock to Europe and far away destinations and bring back an assortment of gifts and mementoes that look innocent but can in fact be illegal.
>
> Most travellers are aware of rules concerning drugs, alcohol and tobacco, but unsuspecting passengers must bear in mind that unusual souvenirs and gifts may be banned in the UK. These include not just the obviously dangerous items like flick knives but goods such as coral, ivory and animal skins, whose trade damages the environment and endangers rare species.

These goods are rightly and commonly seized by Customs Officers. We owe it to each other and future generations to protect the world we live in, so think before you buy.

In 2000, UK Customs officers seized 3,832 derivatives of endangered species. Scottish officers seized reptile skin boots, butterflies, ivory, snakeskin handbags, tortoise shells, crocodile skins, coral, skins of African rock pythons and a live Hyacinth Macaw.

In December 2002 Lerwick and Greenock were named by the World Wildlife Fund as among the top ten UK key smuggling channels. According to the WWF report, whale meat, python skin belts and turtles were among forty-two separate seizures made at Lerwick between 1996 and 2000. During 2002, a stuffed cobra, mongoose and owl, along with three pickled cobras in bottles of Vietnamese snake oil wine were discovered in Lerwick.

According to WWF Scotland spokesman George Baxter, 'We believe the seizures we are seeing are just the tip of the iceberg of illegal wildlife trade in Scotland. Although you can be stopped by Customs on crossing our borders with illegal goods, once in the UK you can't be arrested for selling the world's most endangered wildlife.'

Stuart Chapman, of the WWF's 'Species Programme' noted, 'Although most of the seizures in Shetland and Greenock were individual items being smuggled in on small boats and cruise ships, this is clear evidence of a domestic demand for exotic wildlife items that is fuelling a wider commercial trade.'

In July 2002 a report by ECPAT – which works for the elimination of child pornography, prostitution and trafficking of children for sexual purposes – noted that there was a significant trade in smuggling *people* into Scotland, especially into Glasgow, where women and children, notably from China, Eastern Europe and Africa, were brought to take part in prostitution.

An ECPAT spokeswoman said 'There is a huge prostitution scene in Glasgow and we think this has a lot to do with the rising number of women and children being smuggled there'. Noting that London is no longer the centre for this trade, she said 'we have discovered that more and more of them are being taken to Scotland, notably Glasgow.'

Earlier in 2002, a Scottish Executive spokesman had announced that 'the Executive will add provisions to the Criminal Justice (Scotland) Bill by way of amendment at Stage 2, to introduce an offence of trafficking for the purposes of sexual exploitation'.

'A Glasgow man was fined £300 at Glasgow Sheriff Court for importing video cassettes portraying scenes of bestiality.

David Cameron Petherick, d.o.b. 24/10/65, of Flat 2/1, 1 14 Kelso Street, Yoker, Glasgow, pled guilty to importing three video cassettes and three video spools of the same scenes of bestiality and admitted ordering seven previous video cassettes portraying bestiality over an unspecified period of time.

Dave Clark, Customs' Scottish detection chief said: 'Customs place particular importance to their work in detecting pornographic material, particularly bestiality and paedophilia'.

Customs and Excise press release, 4 April 2002

The development of the North Sea oil industry gave rise to a whole new range of opportunities for smuggling. Offshore, all personnel are officially 'dry', but inevitably, ingenious ways have been found to smuggle alcohol onto rigs.

Perhaps the most intriguing has its origins in the heyday of Hollywood, when the actor Errol Flynn was at one time contractually banned from drinking during the making of movies due to his alcoholic excesses. Flynn would appear on set with a bag of oranges, which he proceeded to devour during filming. What the studio chiefs did not know was that before coming onto the set, Flynn had injected the oranges with as much vodka as they could absorb!

Several decades later, the trick was picked up by offshore workers, and was only rumbled when an alert member of security staff, checking workers for alcohol and drugs as they arrived on a rig, began to wonder just why oranges were so regularly found among the men's luggage when fresh fruit was supplied free of charge by their employers . . . .

# BIBLIOGRAPHY

Allardyce, John (1913), *Bygone Days in Aberdeenshire,* Aberdeen

Arnot, Hugo (1779), *A History of Edinburgh,* Robinson & Co.

Banks, John (1873), *Reminiscences of Smugglers and Smuggling,* London

Barnard, Alfred (1887), *The Whisky Distilleries of the United Kingdom,* Harper's Weekly Gazette

Barrie, David (1890), *The City of Dundee Illustrated,* Winter, Duncan & Co.

Burns, Robert (1867), *The Complete Works,* William P Nimmo

Campbell, J.R.D. (1994), *Clyde Coast Smuggling,* St Maura Press

Cowie, Robert (1871), *Shetland: descriptive and historical,* Aberdeen

Crockett, S.R. (1894), *The Raiders,* T. Fisher Unwin

Cullen, L.M. (1994), *Smuggling and the Ayrshire Economic Boom,* Ayrshire Archaeological and Natural History Society

Dabney, Joseph Earl (1974), *Mountain Spirits,* Bright Mountain Books

Defoe, Daniel, (1991), *A Tour Through the Whole Island of Great Britain,* Yale University Press

Delgarno, James (1897), *From the Brig o' Balgownie to the Bullars o' Buchan*

Denton, Gilbert (1989), *A Brief History of HM Customs & Excise* (unpublished)

Dewar, Thomas (1904), *A Ramble Round the Globe,* Chatto & Windus

Dibdin, James C. (1896), *The Cleekim Inn,* Archibald Constable, London

Fairley, Jan *et al* (1990), *Chambers Scottish Drink Book,* W&R Chambers Ltd

Ferguson, William (1968), *Scotland 1689 to the Present* – Vol. 4, Oliver & Boyd

Forbes, Athol (1909), *The Romance of Smuggling*

Galt, John (1821), *Annals of the Parish,* William Blackwood

Gilfillan, Rev. George (1886), *The Life of Robert Burns,* London

Gillespie, Malcolm (1828), *The Memorial and Case of Malcolm Gillespie*

Graham, H Grey (1899), *The Social Life of Scotland in the Eighteenth Century,* A.&C. Black Ltd

Grant, I.F. (1961), *Highland Folk Ways*, Routledge & Kegan Paul Ltd

Grewar, David (1926), *The Story of Glenisla*, Aberdeen

Hall, Rev. James (1807), *Travels in Scotland*

Hay, George (1876), *The History of Arbroath*, Thomas Buncle

Hunter, Mollie (1971), *The Lothian Run*, Canongate Publishing

Hutchinson, Roger (1990), *Polly – The True Story of Whisky Galore*, Mainstream Publishing

Johnson, Dr Samuel (1755), *A Dictionary of the English Language*

Johnson, Dr Samuel (1775), *A Journey to the Western Islands of Scotland*

Johnstone, C.L. (1878), *The Historical Families of Dumfriesshire and the Border Wars*

Kay, Billy & Maclean, Cailean (1983), *Knee Deep in Claret*, Mainstream Publishing

Lawson, Rev. Roderick (1888), *Ailsa Craig*, Paisley

Lenman, Bruce (1975), *From Esk to Tweed*, Blackie

Leyden, Dr John (1800), *Journal of a Tour in the Highlands and Western Islands of Scotland*, W. Blackwood & Sons

McDowall, Robert (1867), *History of Dumfries*

Mackay, William (ed.) (1915), *The Letter Book of Bailie John Steuart of Inverness 1715-1752*, Scottish Historical Society

Mackenzie, Sir Compton (1947), *Whisky Galore*, Chatto & Windus Ltd

Mackenzie, Osgood (1921), *A Hundred Years in the Highlands*, Geoffrey Bles

Mackenzie, W.M. (1914), *The Book of Arran* – Vol II, The Arran Society of Glasgow/Hugh Hopkins

Mackintosh, W.R. (1898), *Around the Orkney Peat-Fires*, Kirkwall

MacLean, Charles (1985), *The Fringe of Gold*, Canongate Publishing

Miller, Hugh (1854), *My Schools and Schoolmasters*, Edinburgh

Miller, James (1994), *A Wild and Open Sea*, The Orkney Press Ltd

Morley, David (1994), *The Smuggling War*, Alan Sutton Ltd

*The New Statistical Account of Scotland* (1845), various contributors, W. Blackwood & Sons

Nimmo, William (1777) & Gillespie R., (1880), *A History of Stirlingshire*, Hamilton, Adams & Co.

Oliver, Stephen (1835), *Rambles in Northumberland*, Graham

Paterson, James (1847), *A History of the County of Ayr*, J. Dick

Pennant, Thomas (1769), *A Tour of Scotland in 1769*, W. Eyres

Philipson, John (1991), *Whisky Smuggling on the Borders*, Society of Antiquities, Newcastle upon Tyne

Platt, Richard (1991), *The Ordnance Survey Guide to Smugglers' Britain*, Cassell Publishers Ltd

Quinn, Tom (1999), *Smugglers' Tales*, David & Charles Ltd

Ross, David (1998) *Scotland History of a Nation*, Geddes & Grosset

Scott, Sir Walter (1815), *Guy Mannering*, Constable

Scott, Sir Walter (1816), *The Antiquary*, Constable

Scott, Sir Walter (1818), *The Heart of Midlothian*, Constable

Scott, Sir Walter (1824), *Redgauntlet*, Constable

Sillett, Steve (1965), *Illicit Scotch*, Beaver Books

Sinclair, Sir John (ed.) (1791–9), *The Statistical Account of Scotland*

Smith, Adam (1776), *An Inquiry into the Nature and Causes of the Wealth of Nations*

Smith, Alexander (1912), *A Summer in Skye*, W.P. Nimmo, Hay & Mitchell

Smith, Gavin D. (2002), *The Secret Still – Scotland's Clandestine Whisky Makers*, Birlinn Ltd

Smith, Hance D. (1984), *Shetland Life and Trade*, John Donald

Smith-Leask, J.T. (1931), *A Peculiar People and Other Orkney Tales*

Smout, Thomas (1969), *A History of the Scottish People (1560-1830)*, Collins

Southey, Robert (1819), *Journal of a Tour in Scotland*, J. Murray

Stevenson, David (2001), *The Beggar's Benison*, Tuckwell Press

Stevenson, Robert Louis (1889), *The Master of Ballantrae*, London

Thomson, William S. (1910) *The Smuggling Era in Scotland*

Tucker, Thomas (1656), *Report upon the Settlement of the Revenues of Excise and Customs in Scotland*

Watt, Francis (1912), *Edinburgh and the Lothians*, London

Wilkins, Frances (1992), *Strathclyde's Smuggling Story*, Wyre Forest Press

Wilkins, Frances (1993), *The Smuggling Story of Two Firths*, Wyre Forest Press

Wilkins, Frances (1993), *Dumfries & Galloway's Smuggling Story*, Wyre Forest Press

Wilkins, Frances (1995), *The Smuggling Story of the Northern Shores*, Wyre Forest Press

Wood, John Maxwell (1908), *Smuggling in the Solway and Around the Galloway Sea-board*, J. Maxwell & Son, Dumfries


*The Argyllshire Herald, The Dundee Advertiser, The Edinburgh Advertiser, The Glasgow Courant, The Glasgow Herald, The Inverness Courier, The John O'Groats Journal, The Kilmarnock Standard, The Northern Star, The Orcadian, The Press & Journal, Scotland on Sunday, The Scotsman, The Shetland Times, Tocher, The Weekly Scotsman*

# INDEX